ST. THOMAS AQUINAS

Treatise on Happiness

D0144854

NOTRE DAME SERIES IN THE GREAT BOOKS

John Henry Newman, *The Idea of a University* (1982)

ST. THOMAS AQUINAS

Treatise on Happiness

Translated by

JOHN A. OESTERLE

University of Notre Dame Press
Notre Dame, Indiana 46556

University of Notre Dame Press edition 1983
Copyright © 1964 by Prentice Hall, Inc.
All Rights Reserved

To Carl and Margaret

Library of Congress Cataloging in Publication Data

Thomas, Aquinas, Saint, 1225?–1274.
　Treatise on happiness.

　Selected translations from: Summa theologica.
　Reprint. Originally published: Englewood Cliffs, N. J.:
Prentice-Hall, 1964.
　　1. Happiness — Moral and ethical aspects — Early works
to 1800. 2. Christian ethics — Early works to 1800.
I. Oesterle, John A. II. Title.
[BJ1480.T4813 1983]　　171'.2　　83-17091
ISBN 0-268-01848-0
ISBN 0-268-01849-9 (pbk.)

Manufactured in the United States of America

Table of Contents

QUESTION VII   81

The Circumstances of Human Acts

QUESTION VIII   87

What the Will Wills

QUESTION IX   92

What Moves the Will

QUESTION X   101

The Manner in Which the Will Is Moved

The Goodness and Malice of the Interior Act of the Will

PREFATORY NOTE

The Notre Dame Series in the Great Books here proudly presents a republication of John Oesterle's fine translation of the first twenty-one questions of Part I of the Second Part of the *Summa Theologiae* by St. Thomas Aquinas. This translation appeared in 1964 with the title *Treatise on Happiness.* It has become in recent years "a regular" on the seminar reading lists of Notre Dame's Great Books Program, the Program of Liberal Studies.

At mid-century, the Great Books movement, aided by the emergence of paperback technology, began to have a considerable effect on American higher education and specifically Catholic education. One result was the displacement of philosophy textbooks and Thomistic manuals with primary sources. John Oesterle's translation was one of several efforts at this time to present the thought of St. Thomas anew in this changing educational climate. His effort to present a significant portion of the *Summa* in paperback has contributed to the special position the wisdom of St. Thomas Aquinas holds even in the current more pluralistic philosophical atmosphere of the Program of Liberal Studies and Catholic higher education in general.

Special gratitude is due to the Program's Class of 1956 for their founding support for the Notre Dame Series in the Great Books. I also thank Jean Oesterle for her encouragement and approval in this project of republishing her late husband's translation and introduction. I am grateful to Professors Janet Smith and Ralph McInerny of the Notre Dame faculty for their counsel and assistance in the arrangements to republish the *Treatise on Happiness.*

Walter Nicgorski
May, 1983

INTRODUCTION

The phrase "all human beings seek happiness" points to a truth at once obvious and fundamental. It is obvious in the sense that it is a fact about human nature readily observed in the actions and desires of each one of us. It is fundamental in the sense that no human being can avoid acting in terms of attaining complete well-being so far as possible.

The twentieth century is no different in this regard from the thirteenth century, when St. Thomas Aquinas wrote about this matter. The present century may seem to be a much more complicated one, fraught with anxiety over the threat of thermonuclear war, along with many other pressing problems. But all the issues we face, the fears we have, and the frustrations we so often encounter, simply bear witness to that basic tendency in us to achieve happiness; otherwise fears, anxieties, problems, and frustrations are not even intelligible. Inevitably we find ourselves appraising all important matters in terms of fundamental values, and chief among these is the pursuit and attainment of happiness itself.

Problems and difficulties about attaining happiness arise only when we try to ascertain in *what* happiness consists, for though no one can really deny that he seeks well-being, it is quite another matter to realize this state concretely. St. Thomas approached this question as a theologian, and not only as a philosopher, operating in the framework of revealed truths wherein we recognize a supernatural order of knowledge and action over and beyond the natural order, which is perfected by it. He had also discussed the question as a philosopher, particularly in commenting on the *Nicomachean Ethics* of Aristotle, for St. Thomas acknowledges "a twofold ultimate perfection of the rational or intellectual nature. The first is one which it can attain by its own natural power, and this in a measure is called beatitude or happiness." [1] The determination of what natural happiness is and in what it consists is difficult to make, but in his theological work St. Thomas can put this question aside. While natural happiness remains a realizable end in its own order, however difficult and varying, man in fact is ordered to a more perfect and complete happiness beyond anything the human mind could possibly imagine or conceive. "Beyond this happiness [natural happiness] there is still another to which we can look forward in the future, whereby we shall

---

[1] This and the following quotation are taken from *Summa Theologiae* I, question 62, article 1.

see God as He is. This is beyond the nature of every created intellect."
It is such happiness St. Thomas deals with in his *Summa Theologiae*.
    The *Summa Theologiae* is divided into three main sections. Part I
treats of God and the procession of creatures from God.[2] Part II treats
of the movement of rational creatures back to God. Part III treats of the
Incarnate Word Who, both divine and human, is our way to God.[3] Part
II, in turn, is divided into two parts (designated as I-II and II-II). The
first of these treats happiness, human acts, virtues and vices in general;
the second treats virtues and vices, and other moral matters, in particular detail.[4]
    The Treatise on Happiness and the accompanying Treatise on Human
Acts, which this translation covers, comprise the first twenty-one questions of I-II of the *Summa Theologiae*. It must be put in the context,
therefore, of what has been said in Part I about God and creatures, and
what will be said further in the remaining sections of the work. The
Treatise on Happiness occupies the first five questions. This treatise is
not readily available in English translation, since it appears only in complete and costly editions of the *Summa Theologiae*. In this section, St.
Thomas moves from a consideration of an ultimate end for human life
to happiness as such an end; then to what happiness consists in and how
it can be attained. Question II eliminates any created good as completely
and perfectly satisfying man's desire. Question III shows positively that
man's supernatural happiness consists in seeing God as He is in Himself.
Questions IV and V discuss what is required for such happiness and how
it is attained.
    "Since happiness must be attained through certain acts, we must there-
fore consider human acts so as to know by which acts we shall attain
happiness and by which we shall be prevented from attaining happiness."[5] This sentence introduces us to the Treatise on Human Acts,
which is divided into four parts. The first part (Questions VI-X) deals
with the nature of voluntary acts in general, for such acts set man off from
other animals and are therefore acts by which he seeks to achieve happiness. The second part (Questions XI-XVI) deals specifically with acts
that proceed immediately from the will, for example, enjoyment, choice,
and consent. The third part (Question XVII) treats acts commanded by
the will, that is, acts coming from the will by means of other powers.
The last part (Questions XVIII-XXI) considers how human acts are
good or evil. This section includes such pertinent topics as the signifi-

---

[2] Two treatises from this part of the *Summa* have already been published by Prentice-Hall, both translated by Professor James F. Anderson. *Treatise on Man* (questions
75-88) was published in 1962. *Treatise on God* (questions 1-26) was published in 1963.
[3] Cf. the prologue to question 2 of Part I of the *Summa Theologiae*.
[4] Cf. the prologue to II-II of the *Summa Theologiae* for the relation between I-II
and II-II.
[5] Prologue to question 6.

cance of circumstances in moral acts, the problem of erroneous conscience, and the responsibility for consequences of moral acts.

The two treatises have, of course, a theological order in that they draw upon truths of revelation. At the same time, the discussion and argumentation draw largely upon philosophical knowledge; because of this, even those who are not aware of God's revelation of a supernatural end for man, and all this implies, can gather much understanding and benefit from these pages on man's quest for happiness and the acts by which he can gain an ultimate end. Anything human reason can discover which is relevant to happiness and moral action complements what is set forth in these treatises both theologically and philosophically. For those who are Christian, there is no limit to the degree of understanding one can have by way of penetrating the truths revealed to man through the accompanying reasoned grasp of natural truths concerning human happiness and moral action.

Some remarks should be made about the structure of the questions and articles, as well as about the translation. Each question proposes a somewhat general topic or issue. For example, Question I is on *The Ultimate End of Man in General*. The articles of each question raise more specific issues or questions dealing with the general topic. Thus Article 1 of Question I asks: *Does Man Act for an End?* St. Thomas first sets forth arguments on one side of the question, usually stated as "objections." I have not included the word "objection." Instead, after stating in a sentence by itself the position being taken, I have simply numbered the arguments (usually three) supporting this side of the question. After these arguments have been given, a position on the other side of the question is stated; this appears after the phrase *On the contrary*. The body of the article follows and here the resolution of the question is given. This appears after the word *Response* (adapted from the Latin *Respondeo dicendum*). Finally, replies are given to the arguments set forth at the beginning of the article. Over and beyond references, I have added notes wherever I thought further clarification might be desirable either in regard to translation and terminology or to points of exposition.

With respect to the translation, I have endeavored to render the Latin of St. Thomas into as readable English as possible consistent with accuracy of meaning. Some words in English, deriving from Latin, have been kept because their use has become frequent in even ordinary discourse. Other words which have become technical in their philosophical meaning have been supplanted when feasible by more familiar synonyms; when not feasible, a note of explanation is added. No one can hope for a flawless performance in translation, but one may hope for a rendition that will be useful and interesting both for general readers and others more competent in theology and philosophy.

The text from which the translation has been made is the critical Leonine text as it appears in the manual edition of the *Biblioteca de*

Autores Christianos, Madrid, Spain, 1955. Reference has also been made to the Ottawa-Piana edition of 1941. Acknowledgment must be made to the English Dominican translation of the *Summa Theologiae,* which pioneered in this work a half century ago and which renders great assistance to anyone engaged in the same pursuit. I am grateful for the interest and encouragement shown by Mr. Paul E. O'Connell, Assistant Vice-President of Prentice-Hall, not only for stimulating me in preparing this present translation, but for his abiding interest in the series of which this book forms a part and for his general encouragement of many types of academic and scholarly publications. I am indebted also to the unnamed reviewer consulted by Mr. O'Connell, who read various portions of the manuscript and made fruitful suggestions and comments. I must also acknowledge a great debt of gratitude to Professor Charles D. De Koninck, Laval University and Visiting Professor at the University of Notre Dame; he painstakingly read portions of the translation and made many enlightening suggestions which have been incorporated into the translation and some of the notes. Finally, I am grateful to my wife who, an able translator in her own right, read through much of the translation and made countless illuminating observations and alterations.

J. A. O.

PROLOGUE

As Damascene observes,[1] man is said to be made to the image of God, "image" in this context signifying an intellectual being who is free to judge what he shall do and has the power to act or not to act. Now that we have treated the exemplar, God, and the things that have come forth from His divine power in accordance with His will,[2] we should go on to consider His image, that is, man, inasmuch as he too is a principle of his actions, having as he does the freedom to judge what he shall do and control over his actions.

---

[1] *On the Orthodox Faith* II, 22.
[2] This treatment forms the substance of Part I of the *Summa Theologiae.*

The Ultimate End of Man in General

(In Eight Articles)

First we shall consider the ultimate end of human life and secondarily the means by which man can reach this end, or deviate from it, for the end is the measure of things ordered to the end. As to the ultimate end, we will first consider it generally, and then we will consider happiness,[1] since it is said to be the ultimate end of human life.

First Article

DOES MAN ACT FOR AN END?

It seems that man does not act for an end.

1. A cause is naturally prior to its effect. But *end* is conceived as something last, as the meaning of the name indicates. Therefore an end is not conceived as a cause. Now that *from* which man acts is a cause of his action, a relationship of causality being designated by the preposition "from." Therefore man does not act for an end.

2. An ultimate end is not for the sake of an end. But in some cases, actions are an ultimate end, as the Philosopher shows.[2] Therefore not everything man does is for the sake of an end.

3. Man seems to act for an end when he deliberates. But man often does things without deliberation, sometimes even without thinking about them at all, as when he moves his foot or hand while intent on other things, or scratches his beard. Therefore man does not do everything for the sake of an end.

---

[1] The Latin word translated here as "happiness" is *beatitudo*. In Part I of the *Summa Theologiae*, question 62, article 1, St. Thomas explains: "By the name of beatitude is understood the ultimate perfection of rational or intellectual nature, and this is what is naturally desired since everything naturally desires its ultimate perfection. There is a twofold ultimate fulfillment of the rational or intellectual nature. The first is one which it can attain by its own natural power, and this in a measure is called beatitude or happiness. Hence Aristotle says that the ultimate happiness of man consists in the most perfect contemplation, the object of which is God, the highest intelligible thing that can be contemplated in this life. Beyond this happiness there is still another to which we can look forward in the future, whereby we shall see God as He is. This is beyond the nature of any created intellect." In a theological work based on revelation, St. Thomas has supernatural happiness primarily in mind, as will become clear in Question III below.

[2] Aristotle, *Nicomachean Ethics* I, 1 (1094a 4).

3

On the contrary: All things in a given genus are derived from the principle of that genus. But the end is the principle in human actions, as the Philosopher points out.[3] Therefore it is characteristic of man to do everything for an end.

Response: Only those actions of man are properly called human which are characteristic of man as man. Now the difference between man and irrational creatures is that he is the master of his actions. Hence the actions of which man is the master are the only ones that can properly be called human. But man is master of his actions through his reason and will; hence free judgment of choice[4] is said to be "a power of will and reason." [5] Therefore actions that are deliberately willed are properly called human. If there are other actions that belong to man, they can be called *actions of man* but not *human actions* strictly speaking, since they are not actions of man as man. Now it is clear that all actions which proceed from a power are caused by that power in conformity with the nature of its object. But the object of the will is an end and a good. Therefore all human actions are for the sake of an end.

Reply to 1: Although the end is last in execution, it is first in the intention of the agent, and in this way has the aspect of a cause.

Reply to 2: If any human action is an ultimate end it must be a voluntary or willed action, otherwise it would not be human, as we have remarked in the body of this article. Now an action is called voluntary in two ways: first, because it is commanded by the will, as in the instance of walking or speaking; second, because it is elicited by the will, as in the very act of willing. Now it is impossible that the very act elicited by the will be the ultimate end, for the object of the will is an end in the same way as the object of seeing is color. Hence just as it is impossible for the primary thing seen to be the very act of seeing, because all seeing is of some visible object, so too it is impossible that the primary thing desired, which is the end, be the act itself of willing. Consequently, if any human action is an ultimate end it must be commanded by the will, and in that case some action of man, at least willing itself, is for the end. Therefore whatever man does, it is true to say that he does it for an end even when he does an action which is an ultimate end.

Reply to 3: Actions of the kind indicated in the argument are not properly human because they do not result from the deliberation of reason, which is the proper principle of human acts. Such actions, there-

---

[3] Aristotle, *Physics* II, 9 (200a 34).
[4] The Latin expression for "free judgment of choice" is *liberum arbitrium,* which in some contexts can be translated as "free will." This translation, however, is not always adequate. In the present context, the emphasis is on man's free acts deriving from the practical judgment of reason as well as on the free choice which is an act of the will; hence the phrase "free judgment of choice" or, sometimes, just "free judgment" or "free choice."
[5] Peter Lombard, *Sentences* II, d. 24, c. 3.

fore, have a somewhat imaginary end, but not one determined beforehand by reason.

Second Article

DOES ACTING FOR AN END BELONG EXCLUSIVELY TO THOSE BEINGS IN NATURE THAT HAVE REASON?

It seems that to act for an end belongs to a nature that possesses reason.

1. Man, to whom it belongs to act for an end, never acts for an unknown end. But there are many beings who do not know an end, either because they have no cognition at all, as in the case of creatures having no senses, or because they do not apprehend an end as an end, as in the case of irrational animals. Therefore to act for an end seems to belong to a rational nature.

2. To act for an end is to order one's actions to an end. But to order actions in this way is a work of reason. Therefore it does not belong to beings that lack reason.

3. The object of the will is a good and an end. But the will, it is said, depends on reason.[6] Therefore to act for an end belongs to none except a rational nature.

On the contrary: The Philosopher proves that not only an intelligent being, but also nature, acts for an end.[7]

Response: Every agent necessarily acts for an end. For among causes ordered to each other, if the first is withdrawn, the others must also be withdrawn. Now the first of all causes is the final cause. The argument for this is as follows.

Matter does not attain form except insofar as it is moved by an agent, for nothing brings itself from potency to act. But an agent does not move unless it intends an end; for if an agent were not determined to some effect it would not do this rather than that. Therefore to produce a determinate effect it must intend a definite one, which has the nature of an end. This determination as it is in a rational nature is made by rational desire, which is called the will; in others it is by natural inclination, which is called natural appetite.

It should be noted, however, that a thing tends to an end by its action or movement in two ways: in one way, by moving itself to an end, as man does; in another, as moved to an end by something else. An example of the latter would be an arrow, which tends to a determinate end as moved by an archer who directs its action to an end. Now those who have reason move themselves to an end, for they have dominion over their actions through their free judgment, which is a power of will and

---

[6] Cf. Aristotle, *On the Soul* III, 9 (432b 5).
[7] *Physics* II, 5 (196b 21).

reason. Those lacking reason tend to an end by natural inclination, as moved by another and not by themselves, since they do not know an end as end, and consequently cannot order anything to an end but are ordered to it by another. For the whole of irrational nature is compared to God as an instrument is to a principal agent, as was shown above.[8] Hence it is proper to a rational nature to tend to an end by moving or directing itself to an end, whereas it is proper to an irrational nature to tend to an end as moved or directed by another, whether to an apprehended end as with irrational animals, or to an unapprehended end as with things completely devoid of knowledge.

Reply to 1: When man of himself acts for an end, he knows the end, but when he is moved or directed by another, that is, when he acts at another's command or is moved at the instigation of another, he does not have to know the end. So it is with irrational creatures.

Reply to 2: To order to an end belongs to whatever directs itself to an end; to be ordered to an end belongs to whatever is directed by another to an end, and this is the case of an irrational nature, but it is still ordered by an agent possessing reason.

Reply to 3: The object of the will is the end and good universally. Hence there cannot be will in beings that lack reason and intellect since they cannot apprehend universally; but there is in them a natural or sense appetite determined to some particular good. Now it is evident that particular causes are moved by a universal cause; for instance, the mayor of a city, intending the common good, moves by his command all the particular civil officials. Hence all things that lack reason must be moved to particular ends by some rational will which extends to the universal good, namely, by the divine will.

Third Article

ARE HUMAN ACTS SPECIFIED BY THEIR END?

It seems that human acts are not specified by their end.[9]

1. The end is an extrinsic cause. But a thing is what it is because of some intrinsic principle. Therefore human acts are not specified by their end.

2. That which gives a thing its species[10] must be prior to it. But the end is posterior in being. Therefore human acts are not specified by their end.

3. The same thing cannot be in more than one species. But one and

---

[8] *Summa Theologiae* I, question 22, article 2, reply to *4;* question 103, article 1, reply to *3.*

[9] "Specified" or "species" throughout this article means that which makes a thing to be the kind of thing it is. Hence the title of this question may be understood as follows: Are human acts *what* they are by reason of their end?

[10] See preceding note.

the same act can be ordered to diverse ends. Therefore the end does not specify human acts.

On the contrary: Augustine says, "According as the end is blameworthy or praiseworthy, so are our works blameworthy or praiseworthy." [11]

Response: Each thing receives its species from an act,[12] not from a potentiality; hence things composed of matter and form are constituted in their respective species by their proper forms. This also applies to their proper movements. For movement is distinguished in a certain way in terms of action and being-acted-upon, and each of these receives its species from an act, action from the act which is the principle of action, being-acted-upon from the act which is the term of the movement. Heating, for example, as an action is a motion proceeding from heat; as a receiving of an action it is a motion toward heat, the definition in each case manifesting the nature of the species.

In both ways human acts, whether considered in terms of an action or being acted upon, receive their species from the end. Human acts can be considered in both ways because man moves himself and is moved by himself. Now it was stated above that acts are called human insofar as they are deliberately willed.[13] But the object of the will is the good and the end. Clearly, then, the principle of human acts, insofar as they are human, is the end. It is likewise their term, for a human act terminates in what the will intends as an end,[14] just as in natural agents the form of what is generated is conformed to the form of the one generating. And since, as Ambrose says, "moral acts are properly called human acts," [15] moral acts receive their species from the end, for moral acts are the same as human acts.

Reply to 1: The end is not altogether extrinsic to an act, for it is related to an act either as a principle or as a term; and this principle or term is of the very notion of an act, namely, that it be from something, considered as action, and that it be toward something, considered as being received.

Reply to 2: The end as prior in intention pertains to the will, as we have already said,[16] and in this way it gives species to the human or moral act.

Reply to 3: One and the same act, as it proceeds from the agent at any one time, is ordered to but one proximate end, from which it takes its

---

[11] *On the Morals of the Church and the Manicheans* II, c. 13.

[12] "Act" here is taken in the sense of *first* act as distinct from *second* act. *First* act, as this article explains, means the original actual determination given to matter by some form; for example, man's rational soul is the first act of matter constituting man to be a rational animal "in species." *Second* act is the more familiar meaning of "act," for example, this act of thinking or this act of breathing.

[13] Article 1.

[14] The end is the *principle* of human acts insofar as we *first intend* something for itself; the end is a *term* in the sense that it is what we attain *last* in *execution*.

[15] Prologue, *Commentary on Luke.*   [16] Article 1, reply to 1.

species, but it can be ordered to many remote ends of which one is the end of another. However, it is possible for an act which is one in respect to its own species to be ordered to diverse ends of the will. For example, the same act according to its own species—the act of killing a man—can be ordered to the end of upholding justice or the satisfying of anger; this results in acts that are diverse in moral species, for in the one way it will be an act of virtue and in the other an act of vice. For a movement does not receive its species from its accidental term but from its per se term. Now moral ends are accidental to a natural thing and, conversely, the notion of a natural end is accidental to morality. Hence there is no reason why acts that are the same in natural species should not be different with respect to their moral species, and conversely.

Fourth Article

IS THERE AN ULTIMATE END FOR HUMAN LIFE?

It seems that there is not an ultimate end for human life, but an infinite series of ends.

1. The good by its nature communicates itself, as Dionysius states.[17] Therefore if what proceeds from a good is itself good, this good must produce another good, and thus the series of goods is without end. But good has the nature of an end. Therefore there is an infinite series of ends.

2. What is in reason can be multiplied without end. Thus mathematical quantities can be increased without end, and the species of numbers are likewise without end for, given any number, reason can think of another that is greater. But desire of the end follows upon its being grasped by reason. Therefore it seems that there is also an infinite series of ends.

3. The object of the will is the good and the end. But the will can reflect upon itself an infinite number of times, for I can will something, and will to will it, and so on without end. Therefore with respect to ends of the human will one can go on infinitely, and there is not any ultimate end for the human will.

On the contrary: The Philosopher says, "Those who maintain there is an infinite series [of ends] unwittingly destroy the nature of the good." [18] But the good has the nature of an end. Therefore to go on infinitely is contrary to the nature of end. It is necessary, therefore, that there be one ultimate end.

Response: Absolutely speaking, it is impossible to go on infinitely as far as ends are concerned, from any point of view. For in all things which have a per se order, when the first is removed those ordered to the first

---

[17] *The Divine Names* IV, 1.   [18] *Metaphysics* II, 2 (994b 12).

are removed. Accordingly the Philosopher proves that it is impossible to go on without end in moving causes, because then there would not be a first mover; and if there is no first mover the others would not move, since they move only through being moved by the first mover.[19]

Now there is a twofold order in ends, the order of intention and the order of execution, and in either order there must be something first. That which is first in the order of intention is by way of a principle moving the appetite; hence if this principle be removed desire would not be moved at all. The principle in the order of execution is that from which action begins; hence if this principle be removed, no one would begin doing anything.

Now the principle with respect to intention is the ultimate end; the principle with respect to execution is the first means related to the end. To go on without end with respect to either is therefore impossible, for if there were no ultimate end nothing would be desired, nor would any act be terminated, nor would the intention of the agent ever be at rest; and if there were no first means in relation to the end, no one would begin to do anything and deliberation would never end, but go on infinitely. On the other hand, nothing prevents an infinite series in things which do not have a per se order one to another, but are joined accidentally to each other, for accidental causes are indeterminate. In this case, in fact, there may also be an infinity accidentally in ends and in means to the end.

Reply to 1: It is of the nature of the good that something come forth from it but not that it proceed from another. Consequently, since the good is of its very nature an end and the first good is the ultimate end, the argument given does not prove that there is no ultimate end, but that from the end already supposed one may subsequently go on infinitely with respect to things which are for the end. Now this would be all right if only the power of the primary good, which is infinite, were being considered. But because the primary good communicates itself according to intellect, to which it belongs to flow into the caused according to some determined form, it follows that there is a certain measure in the flow of good things from the primary good, from which all other goods share their power of communicating. Therefore the communicating of good does not go on without end but, as is said in Scripture, God disposes all things "in number, weight and measure" (*Wisdom 11:21*).

Reply to 2: With respect to things existing per se, reason begins from principles naturally known and goes on to some term. Hence the Philosopher proves that there is not an infinite regress in demonstrations, for in demonstrations one attends to an order of things per se connected with each other, not accidentally.[20] But nothing prevents reason from

---

[19] *Physics* VIII, 5 (256a 17).   [20] *Posterior Analytics* I, 3 (72b 7).

going on endlessly in accidentally connected things. Now it is accidental to quantity or to a given number, that a quantity or a unit be added. Hence in such things there is nothing to prevent reason from going on endlessly.

Reply to 3: The multiplication of acts of the will as it reflects upon itself is accidental to the order of ends. The evidence for this is that the will reflects on itself indifferently one or several times in regard to one and the same end.

Fifth Article

CAN A MAN HAVE SEVERAL ULTIMATE ENDS?

It seems possible for one man's will to be simultaneously directed to many things as ultimate ends.

1. Augustine says that certain men held that man's ultimate end consisted in four things, pleasure, tranquillity, gifts of nature and virtue.[21] These are clearly many. Therefore a man could set his will on many things as an ultimate end.

2. Things that are not opposed to each other do not exclude each other. But there are many things that are not opposed to each other. Therefore even if one thing is posited as the ultimate end of the will, other things are not thereby excluded.

3. By selecting something as an ultimate end the will does not thereby lose its power of freedom. Now even before selecting something as an ultimate end, say pleasure, it could settle upon something else, say riches. Therefore even after settling upon pleasure as the ultimate end of his will, a man can likewise settle upon riches as his ultimate end. Therefore it is possible for one man's will to be directed to diverse things as ultimate ends.

On the contrary: What man acquiesces in as an ultimate end is master of his affections, since his whole life is regulated by it. Hence it is said of gluttons "Whose god is their belly" (*Philippians 3:19*), because they make pleasures of the belly their ultimate end. But as is also said, "No man can serve two masters" (*Matthew 6:24*), that is, two things not ordered one to the other. Therefore it is impossible that a man have many ultimate ends not ordered to each other.

Response: It is impossible for a man's will to be simultaneously related to diverse things as ultimate ends. Three reasons can be given for this. The first is that each thing desires its own fulfillment and therefore desires for its ultimate end a good that perfects and completes it. Hence Augustine says, "What we here call the end that is a good is not that which is consumed so as not to be, but that which is brought to com-

---

[21] *The City of God* XIX, 1.

pletion so as to be fully." [22] The ultimate end, then, must so entirely satisfy man's desire that there is nothing left for him to desire. It cannot be his ultimate end if something additional is required for his fulfillment. Hence it is not possible for desire to tend to two things as though each were its perfect good.

The second reason is the following. Just as the principle in the functioning of reason is that which is naturally known, [23] so the principle in the functioning of rational desire, which is the will, has to be that which is naturally desired. Now this must be one because nature tends only to one thing. But the principle in the functioning of rational desire is the ultimate end. Hence that to which the will tends as an ultimate end must be one.

The third reason is this. Since voluntary actions receive their species from their end, as we said above, [24] their genus must be assigned from an ultimate end which is common to them all, as in a parallel way natural things are placed in a genus corresponding to a formal notion which is common. Since, then, all things desirable to the will, as desirable, are of one genus, the ultimate end must be one—particularly since in any genus there is one first principle and the ultimate end functions as a first principle, as we have indicated. [25] Now the ultimate end of man absolutely is to the whole human race as the ultimate end of this man is to this man. Hence just as there is by nature one ultimate end for all men, so the will of this man must be ordered to one ultimate end.

Reply to 1: These several objects taken together were considered as one complete good by those who posited them as the ultimate end.

Reply to 2: Although many things can be taken which do not have opposition to each other, still it is opposed to the complete good that there be anything of the perfection of the thing outside of it.

Reply to 3: The power of the will is not such that it can cause opposites to be simultaneously, which would happen if it were to aim at many disparate things as ultimate ends, as shown in this article.

Sixth Article

DOES MAN WILL ALL THAT HE WILLS FOR AN ULTIMATE END?

It seems that man does not will everything that he wills for an ultimate end.

1. Things that are ordered to an ultimate end are said to be something serious, as being useful. But what is done jokingly is distinguished from

---

[22] *Op. cit.,* 2.
[23] That is, known as self-evident and without a process of reasoning.
[24] Article 3. See also footnote 9 above.   [25] Preceding article.

what is serious. Therefore what man does jokingly he does not order to the ultimate end.

2. The Philosopher says that speculative sciences are sought for their own sake.[26] Yet it cannot be said that any of these is an ultimate end. Therefore not everything man desires is desired for the sake of an ultimate end.

3. Whoever orders something to an end is considering[27] that end. But man does not always consider the ultimate end in everything that he desires and does. Therefore man does not desire nor do everything for an ultimate end.

On the contrary: Augustine says, "That is the object of our good for the sake of which we love other things, whereas we love it for its own sake." [28]

Response: All things which man desires he necessarily desires for an ultimate end. This is made clear by two arguments. First, because whatever man desires, he desires under the aspect of a good. If it is not desired as his complete good, which is the ultimate end, he must desire it as tending toward his complete good because a beginning of something is always ordered to its completion, as is evident both in what is brought about by nature and what is made by art. Thus every beginning of fulfillment is ordered to complete fulfillment, which is achieved through the ultimate end.

Second, because the ultimate end as moving the appetite is like the first mover in other motions. But clearly, secondary moving causes move only insofar as they are moved by a first mover. Hence secondary desirable things move the appetite only as ordered to a primary desirable thing, which is the ultimate end.

Reply to 1: What is done jokingly is not ordered to some extrinsic end, but to the good of the one who does it, inasmuch as it affords him pleasure or relaxation. But man's ultimate end is his complete good.

Reply to 2: The reply to this argument is the same as to the first one, for speculative science is desired as a good of the knower and is included in the complete and perfect good which is the ultimate end.

Reply to 3: One need not always be considering the ultimate end when desiring or doing something. In fact, the force of the first intention, which is in view of the ultimate end, remains in the desiring of anything even though one is not actually considering the ultimate end, just as when going somewhere we do not have to think of the end at every step.

---

[26] *Metaphysics* I, 2 (982a 14).   [27] Literally, "cogitating about."
[28] *The City of God* XIX, 1.

Seventh Article

IS THERE ONE ULTIMATE END FOR ALL MEN?

It seems that all men do not have one ultimate end.

1. The ultimate end most of all seems to be an unchanging good. But some turn away from the unchanging good by sinning. Therefore there is not one ultimate end for all men.

2. Man's whole life is regulated in accordance with his ultimate end. But if there were one ultimate end for all men it would follow that there would not be different ways of living, which is clearly false.

3. The end is the term of an action. But actions belong to singulars. Now although men agree in the nature of their species, they differ individually. Therefore all men do not have one ultimate end.

On the contrary: Augustine says, "All men agree in desiring the ultimate end, which is happiness." [29]

Response: We can speak of the ultimate end in two ways, having in mind in one case the notion of the ultimate end, and in the other that in which the notion of the ultimate end is realized. With respect to the notion of the ultimate end, all agree in desiring the ultimate end, since all desire their good to be complete, which is what the ultimate end is, as we have said.[30] But with respect to that in which this kind of thing is realized, all men are not agreed as to their ultimate end, for some desire riches as their complete good, some sense pleasure, and others something else. For example, what is sweet is delightful to every taste, but to some the sweetness of wine is most delightful, to others the sweetness of honey or of something else. But the sweet thing that is more delightful absolutely is the one which most delights him who has the best taste. In like manner, the most complete good absolutely must be what one with well-disposed affections desires for his ultimate end.

Reply to 1: Those who sin turn away from that in which the ultimate end is truly found, but they still intend an ultimate end, which they mistakenly seek in other things.

Reply to 2: Different ways of living come about among men by reason of the different things in which men seek the highest good.

Reply to 3. Although actions belong to individuals, still the first principle of their actions is nature, which tends to one thing, as we have already stated.[31]

---

[29] *The Trinity* XIII, 3.   [30] Article 5.   [31] *Ibid.*

Eighth Article

DO OTHER CREATURES SHARE IN THIS ULTIMATE END?

It seems that all other creatures share in the ultimate end of man.

1. The end corresponds to the beginning. But the principle of man, which is God, is also the principle of all other things. Therefore all others share in man's ultimate end.

2. Dionysius says, "God draws all things to Himself as to their ultimate end." [32] But He Himself is the ultimate end of man, because full enjoyment is derived from Him alone, as Augustine says.[33] Therefore others also share in man's ultimate end.

3. The ultimate end of man is the object of the will. But the object of the will is the universal good, which is the end for all. Therefore all things must share in man's ultimate end.

On the contrary: Man's ultimate end is happiness, which all men desire, as Augustine says.[34] But, he also says, "It is not appropriate to animals devoid of reason that they be blessed." [35] Therefore others do not share with man his ultimate end.

Response: As the Philosopher says, "end" is said in two ways, the end *for the sake of which* and the end *by which*.[36] The former is the object itself in which the good is found; the latter is the use or attainment of that object. For example, we say that the end of the movement of a heavy body is either a lower place, as an *object,* or being in a lower place, as to *use;* the end of a greedy man is either money, as an *object,* or the possession of money, as to *use.*

If we speak of man's ultimate end as meaning the object which is the end, all other things share in man's ultimate end since God is the ultimate end of man and of all other things. But if we speak of man's ultimate end with respect to possession of the end, irrational creatures do not share in this end of man. For man and other rational creatures reach their ultimate end by knowing and loving God. This is not possible for other creatures, who acquire the ultimate end insofar as they participate in some likeness to God, in proportion as they exist, or live, or even know.

Hence the replies to the arguments are clear, for happiness signifies the possession of the ultimate end.

---

[32] *The Divine Names* IV, 4.
[33] *On Christian Doctrine* I, 1.
[34] *The Trinity* XIII, 3.
[35] *Book of Eighty-Three Questions,* question 5.
[36] *Physics* II, 2 (194a 35) .

QUESTION II

In What Man's Happiness Consists

(In Eight Articles)

First Article

DOES MAN'S HAPPINESS CONSIST IN WEALTH?

It seems that man's happiness consists in wealth.

1. Since happiness is the ultimate end of man, his happiness must consist in whatever has the greatest hold on his affections. Now wealth is a thing of this kind, for as it is said in Scripture, "All things obey money" *(Ecclesiastes 10:19).* Therefore man's happiness consists in wealth.

2. According to Boethius, happiness is "a state brought to completion by the aggregation of all goods." [1] Now money seems to be the means of possessing all things, for, as the Philosopher says, money was devised so that it might be a sort of guarantee for the having of anything whatever that man wills.[2] Therefore happiness consists in wealth.

3. Since the desire for the utmost good is without limit, it seems to be infinite. But the desire for wealth is most of all without limit, for "an avaricious man will not be satisfied with riches" *(Ecclesiastes 5:9).* Therefore happiness consists in wealth.

On the contrary: Man's good consists in keeping happiness rather than losing it. But as Boethius says, "wealth flourishes more by being poured forth than by being amassed, for avarice makes men loathsome whereas generosity makes them illustrious." [3] Therefore happiness does not consist in wealth.

Response: It is impossible for man's happiness to consist in wealth. For, as the Philosopher says, there are two kinds of wealth, natural and artificial.[4] Natural wealth is that which relieves man's natural needs, such as food, drink, clothing, travel, shelter, and so on. Artificial wealth, such as money, is not in itself an aid to nature, but has been devised by human art to facilitate exchange and as a measure of things for sale.

Now it is evident that man's happiness cannot consist in natural wealth, for wealth of this kind is sought for the sake of something else, that is, for human sustenance. Hence it cannot be man's ultimate end,

---

[1] *The Consolation of Philosophy* III, prose 2.
[2] Aristotle, *Nicomachean Ethics* V, 5 (1133b 12).
[3] *The Consolation of Philosophy* II, prose 5.
[4] Aristotle, *Politics* I, 9 (1257a 4).

15

but rather is ordered to man as an end. Consequently, in the order of nature, everything of this kind is below man and made for him, as is said in Scripture, "Thou hast subjected all things under his feet" (*Psalms 8: 8*).

Artificial wealth, on the other hand, is sought only for the sake of natural wealth. In fact, it would not be sought unless what is necessary for life could be bought with it. Hence it has even less the nature of an ultimate end. Therefore it is impossible that happiness, man's ultimate end, consist in wealth.

Reply to 1: Many foolish men think that all corporeal things obey money, but these are men who are conscious only of goods which can be acquired with money. But our judgment about human goods should be taken, not from the foolish but from the wise, just as we should take our judgment about taste from those with a well-ordered sense of taste.

Reply to 2: All things for sale can be had for money, but not spiritual things. These cannot be bought. Hence it is said in *Proverbs 17:16* "What does it avail a fool to have riches, seeing he cannot buy wisdom?"

Reply to 3: The desire for natural wealth is not infinite because at a certain point the needs of nature are satisfied. But the desire for artificial wealth is infinite because it is subject to disordered concupiscence which observes no measure, as the Philosopher shows.[5] There is a difference, however, between the infinite desire for wealth and the infinite desire for the ultimate good, since the more perfectly the ultimate good is possessed the more it is loved and other things despised, for the more it is possessed the more it is known. Hence it is said in *Ecclesiasticus 24: 29* "They that eat me shall yet hunger." But with respect to desire for wealth and any temporal good it is the converse, for as soon as any such thing is possessed it is despised and other things are desired. This is what is signified in *John 4:13* when Our Lord says, "Whosoever drinks of this water," by which temporal things are signified, "shall thirst again." The reason for this is that we recognize their insufficiency more when we possess them; this very fact shows their imperfection and that the ultimate good does not consist in them.

Second Article

DOES MAN'S HAPPINESS CONSIST IN HONORS?

It seems that man's happiness consists in honors.

1. Happiness is "the reward of virtue," as the Philosopher says.[6] But honor most of all seems to be the reward of virtue, as the Philosopher also says.[7] Therefore happiness consists principally in honor.

---

[5] *Ibid.* (1258a 1).

[6] Aristotle, *Nicomachean Ethics* I, 8 (1099a 16).

[7] *Op. cit.* IV, 3 (1123b 35).

2. Happiness, which is the perfect good, seems to belong to God and to persons of great excellence. But honor is of this sort, as the Philosopher says.[8] And even the Apostle says (*I Timothy 1:17*), "To . . . the only God be honor and glory." Therefore happiness consists in honor.

3. Happiness is what men most of all desire. But nothing seems to be more desirable to men than honor, for men suffer the loss of all other things rather than suffer any loss of honor. Therefore happiness consists in honor.

On the contrary: Happiness is in the one who is happy. But honor is not in the one who is honored but, rather, in the one honoring, who shows deference to him, as the Philosopher says.[9] Therefore happiness does not consist in honor.

Response: It is impossible that happiness consist in honor, for honor is conferred on someone because of some excellence he has, and so is a sign and a kind of testimony of the honored person's excellence. A man's excellence is measured in terms of happiness, which is his complete good, and in relation to its parts, that is, to those goods by which he has some share in happiness. Therefore honor may follow upon happiness, but happiness cannot consist principally in honor.

Reply to 1: As the Philosopher says in the same place, honor is not the reward of virtue in the sense that virtuous works are done for the sake of honor. On the contrary, such works receive honor from men in place of reward, as from those who have nothing greater to give. But the true reward of virtue is happiness, for which the virtuous work is done. If such works were done for honor, this would no longer be virtue but ambition.

Reply to 2: Honor is owed to God and to persons of great excellence as a sign or testimony of the excellence they already have; honor does not make them excellent.

Reply to 3: Because of the natural desire for happiness, of which honor is a consequence, as we have said, it is possible for men to desire honor especially. Hence men seek particularly to be honored by the wise, by whose judgment they believe themselves to be excellent or happy.

Third Article

DOES MAN'S HAPPINESS CONSIST IN FAME OR GLORY?

It seems that man's happiness consists in glory.

1. Happiness seems to consist in that which is conferred upon the saints for the tribulations they suffered in this world. This is what glory is, for the Apostle says (*Romans 8:18*), "the sufferings of the present time are not worthy to be compared with the glory to come that will be revealed in us." Therefore happiness consists in glory.

---

[8] *Op. cit.* IV, 3 (1123b 20). [9] *Op. cit.* I, 5 (1095b 25).

2. Good is diffusive of itself, as Dionysius states.[10] But by glory, more than anything else, the goodness of a man is diffused through others knowing of him, since glory, according to Ambrose, consists in "being well known and praised." [11] Therefore happiness consists in glory.

3. Happiness is the most stable good. But this is what fame and glory seem to be, for through fame and glory men in some way achieve immortality. Hence Boethius says, "You seem to beget immortality for yourselves when you consider the renown of future time." [12] Therefore man's happiness consists in fame or glory.

On the contrary: Happiness is man's true good. But fame or glory may be false for, as Boethius says, "Many often owe their great name to the false opinions of the multitude. Can anything be more shameful? For they who are falsely acclaimed ought to blush at their own praises." [13] Therefore man's happiness does not consist in fame or glory.

Response: It is impossible that man's happiness consist in human fame or glory, for glory is "being well known and praised," as Ambrose says.[14] Now a thing known is related to human knowledge in one way and to divine knowledge in another, for human knowledge is caused by things known whereas divine knowledge is the cause of things that are known. Hence the fullness of human good which is called happiness cannot be caused by human knowledge; rather, human knowledge of someone's happiness proceeds and is in some way caused by human happiness itself, whether in a beginning or a perfect stage. Consequently man's happiness cannot consist in fame or glory. However, man's good depends on God's knowledge as its cause; therefore man's happiness depends, for its cause, on the glory man has before God, in accordance with *Psalms 90:15-16,* "I will deliver him and I will glorify him. I will fill him with length of days, and I will show him my salvation."

We should also take into account that human knowledge is often in error, especially in regard to singular contingent things, which is what human acts are. For this reason, human glory is frequently fallacious. But because God cannot be in error, the glory coming from Him is always true. Therefore it is said (*II Corinthians 10:18*), "He is approved whom God commends."

Reply to 1: The Apostle is not speaking of the glory which is from men but of the glory which is from God before His angels. Hence it is said, "The Son of Man shall confess him in the glory of His Father, before His angels." [15]

Reply to 2: If the knowledge many have of the goodness of a man

---

[10] *The Divine Names* IV, 1.

[11] Cf. Augustine, *Contra Maximin. Arian.* II, 13.

[12] *The Consolation of Philosophy* II, prose 7.

[13] *Op. cit.* III, prose 6.   [14] See note 11 above.

[15] This quotation combines passages from *Mark 8:38* and *Luke 12:8.* St. Thomas may also be quoting from memory

through fame or glory is true knowledge, it must be derived from the goodness in that man and so presuppose either complete happiness or happiness in a beginning state. If the knowledge is false, it does not correspond to reality, and so goodness is not in him whose fame is celebrated. Hence it is evident that fame by no means makes a man happy.

Reply to 3: Fame is not stable; in fact it is easily lost by false rumor. And if it sometimes remains stable, this is accidental. But happiness has stability of itself and always.

Fourth Article

DOES MAN'S HAPPINESS CONSIST IN POWER?

It seems that man's happiness consists in power.

1. All things seek to be conformed to God, as to an ultimate end and first principle. But men who hold power seem most of all to resemble God by reason of likeness of power. Hence in Scripture they are called gods, "Thou shalt not speak ill of the gods" (*Exodus 22:28*). Therefore happiness consists in power.

2. Happiness is the perfect good. But the most perfect thing for man is to be able to rule others, which belongs to those who are established in power. Therefore happiness consists in power.

3. Happiness, since it is most of all desirable, is opposed above everything else to what is to be shunned. But men most of all flee from servitude, which is opposed to power. Therefore happiness consists in power.

On the contrary: Happiness is the perfect good. But power is most imperfect for, as Boethius says, "human power cannot drive away the gnawing of cares, evade the pain of fears," and further on, "Think you a man is powerful who is surrounded by attendants, whom he inspires with fear, but whom he fears more." [16] Happiness, then, does not consist in power.

Response: It is impossible, for two reasons, that happiness consists in power. First because power has the nature of a principle, as is evident in the *Metaphysics*,[17] whereas happiness has the nature of an ultimate end. Second, because power is related both to good and evil, whereas happiness is the proper and perfect good of man. Consequently there might be some happiness in the good use of power—which would be through virtue—rather than in power itself.

Now four general reasons can be given to show that happiness does not consist in any of the foregoing external goods.[18] First, since happiness is man's highest good, it is not compatible with any evil. But all of the foregoing are found in both good and evil men. Second, it is of the

---

[16] *The Consolation of Philosophy* III, prose 5.

[17] Aristotle, *Metaphysics* V, 12 (1019a 15).

[18] Namely, wealth, honor, glory, and power.

nature of happiness that it be self-sufficient, as is evident in the *Ethics*.[19] Having gained happiness, therefore, man cannot lack any necessary good. But after gaining any one of the foregoing, man may still lack many necessary goods, for instance, wisdom, health, and such things. Third, since happiness is the perfect good, no evil can come to man from it. This does not apply to the foregoing goods for, as is said in *Ecclesiastes 5:12*, riches are sometimes kept "to the hurt of the owner," and the same is true of the other three. Fourth, man is ordered to happiness by principles which are within him since he is ordered to it naturally. But the four goods we have dealt with are attributed more to exterior causes, and for the most part to fortune. Clearly, then, happiness can in no way consist in any of these.

Reply to 1: God's power is His goodness; hence He cannot use His power otherwise than well. But it is not so with men. Hence it would not be sufficient for man's happiness to become like God with respect to power unless man also became like God in goodness.

Reply to 2: Just as it is a most excellent thing for someone to use power well in ruling others, so also it is evil in the highest degree to use it badly. Therefore power is related to both good and evil.

Reply to 3: Servitude is an impediment to the good use of power. This is why men naturally flee from servitude, not because power is man's highest good.

Fifth Article

DOES MAN'S HAPPINESS CONSIST IN SOME GOOD OF THE BODY?

It seems that man's happiness consists in a good of the body.

1. It says in Scripture: "There is no riches above the riches of health of the body" (*Ecclesiasticus 30:16*). But happiness consists in what is best. Therefore it consists in health of the body.

2. Dionysius says that to be is better than to live and to live is better than the other things following upon it.[20] But for man, to be and to live require health of the body. Therefore, since happiness is man's highest good, it seems that health of body particularly belongs to happiness.

3. The more universal something is the more it depends on a higher principle, because the higher the cause the more extensive its power. Now just as the causality of an efficient cause has reference to what flows from it, so the causality of the final cause has reference to desire. Therefore, just as the first efficient cause is that which flows into all things, so the ultimate final cause is what is desired by all things. But all things desire most of all to be. Therefore man's happiness consists more than anything else in those things which belong to his being, such as health of the body.

---

[19] Aristotle, *Nicomachean Ethics* I, 7 (1097b 8).
[20] *The Divine Names* V, 3.

On the contrary: Man surpasses all other animals as far as happiness is concerned. But he is surpassed by many animals in bodily goods, by the elephant in longevity, by the lion in strength, and by the deer in speed. Therefore man's happiness does not consist in some good of the body.

Response: It is impossible, for two reasons, that man's happiness consists in some good of the body. First, it is impossible for the ultimate end of one thing ordered to another, as to its end, to consist in the preservation of that thing's being. For example, the captain of a ship does not intend, as an ultimate end, the preservation of the ship entrusted to him, because the ship is ordered to something else as an end, namely, to navigation. Now just as the ship is committed to the captain for steering a course so man is committed to his reason and will, according to Scripture: "God made man from the beginning and left him in the hand of his own counsel" *(Ecclesiasticus 15:14)*. But clearly man is ordered to something else as an end, since man is not the supreme good. Hence it is impossible that the ultimate end of man's reason and will be the preservation of the human being.

The second reason is as follows. Even granting that the end of man's reason and will is the preservation of the human being, it still could not be said that the end of man is some good of the body. For a human being consists of soul and body, and although the existence of the body depends upon the soul, the existence of the soul does not depend on the body, as we have already shown.[21] Accordingly, the body is for the sake of the soul, as matter is for the sake of form, and instruments for the sake of the moving agent so that by their means he may do his work. Hence all goods of the body are ordered to goods of the soul as to an end. Therefore happiness, which is the ultimate end of man, cannot consist in goods of the body.

Reply to 1: As the body is ordered to the soul as to an end, so exterior goods are ordered to the body. It is reasonable, therefore, to prefer goods of the body to exterior goods, which is signified here by "riches," and to prefer the good of the soul to all goods of the body.

Reply to 2: "Being," taken absolutely, as including every perfection of being, surpasses life and all ensuing perfections, for taken in this way it includes in itself all of these. This is the point of view Dionysius is taking. But if being is considered as participated in by this or that thing which does not possess the whole perfection of being, but only imperfect being, such as the being of any creature, then clearly "being" along with additional perfections is more excellent. Hence Dionysius says in the same passage that living things are better than those that just exist and intelligent things are better than living things.

Reply to 3: Since the end corresponds to the beginning, this argument

[21] Part I, question 75, article 2; question 76, article 1, replies to 5 and 6; question 90, article 2, reply to 2.

proves that the ultimate end is the first principle of being, in Whom is every perfection of being, Whose likeness all things in proportion desire —some by being only, some by being alive, some by being alive and intelligent and happy, and this belongs to few.

Sixth Article

DOES MAN'S HAPPINESS CONSIST IN PLEASURE?

It seems that man's happiness consists in pleasure.[22]

1. Happiness, since it is an ultimate end, is not desired for something else, but other things for it. But this belongs more to delight[23] than to anything else, "for it is absurd to ask someone why he wishes to be pleased." [24] Therefore happiness consists most of all in pleasure and delight.

2. "The primary cause makes a more forceful impression than the second." [25] Now the influence of the end is thought of as attracting desire for it. Therefore that which more than anything else moves desire seems to have the notion of an ultimate end. But this is pleasure, and a sign of this is that the delight in it so absorbs man's reason and will that it causes him to despise other goods. It seems, therefore, that man's ultimate end, which is happiness, consists in pleasure.

3. Since desire is of the good, it seems that all desire what is best. But all desire the delight of pleasure, both the wise and the foolish, and even irrational creatures. Therefore such delight is better than all other goods. Accordingly happiness, which is the highest good, consists in pleasure.

On the contrary: Boethius says, "Anyone who chooses to look back at his past excesses would perceive that such pleasures have a sad ending, and if these can make men happy, there is reason for saying that beasts too are happy." [26]

Response: "Because bodily delights are more known, the name "pleasure" has been appropriated to them," [27] although other delights excel

---

[22] The Latin word is "voluptas." The meaning intended, therefore, is sense pleasure or gratification of the senses—not immoderate gratification or delight. The body of this article explains how and why "pleasure" first means sense delight, although the name can be extended to signify intellectual delight as well, which, however, is not the principal concern here.

[23] The Latin word is "delectatio" and means "delight," "satisfaction," or sometimes "gratification." A certain sort of delight is what St. Thomas usually means by "delectatio," though, like "pleasure," it may belong either to intellect or sense. The latter is primarily intended here.

[24] Aristotle, *Nicomachean Ethics* X, 2 (1172b 23).

[25] *The Book on Causes (Liber De Causis)* prop. I. This is the opening sentence of the work. Cf. *Expositio Super Librum De Causis*, Lesson I, by St. Thomas (Opusculum X in the Mandonnet edition).

[26] *The Consolation of Philosophy* III, prose 7.

[27] Aristotle, *op. cit.* VII, 13 (1153b 33).

them. Happiness, however, does not consist in them. For there is a distinction between what pertains to the essence of a thing and its proper accident; thus, in man, to be a mortal rational animal is other than to be risible. It must be noted, then, that delight is a proper accident which follows upon happiness or some part of happiness, for a man is delighted when he possesses some good suitable to him, either in fact or in hope, or at least in memory. Now a suitable good, if it is the perfect good, is precisely man's happiness; and if imperfect it is a certain participation in happiness, either proximate or remote, or at least seemingly so. Clearly, then, even the delight which follows upon the perfect good is not the essence of happiness, but something resulting from it as a proper accident.

But bodily pleasure cannot follow upon the perfect good even in that way, for such pleasure follows upon a good apprehended by sense, which is a power of the soul using the body. Now a good pertaining to the body, which is apprehended by sense, cannot be man's complete good. For the rational soul exceeds the proportion of corporeal matter, and therefore that part of the soul which is independent of a corporeal organ has a certain infinity with respect to the body and to the parts of the soul concretized in the body, just as immaterial things are in a certain way infinite as compared to material things, because through matter forms are in a certain way contracted and limited, and hence a form independent of matter is in a way infinite. For this reason sense, which is a corporeal power, knows the singular which is determined by matter; whereas the intellect, which is a power free from matter, knows the universal which is separated from matter and contains under it an infinity of singulars. Hence it is evident that a good suitable to the body, which being apprehended by sense, causes bodily delight, is not the complete good of man but a certain minimal part as compared to the good of the soul. Hence it is said that "all gold in comparison to wisdom is as a little sand" (*Wisdom 7:9*). Therefore bodily pleasure is neither happiness itself nor a proper accident of happiness.

Reply to 1: We desire good for the same reason we desire delight, which is simply the resting of the appetite in a good, just as it is due to the same natural force that a heavy body is borne downward, and rests there. Hence just as good is sought for itself, so also delight is sought for itself and not for anything else, if "for" expresses a final cause. But if "for" expresses a formal cause, or more the moving cause, delight is desirable for something else—for the good—which is the object of delight and consequently its principle, and gives it its form; for delight is desired because it is a resting in the desired good.

Reply to 2: The vehemence of desire for sense delight arises from the fact that the operations of the senses, because they are principles of our knowledge, are more receptive. This is the reason sense delights are desired by the majority.

Reply to 3: All desire delight in the same way as they desire good; yet they desire delight by reason of the good and not conversely, as said in the first reply above. Hence it does not follow that delight is a maximum and per se good, but that every delight results from some good, and that some delight follows upon a per se and maximum good.

Seventh Article

DOES MAN'S HAPPINESS CONSIST IN SOME GOOD OF THE SOUL?

It seems that happiness consists in some good of the soul.

1. Happiness is a certain kind of human good. Such good is divided into three kinds: external goods, goods of the body, and goods of the soul. But happiness does not consist in external goods nor goods of the body, as we have already shown.[28] Therefore happiness consists in goods of the soul.

2. We love that for which we desire some good more than the good we desire for it. For example, we love a friend for whom we desire money more than we love the money. But each one desires every good for himself. Therefore he loves himself more than all other goods. Now happiness is what is loved above all, and this is evident from the fact that for its sake all other things are loved and desired. Therefore happiness consists in a good of man himself; but not in goods of the body, and therefore in goods of the soul.

3. Perfection or fulfillment is something belonging to that which is fulfilled. But happiness is a perfection of man. Therefore happiness is something belonging to man. But it is not something of the body. Therefore happiness is something pertaining to the soul, and so consists in goods of the soul.

On the contrary: Augustine says, "That which constitutes a life of happiness is to be loved for itself." [29] Man, however, is not to be loved for his own sake, but whatever is in man is to be loved for the sake of God. Therefore happiness does not consist in any good of the soul.

Response: As we have already said,[30] "end" is said in two ways, of the thing itself which we desire to obtain, and of the use, attainment, or possession of that thing. If we are speaking of the ultimate end of man as the thing itself that we desire as an ultimate end, it is impossible that the ultimate end of man be the soul or something pertaining to the soul. For the soul, considered in itself, is like a being in potency, for it becomes knowing in act from knowing in potency, and virtuous in act from virtuous in potency. But since potency is for the sake of act, as its fulfillment, it is impossible that what is in itself a being which is in potency have the nature of an ultimate end. Hence it is impossible that the soul be its own ultimate end.

---

[28] Articles 4 and 5.   [29] *On Christian Doctrine* I, 22.
[30] Question I, article 8.

Nor can anything belonging to the soul be the ultimate end, whether power, habit, or act, for the good which is the ultimate end is a complete good fulfilling the appetite. Now human appetite, or will, is for a universal good. But any good inhering in the soul is a participated good, and hence a partial good. Consequently none of the goods belonging to the soul can be the ultimate end of man.

But if we are speaking of the ultimate end of man as the attainment, possession, or any use of the thing which is desired as an end, then something on the part of the soul of man does pertain to the ultimate end, since man attains happiness through the soul. Therefore the thing itself, desired as an end, is that in which happiness consists and which makes men happy, but the attainment of that thing is called happiness. Hence we must say that happiness is something belonging to the soul, but that the object of happiness is something outside the soul.

Reply to 1: Inasmuch as this division comprehends all the goods that man can desire, the good of the soul includes not only power, habit, or act, but even the object which is extrinsic. And in this way nothing prevents us from saying that happiness consists in some good of the soul.

Reply to 2: With respect to this objection, happiness is taken as that which is loved above everything else, as the good that is desired. But a friend is loved as that for whom good is desired, and thus also man loves himself. Hence there is not the same kind of love in both instances. There will be occasion to consider whether man loves anything more than himself with a love of friendship when we treat of charity.

Reply to 3: Happiness itself, since it is a perfection of the soul, is a good inhering in the soul. But that in which happiness consists, which makes man happy, is something outside the soul, as we have said.

Eighth Article

DOES MAN'S HAPPINESS CONSIST IN ANY CREATED GOOD?

It seems that man's happiness consists in some created good.

1. Dionysius says that divine wisdom joins the ends of first things to the beginnings of second things,[31] from which we may gather that the highest of a lower nature touches the lowest of the higher nature. But man's highest good is happiness, and since the angel is above man in the order of nature, as we have already shown,[32] it seems that the happiness of man consists in his becoming in some way like an angel.

2. The ultimate end of anything is realized in the complete whole, and thus the part is for the whole as for its end. But the whole universe of creatures, which is called a macrocosm, is compared to man who is

---

[31] *The Divine Names* VII, 3.
[32] Part I, question 96, article 1, reply to *1;* question 108, article 2, reply to *3;* article 8, reply to *2;* question 111, article 1.

called a microcosm,[33] as perfect to imperfect. Therefore man's happiness consists in the whole universe of creatures.

3. Man is made happy by that which brings to rest his natural desire. But man's natural desire does not extend to a greater good than he is capable of, and since man is not capable of a good which exceeds the limits of the creature entirely, it seems that man can be made happy by some created good; and thus the happiness of man consists in some created good.

On the contrary: Augustine says, "As the soul is the life of the body, so God is man's life of happiness, concerning which it is said, 'Happy is that people whose God is the Lord'" (*Psalms 143:15*).[34]

Response: It is impossible for man's happiness to consist in a created good, for happiness is the perfect good which wholly brings desire to rest, for it would not be an ultimate end if something should still remain to be desired. Now the object of the will, or human appetite, is the universal good, just as the object of the intellect is universal truth. Hence it is evident that nothing can bring the will of man to rest except the universal good. This is not found in any created thing but only in God, for all creatures have goodness by participation. Hence only God can satisfy the will of man, as is said (*Psalms 102:5*), "Who satisfieth thy desire with good things." Therefore man's happiness consists in God alone.

Reply to 1: A man who is superior does approach the lowest in angelic nature by a kind of likeness, yet he does not stop there as though this were the ultimate end, but goes on to that universal source of good, who is the universal object of happiness of all the blessed, since He is the infinite and perfect good.

Reply to 2: If some whole is not the ultimate end but is ordered to a further end, the ultimate end of a part of that whole is not the whole itself, but something else. Now the whole universe of creatures, to which man is compared as a part to a whole, is not the ultimate end, but is ordered to God as to an ultimate end. Hence God Himself, not the good of the universe, is the ultimate end of man.

Reply to 3: A created good, as an intrinsic and inherent thing, is not less than the good that man is capable of, but as an object it is less than the good he is capable of, since he has the capacity for an infinite good. The good which is participated in by an angel and by the whole universe is a finite and restricted good.

---

[33] Cf. Aristotle, *Physics* VIII, 2 (252b 24).
[34] *The City of God* XIX, 26.

What Is Happiness

(In Eight Articles)

IS HAPPINESS SOMETHING UNCREATED?

It seems that happiness is something uncreated.

1. Boethius says, "We must acknowledge that God is happiness itself." [1]

2. Happiness is the supreme good. But only God is the supreme good. Since there cannot be several supreme goods, it therefore seems that happiness is identified with God.

3. Happiness is the ultimate end to which the human will tends naturally. But the will should not tend to anything else as an end except God, in Whom alone we should take delight, as Augustine remarks.[2] Therefore happiness is identified with God.

On the contrary: What is not made is uncreated. But man's happiness is something produced, for, according to Augustine, "The things we are to enjoy are those that produce happiness." [3] Therefore happiness is not something uncreated.

Response: "End" is said in two ways, as we have already pointed out.[4] It may refer to the object we wish to obtain, for example, money in the case of an avaricious man. Or it may refer to the attainment or possession, that is, the use or enjoyment of the object desired; for example, we say that possession of money is the end of the avaricious man, and enjoyment of sense pleasure the end of the intemperate man. In the first sense, the ultimate end of man is an uncreated good, namely, God, Who alone by His infinite goodness can perfectly fulfill man's will. In the second sense, the ultimate end of man is something created existing in him, that is, the attainment or enjoyment of the ultimate end. Now the ultimate end is called happiness. Therefore, if man's happiness is considered with respect to the cause or object, it is something uncreated; but if with respect to precisely what happiness is, it is something created.

Reply to 1: God is happiness by His own essence, for it is not by the attainment or participation of something else that He is happy, but by His own essence. Men, on the other hand, are happy by participation,

---

[1] *The Consolation of Philosophy* III, prose 10.

[2] *On Christian Doctrine* I, 5 and 22.   [3] *Op. cit.,* 3.

[4] Question 1, article 8; question 2, article 7.

as Boethius says;[5] so too they are called "gods" by participation. And this participation of happiness with respect to which man is called happy is something created.

Reply to 2: Happiness is said to be the supreme good of man because it is the attainment or enjoyment of the supreme good.

Reply to 3: Happiness is called an ultimate end in the same way as the attainment or enjoyment of the end is called an end.

Second Article

IS HAPPINESS AN ACTIVITY?

It seems that happiness is not an activity.[6]

1. The Apostle says (*Romans 6:22*), "You have your fruit unto sanctification, and as your end, life everlasting." Now life is not an activity but the very being of living things. Therefore the ultimate end, happiness, is not an activity.

2. Boethius says that happiness is "a state brought to completion by the aggregation of all goods." [7] But a state does not signify an activity. Therefore happiness is not an activity.

3. "Happiness" signifies something existing in the one who is happy, since it is the ultimate fulfillment or perfection of man. But "activity" does not signify something existing in the one acting, but rather something proceeding from him. Therefore happiness is not an activity.

4. Happiness is lasting in the one who is happy, while activity does not remain in the one who acts but is transitory. Therefore happiness is not an activity.

5. For one man there is one happiness. But his activities are many. Therefore happiness is not an activity.

6. Happiness is present without interruption in the one who is happy. But human activity is often interrupted, for example by sleep, by some other occupation, or by ceasing. Therefore happiness is not an activity.

On the contrary: The Philosopher says that "happiness is activity in accordance with complete virtue." [8]

Response: Man's happiness, inasmuch as it is something created that exists in him, must be an activity, for happiness is man's ultimate perfection. Now the perfection of a thing corresponds to its actuality, for potentiality without act is imperfect. Therefore happiness must consist in man's ultimate act. Now it is clear that activity is the ultimate act

---

[5] *Loc. cit.*

[6] The Latin word is "operatio," but "operation" in English would not always convey the proper meaning. "Activity" is used here in the sense of *immanent* action, that is, action originating within an agent but terminating there also, as for example, thinking, willing, or sensing. See the reply to 3 of this article.

[7] *The Consolation of Philosophy* III, prose 2.

[8] Aristotle, *Nicomachean Ethics* I, 13 (1102a 5).

of the one acting. Hence Aristotle calls it "second act," [9] because that which has a form is potentially capable of acting, just as one who possesses knowledge is in potency to considering that knowledge. This is also the reason in regard to other things as well, that each is said to be "for its activity." [10] Therefore man's happiness must consist in activity.

Reply to 1: "Life" is said in two ways. First, it is said of the very being of a living thing and thus happiness is not life, for we have already seen that the being of a man, no matter what it consists in, is not man's happiness;[11] only of God is His happiness His being. Second, it is said of the activity of the living being by which a principle of life is made actual; and thus we speak of the active life, the contemplative life or the life of pleasure. It is in this sense that eternal life is said to be the ultimate end, as is evident in Scripture: "This is everlasting life, that they may know thee, the only true God" (*John 17:3*).

Reply to 2: In defining happiness, Boethius considered the general notion of happiness. As a general notion, happiness is a complete universal good, which he signified by saying happiness is "a state brought to completion by the aggregation of all goods." What is signified by this is simply that the happy man is in a state of possessing complete or perfect good. Aristotle, on the other hand, expresses the very essence of happiness; he shows what it is that establishes man in such a state, because it is by some kind of activity. Hence he also shows that happiness is the complete good.[12]

Reply to 3: Action is of two kinds, as is said in the *Metaphysics*.[13] One kind proceeds from an agent into exterior matter, such as to burn and to cut. Such cannot be happiness, for it is not an actuality and perfection of the agent, but rather of what receives the action. The other kind of action remains in the agent. To sense, to think, or to will are examples of this. Activity of this kind is a perfection and actuality of the agent, and such an activity can be happiness.

Reply to 4: Since happiness signifies some ultimate perfection, it must be said in different ways corresponding to the diverse grades of perfection attainable by the diverse beings capable of happiness. In God there is happiness essentially, for His very being is His activity by which He delights in nothing other than Himself. The ultimate perfection of the angels who are happy is an activity whereby they are united to the uncreated good. In them this action is one and everlasting. In man's present state of life, his ultimate perfection is in the activity whereby he is united to God, but this activity cannot be continual and, consequently, is not just one, because activity is multiplied by being discontinuous. For this reason, man cannot have complete happiness in this life. Hence the Philosopher, when he considers man's happiness in this life, says it is imperfect, and after much discussion concludes that "we call men happy, but as *men*." [14] But God has promised us complete happiness, when we shall be "as the angels . . . in heaven" (*Matthew 22:30*).

The argument raised does not hold with respect to complete happiness, for in that state of happiness the mind of man will be united to God in one, continual, everlasting activity. In the present life, however, we lack complete happiness in proportion as we lack the unity and the continuity of that activity. Yet there is a participation in happiness, and it is greater in proportion as the activity can be more continuous and more one. Consequently there is less of the nature of happiness in the active life, which is occupied with many things, than in the contemplative life, which is concerned with one thing, the contemplation of truth. And although man is not always actually engaged in such activity, yet because he can easily return to it and because he even orders its ceasing, by sleep or some other natural occupation, such activity almost seems to be continual.

It is clear from this explanation what the replies are to the fifth and sixth arguments.

Third Article

IS HAPPINESS AN ACTIVITY OF THE SENSES OR ONLY OF THE INTELLECT?

It seems that happiness consists also in the activity[15] of the senses.

1. There is no activity in man more noble than that of the senses except intellectual activity. But intellectual activity in man depends upon the activity of the senses "because we cannot understand without a phantasm." [16] Therefore happiness consists also in the activity of the senses.

2. Boethius says that happiness is "a state brought to completion by the aggregation of all goods." [17] But some goods are sense goods which we attain by the activity of the senses. It seems, therefore, that the activity of the senses is required for happiness.

3. Happiness is "the perfect good," as is proved in the *Ethics*.[18] It could not be this unless man were perfected by it with respect to all his parts. But some parts of the soul are perfected by activity of the senses. Therefore sense activity is required for happiness.

On the contrary: Sense activity is common to man and brute animal. Happiness is not. Therefore happiness does not consist in sense activity.

---

[14] Aristotle, *Nicomachean Ethics* I, 10 (1101a 20).

[15] Here again "activity" is generally used for "operatio." See note 6 above.

[16] Aristotle, *On the Soul* III, 7 (431a 16).

[17] *The Consolation of Philosophy* III, prose 2.

[18] *Nicomachean Ethics* I, 7 (1097a 15-1098a 20).

Response: Something can pertain to happiness in three ways: (1) essentially, (2) antecedently, (3) consequently. The activity of the senses cannot pertain to happiness essentially, for man's happiness consists essentially in his being united with the uncreated good, which is his ultimate end, as we have already shown.[19] But man cannot be united with the uncreated good by his senses. Likewise, as we have shown,[20] man's happiness does not consist in goods of the body, which we attain only by sense activity, and therefore the activity of the senses does not belong to man's happiness essentially.

However, sense activity can belong to man's happiness antecedently and consequently. It belongs antecedently with respect to imperfect happiness, which can be had in this life, since sense activity is required for the operation of the intellect. It belongs consequently to that perfect happiness which we look for in heaven, because after the resurrection, "from the very happiness of the soul," as Augustine says, "there will come about a certain overflow in the body and the bodily senses such that they will be perfected in their operations." [21] This will be explained later, in treating the resurrection.[22] Then, however, the operation by which the human mind is united to God will not depend on the senses.

Reply to 1: This argument proves that the activity of the senses is required antecedently for the imperfect happiness which can be had in this life.

Reply to 2: Perfect happiness, such as the angels have, involves an aggregation of all goods through union with the universal source of all good; this does not require each particular good. But in imperfect happiness we need an accumulation of goods sufficient for the most perfect operation of this life.

Reply to 3: In perfect happiness the whole man is perfected, in the lower part of his nature by the overflow from the higher. But the reverse is true in the imperfect happiness of the present life; here we go from the perfection of the lower part to the perfection of the higher.

Fourth Article

GIVEN THAT HAPPINESS IS AN ACTIVITY OF THE
INTELLECTUAL PART, IS IT AN ACT OF
THE INTELLECT OR OF THE WILL?

It seems that happiness consists in an act of the will.

1. Augustine says that the happiness of man consists in peace.[23] Hence it says in Scripture: "Who hath placed peace in thy borders" [24] (*Psalms*

---

[19] Article 1.   [20] Question 2, article 5.
[21] *Epistle to Discorus* (Epistle 118, 3).
[22] This is treated in the *Supplement*, question 82.
[23] *The City of God* XIX, 10, 11.
[24] St. Thomas has *fines* for "borders," suggesting "ends" or "goals."

147:14). But peace belongs to the will. Therefore man's happiness consists in an act of the will.

2. Happiness is the supreme good. But good is the object of the will. Therefore happiness consists in an act of the will.

3. The ultimate end corresponds to the first mover; thus the ultimate end of the whole army is victory, which is the end of the general who moves all the men under his command. But the first mover in regard to operation is the will, since it moves the other powers, as we shall say later.[25] Therefore happiness pertains to the will.

4. If happiness is an activity, it must be man's most excellent activity. But love of God, which is an act of the will, is superior to knowledge, which is an act of the intellect; this is evident from what the Apostle says in *I Corinthians 13*. It seems, therefore, that happiness consists in an act of the will.

5. Augustine says, "Happy is he who has all that he wills and wills nothing evil;" and a little further on he adds, "He approaches being happy who wills well whatever he wills, for good things make him happy and such a man already possesses something good, namely, a good will." [26] Therefore, happiness consists in an act of the will.

On the contrary: Our Lord says: "This is eternal life, that they know thee, the one true God" (*John 17:3*). But eternal life is the ultimate end, as we have already said.[27] Man's happiness, therefore, consists in knowledge of God, which is an act of the intellect.

Response: Two things are required for happiness, as we have stated.[28] One refers to the very being of happiness and the other is a sort of per se accident of it, namely, the delight connected with it. Now with respect to what happiness is essentially, I maintain that it is impossible for it to consist in an act of the will. For it is evident from what has been said,[29] that happiness is the attainment of the ultimate end. But the attainment of the end does not consist in an act itself of the will, for the will is directed to the end both as absent and present—absent, when it desires it; and present, when it delights in resting in it. Now it is clear that desire for the end is not attainment of it, but a movement toward the end. Now delight is in the will as a result of the end being present; but the converse is not true, that a thing becomes present because the will delights in it. Therefore it must be something other than an act of the will by which the end becomes present to the one willing it.

This is clearly the case in regard to ends which are sensed, for if the acquiring of money were a result of an act of the will, an avaricious man would have it from the very moment he willed to have it. But as the out-

---

[25] Question 9, article 1, reply to 3.   [26] *The Trinity* XIII, 5.
[27] Article 2, reply to 1.   [28] Question 2, article 6.
[29] Articles 1 and 2; question 2, article 7.

set he does not have it; he attains it when he gets it in his hands or in some such way, and then he takes delight in the money possessed. It is the same with an intelligible end. At the outset, we wish to attain it; we attain it when it becomes present to us by an act of the intellect, and then the delighted will rests in the end now attained.

Consequently the essence of happiness consists in an act of the intellect, but the delight resulting from happiness belongs to the will. As Augustine says, happiness is "joy in the truth," [30] because joy itself is the fulfillment of happiness.

Reply to 1: Peace pertains to the ultimate end of man, not as though it were the essence of happiness, but because it is antecedent and consequent to it. It is antecedent insofar as all the things are removed which disturb and hinder man in attaining the ultimate end; it is consequent inasmuch as man is at peace when he has attained the ultimate end, all his desires being at rest.

Reply to 2: The will's first object is not its act, just as the first object of sight is not the act of seeing but a visible object. Hence, from the fact that happiness belongs to the will as its first object, it follows that it does not belong to it as its act.

Reply to 3: The intellect apprehends the end before the will does; movement toward the end, however, begins in the will. Therefore the delight or enjoyment, i.e., what last of all follows the attainment of the end, is due to the will.

Reply to 4: Love surpasses knowledge with respect to moving, but knowledge precedes love with respect to attaining, "for nothing is loved unless it is known," as Augustine says.[31] Hence we first come in contact with an intelligible end by an act of the intellect just as we first come in contact with a perceptible end by an act of the senses.

Reply to 5: The person who has whatever he wills is happy because he has what he desires; this in fact is through something other than an act of the will. But to will nothing evil is also required for happiness as a certain necessary disposition for it. And a good will, inasmuch as it is an inclination of the will, is posited among the good things that make a man happy, just as a movement is reduced to the genus of its term, for instance, alteration to quality.

---

[30] *Confessions* X, 23.　　　　　[31] *The Trinity* X, 1.

Fifth Article

IS HAPPINESS AN ACTIVITY OF THE SPECULATIVE
OR PRACTICAL INTELLECT? [32]

It seems that happiness consists in activity of the practical intellect.
1. The ultimate end of any creature consists in becoming like God.
But man is more like God with respect to his practical intellect, which is
the cause of things thought of, than his speculative intellect, which derives knowledge from things. Therefore man's happiness consists in
activity of his practical rather than his speculative intellect.

2. Happiness is man's complete good. But it is the practical intellect
that is ordered to the good, whereas the speculative intellect is ordered
to what is true. Hence we are said to be good with reference to a perfection of the practical intellect, not of the speculative, by which we are said
to be knowledgeable and intelligent. Consequently man's happiness consists in activity of the practical intellect rather than of the speculative intellect.

3. Happiness is the good of man himself. But the speculative intellect
is taken up with things outside of man while the practical intellect is
concerned with things belonging to man himself, that is, his actions and
passions. Therefore man's happiness consists in activity of his practical
intellect rather than of his speculative intellect.

On the contrary: Augustine says that "contemplation is promised us
as the goal of all our actions and the everlasting fulfillment of our
joys." [33]

Response: Happiness consists in activity of the speculative intellect
rather than the practical. This is evident for three reasons. First, if man's
happiness is an activity, it must be man's highest activity; his highest
activity is that of his highest power with respect to its highest object; his
highest power is his intellect and its highest object is the divine good,
which is an object of the speculative, not the practical, intellect. Hence
happiness consists in such an activity, that is, in the contemplation of
divine things principally. And since "each man seems to be what is best
in him," [34] such an activity is more proper and satisfying to man than
any other.

Second, contemplation is most of all sought for itself. The act of the
practical intellect, on the other hand, is sought not for its own sake but
for the sake of action; and these actions too are for the sake of some end.

---

[32] On the distinction between speculative and practical intellect, see I, question 79,
article 11. They are not distinct powers, but one power related to different ends; the
intellect as speculative to knowing truth, as practical to action.

[33] *The Trinity* X, 8.

[34] Aristotle, *Nicomachean Ethics* IX, 8 (1169a 1); X, 7 (1178a 2).

Clearly, then, the ultimate end cannot consist in the active life, which belongs to the practical intellect.

Third, in the contemplative life man has something in common with higher beings, with God and the angels, to whom he is assimilated through happiness. But the other animals share with man in some way, though imperfectly, what belongs to the active life.

Therefore, ultimate and complete happiness, which we look for in a future life, consists entirely in contemplation. Imperfect happiness, such as can be had in this life, consists principally in contemplation, but secondarily in the operation of the practical intellect directing human actions and passions, as is said in the *Ethics*.[35]

Reply to 1: The likening of the practical intellect to God, spoken of in the objection, is according to proportionality, that is, the practical intellect is related to what it knows as God to what He knows. But the likening of the speculative intellect to God is according to union or representation, which is a much greater likeness. In addition, we may answer that with respect to the principal thing known, which is His essence, God has only speculative knowledge, not practical.

Reply to 2: The practical intellect is ordered to a good outside of itself, whereas the speculative intellect has a good within it, the contemplation of truth. And if this good is perfect, the whole man is thereby perfected and made good; the practical intellect does not have such a good but directs man to it.

Reply to 3: This argument would be valid if man were his own ultimate end, for in that case the consideration and ordering of his actions and passions would be his happiness. But since man's ultimate end is an extrinsic good—God, whom we attain by an act of the speculative intellect—his happiness consists in activity of the speculative rather than of the practical intellect.

Sixth Article

DOES HAPPINESS CONSIST IN SCIENTIFIC KNOWLEDGE?

It seems that man's happiness consists in scientific knowledge.[36]

1. Aristotle says that "happiness is activity in accordance with complete virtue." [37] When he distinguishes the virtues he lists only the three speculative virtues—science, wisdom and understanding—all of which pertain to theoretical knowledge. Therefore man's happiness consists in knowledge of the theoretical sciences.

2. That which everyone desires for its own sake seems to be man's ul-

---

[35] *Op. cit.* X, 7 (1177a 12); 8 (1178a 9).

[36] The Latin word is "consideratio," which can be taken as "knowledge" throughout this article.

[37] *Nicomachean Ethics* I, 13 (1102a 5).

timate happiness. But such is the knowledge of science, for "all men by nature desire to know," as is said in the *Metaphysics*,[38] and a little farther on it is stated that theoretical science is sought for its own sake.[39] Happiness therefore consists in scientific knowledge.

3. Happiness is the ultimate perfection of man. Now a thing is perfected to the degree that it is brought from potency to act, and the human intellect is actualized by knowledge of the theoretical sciences. Therefore man's ultimate happiness seems to consist in scientific knowledge.

On the contrary: It is said in Scripture, "Let not the wise man glory in his wisdom" (*Jeremias 9:23*), and this is said in reference to the wisdom of theoretical science. Consequently man's ultimate happiness does not consist in such knowledge.

Response: Man's happiness is twofold, as we have already said.[40] One is perfect or complete, the other imperfect. By perfect happiness we understand that which attains the true nature of happiness; imperfect happiness, that which does not attain this but participates in some partial likeness of happiness. Thus perfect prudence is found in man, who reasons about things to be done; imperfect prudence is found in some of the brute animals who have certain particular instincts for works similar to those of prudence.

Consequently perfect happiness cannot consist essentially in scientific knowledge. To establish this we must note that scientific knowledge does not extend beyond the power of its principles. Now the first principles of sciences are gotten through the senses, as Aristotle clearly states at the beginning of the *Metaphysics* and at the end of the *Posterior Analytics*.[41] Hence the knowledge of science can only extend as far as the knowledge of sensed things can lead.[42] But man's ultimate happiness, which is his ultimate fulfillment, cannot consist in the knowledge of perceptible things, for a thing is not perfected by something lower except insofar as the lower participates in something higher. Now it is clear that the form of a stone or of any perceptible thing is lower than man. Hence the intellect is not perfected by the form of a stone insofar as it is the form of a stone, but insofar as the form shares a likeness of something above the human intellect, namely, the intelligible light,[43] or something of this kind. Now whatever is by reason of something else is led back to what is per se. Therefore man's ultimate perfection has to be through knowledge of something above the human intellect. But it has been shown above[44]

---

[38] *Metaphysics* I, 1 (980a 21).   [39] *Op. cit.*, 2 (982a 15).

[40] Question 2, article 4.

[41] *Metaphysics* I, 1 (981a 1); *Posterior Analytics* II, 15 (100a 7).

[42] This is another way of saying that all human knowledge originates with sense knowing.

[43] See II-II, question 173, article 2, for the meaning of "intelligible light," which refers to understanding as strengthened by revelation.

[44] I, question 88, article 2.

that through things that can be sensed man cannot arrive at knowledge of the separated substances, which are above the human intellect. Hence it follows that the ultimate happiness of man cannot be in the knowledge of theoretical science. But just as in forms that can be sensed there is shared a certain likeness to higher substances, so the knowledge of theoretical science is a certain participation in true and perfect happiness.

Reply to 1: Aristotle is speaking in the *Ethics* of imperfect happiness, such as can be had in this life, as we have said above.[45]

Reply to 2: Not only is complete happiness desired naturally, but also any likeness or participation of it.

Reply to 3: Our intellect is actualized in some measure by knowledge of theoretical science, but it does not reach its ultimate and complete actuality through such knowledge.

Seventh Article

DOES HAPPINESS CONSIST IN KNOWLEDGE ABOUT THE SEPARATED SUBSTANCES, NAMELY, THE ANGELS?

It seems that the happiness of man consists in knowledge about the separated substances,[46] namely, the angels.

1. Gregory says, "It profits us nothing to take part in the feast of men if we may not take part in the feast of the angels," [47] designating by this final happiness. But we can take part in the feasts of the angels by contemplating them. Therefore the ultimate happiness of man seems to consist in contemplation of the angels.

2. The ultimate perfection of each thing is to be united to its principle. Thus a circle is said to be a perfect figure because its beginning is the same as its end. But the principle by which men know is from the angels by whom men are illumined, as Dionysius says.[48] Therefore the ultimate perfection of the human intellect is in contemplation of the angels.

3. Each nature is perfected when it is joined to a superior nature; thus, the ultimate perfection of a body is to be joined to a spiritual nature. But in the order of nature angels are above the human intellect. Therefore the ultimate perfection of the human intellect consists in contemplating the angels.

On the contrary: It is written, "Let him that glorieth, glory in this, that he understandeth and knoweth Me" (*Jeremias 9:24*). Therefore the ultimate glory of man, or happiness, consists only in the knowledge of God.

---

[45] Article 2, reply to *4*.

[46] Angels are understood in philosophy as separated substances because they are wholly separated from matter, and consequently are totally immaterial or spiritual substances.

[47] *Homily 26.*   [48] *On the Celestial Hierarchy* IV, 2.

Response: As we said in the preceding article, man's complete happiness does not consist in what perfects the intellect by way of participation in something, but in that which perfects it essentially. Now it is evident that whatever is the perfection of a power is so inasmuch as it has the nature of the proper object of that power. Now the proper object of the intellect is the true. Therefore the contemplation of whatever has participated truth does not perfect the intellect with its final perfection. Since the order of things with respect to being and truth is the same,[49] whatever are beings by participation are true by participation. But the angels have participated being, for in God alone is His being His essence, as we have already shown.[50] It follows, then, that God alone is truth by essence and that contemplation of Him makes man perfectly happy. However there is no reason why we should not admit some kind of imperfect happiness in the contemplation of the angels, and an even greater happiness than in the knowledge of speculative science.

Reply to 1: We take part in the feasts of the angels when we contemplate not only the angels but, together with them, God.

Reply to 2: According to those who hold that human souls are created by angels, it seems appropriate enough that the happiness of man should be in the contemplation of the angels, which is a kind of union of man with his first principle. But this is erroneous, as we have already said.[51] Hence the ultimate perfection of the human intellect is through union with God, who is the first principle both of creation of the soul and illumination of it. The angel illumines as ministering, a point we have already made.[52] By his ministration, then, the angel aids man in attaining happiness, but he is not the object of human happiness.

Reply to 3: A higher nature may be attained by a lower in two ways. In one way, according to the degree of the power of participating, and thus man's ultimate perfection will be in his attaining to a contemplation such as that of the angels. In another way, as the object is attained by the power, and thus the ultimate perfection of any power is to attain that in which its object is fully found.

Eighth Article

DOES THE HAPPINESS OF MAN CONSIST IN THE VISION
OF THE DIVINE ESSENCE?

It seems that the happiness of man does not consist in the vision of the divine essence.

1. Dionysius says that man by the highest part of his intellect is united

---

[49] Cf. Aristotle, *Metaphysics* II, 1 (993b 30).

[50] I, question 44, article 1; cf. I, question 3, article 4; question 7, article 1, reply to 3; article 2.

[51] I, question 90, article 3.   [52] I, question 111, article 2, reply to 2.

to God as to something wholly unknown.[53] But what is seen essentially is not wholly unknown. Therefore the ultimate perfection of the intellect, happiness, cannot consist in God's being seen essentially.

2. A perfection in a higher nature is higher. But to see His own essence is a perfection proper to the divine intellect. Therefore the ultimate perfection of the human intellect does not extend this far, but stops with something else.

On the contrary: "When He shall appear, we shall be like Him; because we shall see Him as He is" (*I John 3:2*).

Response: Ultimate and perfect happiness can only be in the vision of the divine essence. To make this evident, two points must be noted. First, man is not perfectly happy as long as something remains for him to desire and seek; second, the perfection of a power is judged in terms of its object. Now the object of the intellect is *what a thing is,* that is, the essence of a thing.[54] Hence the intellect is perfected in the measure that it knows the essence of a thing. If, then, an intellect knows the essence of some effect but through it is not able to know the essence of the cause, that is, to know the *what it is* of the cause, that intellect is not said to know the cause absolutely, although it may be able to gather from the effect the knowledge that the cause exists. Consequently, when man knows an effect and knows that it has a cause, he still has a natural desire to know the cause as to *what it is.* And that desire is one of wonder, and is a cause of inquiry, as is said in the *Metaphysics.*[55] For example, if a man, knowing that the sun is eclipsed, takes into account that it comes from some cause which he does not know as to what it is, he wonders about it, and from wondering begins to inquire about it, and he goes on inquiring until he comes to know the essence of the cause.

If therefore the human intellect knows the essence of some created effect and knows no more about God than that He exists, the perfection of that intellect has not reached the point of knowing the first cause absolutely, and there still remains in it a natural desire to seek out the cause. Hence it is not yet completely happy. Consequently, for perfect happiness, the intellect must reach the very essence of the first cause. Thus its perfection will be had by its union with God as an object, and only in this does man's happiness consist, as has been pointed out.[56]

Reply to 1: Dionysius is speaking here of the knowledge of those who are on the way to happiness.

Reply to 2: As we have said,[57] an end can be taken in two ways. First, of the thing itself which is desired, and taken in this way a higher and a lower nature, and indeed all things, have the same end, as we have said

---

[53] *Mystical Theology* I, 3.
[54] Cf. Aristotle, *On the Soul* III, 6 (430b 27).
[55] *Metaphysics* I, 2 (982b 12; 983a 12).   [56] Articles 1 and 7; question 2, article 8.
[57] Question 1, article 8.

before.[58] Second, of the attainment of that thing, and taken in this way the end of a higher nature and a lower nature are diverse, corresponding to their different relationship to that thing. Thus the happiness of God, comprehending His essence, is higher than man's or an angel's who see but do not comprehend it.

------

[58] *Ibid.*

What Is Required for Happiness

(In Eight Articles)

IS DELIGHT REQUIRED FOR HAPPINESS?

It seems that delight is not required for happiness.

1. Augustine says that "vision is the entire reward of faith."[1] But the prize or reward of virtue is happiness, as Aristotle shows.[2] Therefore nothing besides vision is required for happiness.

2. Happiness is "the most self-sufficient of all goods," as the Philosopher says.[3] But that which needs something else is not self-sufficient. Since, then, the essence of happiness consists in the vision of God, as we have already shown,[4] it seems that delight is not required for happiness.

3. "The activity of felicity," or happiness, "has to be one that is not impeded," as is said in the *Ethics*.[5] But delight hinders the action of the intellect, for "it destroys the judgment of prudence," as is said in the *Ethics*.[6] Therefore delight is not required for happiness.

On the contrary: Augustine says that happiness is "joy in the truth."[7]

Response: One thing may be required for another in four ways. First, as preliminary and a preparation for it, and thus teaching is necessary for science. Second, as perfecting it, and thus the soul is necessary for life of the body. Third, as an extrinsic aid, and thus friends are needed for some undertaking. Fourth, as something concomitant, and thus we might say that heat is needed for fire. It is in this last way that delight is required for happiness. For it is caused by desire being at rest in the good attained, and since happiness is the attainment of the highest good, it cannot be without a concomitant delight.

Reply to 1: When a reward is given to someone, the will of the one rewarded is at rest, and this is what delight is. Delight is therefore included in the very notion of a reward given.

Reply to 2: The very sight of God causes delight. Hence he who sees God cannot be without delight.

Reply to 3: The delight accompanying the activity of the intellect does not hinder it but, rather, strengthens it, as is said in the *Ethics*,[8] for what

---

[1] *The Trinity* I, 8.
[3] *Op. cit.,* 7 (1097b 8).
[5] VII, 13 (1153b 16).
[7] *Confessions* X. 23.

[2] *Nicomachean Ethics* I, 9 (1099b 16).
[4] Question 3, article 8.
[6] VI, 5 (1140b 12).
[8] X, 4 (1174b 23).

we do with delight we do with greater care and perseverance. But a delight that is extraneous to the intellect's activity is a hindrance. Sometimes it is because it distracts our attention, since, as we have said, we are more attentive to things that delight us; and when we are very intent on one thing, of necessity our attention is withdrawn from another. Other times it is a hindrance because it is contrary; thus a sensual delight that is contrary to reason hinders the judgment of prudence more than it hinders the judgment of the speculative intellect.

Second Article

IS VISION OR IS DELIGHT PRIMARY IN HAPPINESS?

It seems that in happiness delight is primary rather than vision.

1. Delight is the fulfillment of activity, as is said in the *Ethics*.[9] But fulfillment is more important than what can be fulfilled. Therefore delight is primary rather than the activity of the intellect, which is vision.

2. That by reason of which something is desirable is more desirable. But activity is desired because of the delight it gives; hence nature has joined delight to activities necessary for the preservation of the individual and the species, so that such activities would not be neglected by animals. Therefore, in happiness, delight is more important than the activity of the intellect, which is vision.

3. Vision corresponds to faith while delight or enjoyment corresponds to charity. But charity is greater than faith, as the Apostle says.[10] Therefore delight or enjoyment is superior to vision.

On the contrary: A cause is more important than its effect. But vision is the cause of delight. Therefore vision is superior to delight.

Response: The Philosopher proposes this question in the *Ethics* and leaves it unsolved,[11] but a careful consideration of the matter will show that the activity of the intellect, which is vision, is primary. Delight consists in a certain repose of the will. Now the will rests in something only because of the goodness of that in which it rests. If therefore the will rests in some activity, its rest results from the goodness of that activity. Nor does the will seek good for the sake of repose, for if this were the case the very act of the will would be the end, which has already been disproved.[12] Rather it seeks to be at rest in the activity because that activity is its good. Hence it is clear that the activity in which the will rests is a greater good than the resting of the will in that good.

Reply to 1: The Philosopher says in the same passage that "delight complements activity as the bloom of youth," which is a result of youth, "complements youth." Consequently delight is a certain perfection ac-

---

[9] *Ibid.*
[10] *I Corinthians 13:13.*
[11] Cf. *Nicomachean Ethics* X, 4 (1175a 18).
[12] Question I, article 1, reply to 2; question 3, article 4.

companying vision, not a perfection making vision perfect as to the kind of thing it is.

Reply to 2: The apprehending by sense does not attain the universal notion of good but some particular good which is delectable. Hence animals seek activities corresponding to their sense appetites for the sake of the delight involved. But the intellect apprehends the universal notion of good, and the attainment of this results in delight. Hence it intends the good principally rather than the delight. This is the reason the divine intellect, which is the author of nature, joined delight to activities on account of the activities. But our estimate of things should be made not simply in terms of the order of sense desire, but rather in terms of the order of intellectual desire.

Reply to 3: Charity does not seek the good it loves for the sake of the delight; that it delights in the good it gains is a consequence for charity. Thus vision rather than delight is correlative to charity as an end, for thereby the end is first made present to it.

Third Article

IS COMPREHENSION REQUIRED FOR HAPPINESS?

It seems that comprehension is not required for happiness.

1. Augustine says, "To attain God by the mind is great happiness, but to comprehend Him is impossible." [13] Therefore happiness is without comprehension.

2. Happiness is the perfection of man as to the intellectual part of his soul, in which there are no other powers than intellect and will, as we have shown above.[14] But the intellect is sufficiently perfected by seeing God and the will by delight in Him. Therefore some third thing like comprehension is not required.

3. Happiness consists in activity, and activities are specified by their objects. Now there are two universal objects, the true and the good; the true corresponds to vision and the good to delight. Therefore comprehension is not required as some third thing.

On the contrary: The Apostle says, "So run as to comprehend" [15] (*I Corinthians 9:24*). But a spiritual race terminates in happiness; hence he says, "I have fought the good fight, I have finished the course, I have kept the faith. For the rest, there is laid up for me a crown of justice" (*II Timothy 4:7-8*). Therefore comprehension is required for happiness.

Response: Since happiness consists in attaining the ultimate end, what is required for happiness must be gathered from the way man is ordered to an end. Now man is ordered to an intelligible end partly through the intellect and partly through the will; through the intellect insofar as some

---

[13] *De verbis Evang.*, Sermon 117, 3.   [14] I, question 79, and following.
[15] The usual translation of this passage is; "So run as to obtain it."

imperfect knowledge of the end exists beforehand in the intellect; through the will, first by love, which is the will's first movement toward something, secondly by the real relationship of the one loving to the thing loved, which may be threefold. Sometimes the thing loved is present to the one who loves it, and then it is no longer sought. Sometimes it is not present, but is impossible to attain, and then again it is not sought. Sometimes it is possible to attain it, yet it is beyond the capacity of the one seeking to attain it so that he cannot have it at present; this is the relationship of one who hopes to what he hopes for, and only this relationship causes a search for the end.

Something in happiness itself corresponds to these three. Perfect knowledge of the end corresponds to imperfect; presence of the end corresponds to the relationship of hope; but delight in the end already present arises from love, as we have said.[16] Consequently, there must be a concurring of these three for happiness: vision, which is perfect knowledge of the intelligible end; comprehension, which implies presence of the end; and delight or enjoyment, which implies repose of the one loving in what is loved.

Reply to 1: Comprehension can be understood in two ways. First, as including what is comprehended in the one comprehending, and in this way whatever is comprehended by someone finite is finite, and thus God cannot be comprehended by any created intellect. In another way, comprehension means nothing other than the grasping of something now directly possessed; thus a person who runs after another is said to comprehend [17] him when he gets hold of him. In this way comprehension is required for happiness.

Reply to 2: Just as hope and love pertain to the will, because it belongs to the same thing to love something and strive for it when not possessed, so also comprehension and delight pertain to the will, since it belongs to the same thing to possess something and rest in it.

Reply to 3: Comprehension is not some activity in addition to vision, but a certain relationship to the end already possessed. Hence the vision itself, or the thing seen inasmuch as it is present, is the object of comprehension.

Fourth Article

IS RECTITUDE OF THE WILL REQUIRED FOR HAPPINESS?

It seems that rectitude of the will is not required for happiness.

1. Happiness consists essentially in an act of the intellect, as we have said.[18] But rectitude of the will by which men are called clean of heart

---

[16] Article 2, reply to 3.

[17] In the sense of "grasping." In English, the word "apprehend" would be more appropriate since it means both to "comprehend" and to "lay hold of."

[18] Question 3, article 4.

is not required for the perfect activity of the intellect, for Augustine says, "I do not approve what I have said in a prayer: O God, Who didst will none but the clean of heart to know the truth. For it can be answered that many who are not clean of heart know what is true." [19] Therefore rectitude of the will is not required for happiness.

2. What is prior does not depend upon what is posterior. But activity of the intellect is prior to activity of the will. Therefore happiness, which is the perfect activity of the intellect, does not depend upon rectitude of the will.

3. Whatever is ordered to an end is not necessary when the end is already attained, just as a ship is not necessary when one has reached port. But rectitude of the will, which is effected by virtue, is ordered to happiness as to an end. Therefore, with happiness attained, rectitude of the will is no longer necessary.

On the contrary: "Blessed are the pure of heart, for they shall see God" (*Matthew 5:8*). And "Strive for peace with all men, and for that holiness without which no man will see God" (*Epistle to Hebrews 12:14*).

Response: Rectitude of the will is required for happiness both antecedently and concomitantly. Antecedently, because rectitude of the will consists in being properly ordered to the ultimate end. Now the end is compared to what is ordered to the end as form to matter. Hence just as matter cannot attain form unless it is disposed in an appropriate way for form, so nothing attains the end unless it is rightly ordered to it. Consequently no one can attain happiness unless he have rectitude of the will.

Concomitantly because, as has been said,[20] ultimate happiness consists in the vision of the divine essence, which is the very essence of goodness. Thus the will of one who sees the essence of God necessarily loves whatever he loves in subordination to God, just as the will of one who does not see the essence of God necessarily loves whatever he loves under the common notion of the good which he knows. Now this is precisely what makes the will right. Hence it is clear that happiness is not possible without rectitude of the will.

Reply to 1: Augustine is speaking of a knowledge of the true which is not the very essence of goodness.

Reply to 2: Every act of the will is preceded by some act of the intellect. But there is an act of the will that is prior to an act of the intellect, for the will moves toward the final act of the intellect, which is happiness. Hence a right inclination of the will is required beforehand for happiness, just as an arrow must follow a right course in order to hit the target.

Reply to 3: Not everything which is ordered to the end ceases with the attaining of the end, but only whatever has the nature of something imperfect, such as movement. Consequently the means for movement are

---

[19] *Retractions* I, 4.   [20] Question 3, article 8.

not necessary after the end has been attained, but a due order to the end is necessary.

Fifth Article

IS THE BODY NECESSARY FOR MAN'S HAPPINESS?

It seems that the body is necessary for happiness.

1. The perfection of virtue and grace presupposes perfection of nature. But happiness is the perfection of virtue and grace. Now the soul without the body does not have perfection of nature since the soul is a natural part of human nature, and every part is imperfect when separated from its whole. Therefore the soul without the body cannot be happy.

2. Happiness is a perfect activity, as we have said.[21] But perfect activity follows upon perfect being, because nothing acts unless it is an actual being. Since therefore the soul does not have perfect being when separated from the body, as a part does not when separated from the whole, it seems that the soul cannot be happy without the body.

3. Happiness is the perfection of man. But the soul without the body is not man. Therefore happiness cannot be in the soul without the body.

4. According to Aristotle, "the activity of felicity," in which happiness consists, "has to be one that is not impeded." [22] But the activity of the separated soul is impeded because, as Augustine says, the soul "has a natural desire to rule the body, the result of which is that it is held back in a certain way from wholly tending to its journey to heaven," [23] that is, to the vision of the divine essence. Therefore the soul cannot be happy without the body.

5. Happiness is a satisfying good and fulfills desire. But this does not belong to the separated soul since it still seeks union with the body, as Augustine says.[24] Therefore the soul is not happy separated from the body.

6. In happiness, man is equal with the angels. But the soul without the body is not equal to the angel, as Augustine says.[25] Therefore the separated soul is not happy.

On the contrary: "Blessed [i.e., happy] are the dead who die in the Lord" (*Apocalypse 14:13*).

Response: Happiness is of two kinds; an imperfect one which is had in this life, and a perfect one which consists in the vision of God. Now it is clear that the body is necessary for happiness in this life. For the happiness of this life consists in activity of the intellect, whether speculative or practical. But the activity of the intellect in this life cannot go on without a phantasm, which can only belong to a corporeal organ, as we have

---

[21] Question 3, articles 2 and 5.   [22] *Nicomachean Ethics* VII, 13 (1153b 16).
[23] *A Literal Commentary on "Genesis"* XII, chapter 35.
[24] *Ibid.*   [25] *Ibid.*

noted.[26] Thus the happiness which we can have in this life depends in a certain way on the body.

But with respect to perfect happiness, which consists in the vision of God, some have maintained that it cannot take place in the soul without the body, saying that the souls of the saints, separated from the body, do not attain this happiness until the Day of Judgment when their bodies are restored. This appears to be false both from authority and from reason. It is false on the authority of the Apostle who says, "knowing that while we are in the body we are exiled from the Lord," pointing out the reason for this exile when he adds, "for we walk by faith and not by sight." [27] It is apparent from this that as long as one walks by faith and not by sight, lacking the vision of the divine essence, one is not present to God. But the souls of the saints, separated from their bodies, are present to God, and hence he adds, "we even have the courage to prefer to be exiled from the body and to be at home with the Lord." [28] Hence it is clear that the souls of the saints, separated from their bodies, walk by sight, seeing the essence of God, wherein is true happiness.

This can also be shown by reason. The intellect in its activity does not need the body save for phantasms, in which it beholds intelligible truth, as we have stated.[29] Now it is clear that the divine essence cannot be seen by means of phantasms, as we have said.[30] Hence, since the perfect happiness of man consists in the vision of the divine essence, it does not depend upon the body. Consequently the soul can be happy without the body.

But we must take into account that something pertains to a thing's perfection in two ways: in one way, so as to constitute the essence of the thing, as the soul is necessary for the perfection of man; in another way, as necessary for its well-being, and thus beauty of the body and quickness of mind belong to the perfection of man. Now although the body does not belong in the first way to the perfection of human happiness, it does in the second. For activity depends on the nature of a thing, and hence the more perfect the soul in its nature the more perfectly will it have its characteristic activity, in which happiness consists. Hence Augustine, after inquiring "whether perfect happiness can be ascribed to the souls of the dead separated from their bodies," answers that "they cannot see the Unchangeable Substance as the blessed angels see it, either for some other more hidden reason or because they have a natural desire to rule the body." [31]

Reply to 1: Happiness is a perfection of the soul relative to the intellect, according to which the soul transcends a corporeal organ, not a per-

---

[26] I, question 84, articles 6 and 7.   [27] *II Corinthians* 5:6-7.
[28] V. 8.   [29] I, question 84, article 7.
[30] I, question 12, article 3.
[31] *A Literal Commentary on "Genesis"* XII, chapter 35.

fection of the soul as it is the form of a natural body. Hence that perfection of nature with respect to which happiness is owed to it remains,
though the perfection of nature in respect to which it is the form of a
body does not.

Reply to 2: The soul is related in a different way to being than other
parts are. For the being of a whole is not that of any of its parts, and
hence the part either entirely ceases to be with the destruction of the
whole, as the parts of the animal with the destruction of the animal, or if
the parts remain they have some other actual being, as a part of a line
has an existence other than that of the whole line. But the being of the
composite still belongs to the human soul after the destruction of the
body, and this is because the being of the form is the same as that of its
matter, and this is the being of the composite. Now the soul is self-sub-
sistent, as we have shown.[32] Hence it follows that after separation from
the body it has complete being, and thus can function completely, though
it does not have the complete specific nature.

Reply to 3: The happiness of man is with respect to his intellect and
since the intellect remains, happiness can exist in it. In a similar way, the
teeth of an Ethiopian, with respect to which he is said to be white, can
remain white even after extraction.

Reply to 4: One thing can be impeded by another in two ways. In one
way by contrariety, as cold impedes the action of heat, and such an impediment to action is opposed to happiness. In another way by some kind
of defect, in that what is impeded does not have whatever is necessary for
its perfection in all respects. Such an impediment to activity is not in-
compatible with happiness, but does prevent it from being perfect in all
respects. Thus separation from the body is said to restrain the soul so that
it does not wholly tend to the vision of the divine essence. For the soul
seeks to enjoy God in such a way that the enjoyment may overflow into
the body so far as possible. Therefore as long as the soul enjoys God without the body, its desire is at rest in what it has, yet in such a way that it
would still wish the body to participate in it.

Reply to 5: The desire of the separated soul is wholly at rest with respect to what it desires, since it has that which fulfills it. But desire is not
wholly at rest on the part of the one desiring, for he does not possess that
good in every way he could wish. Hence, with reunion of the body, happiness will increase, not intensively, but extensively.

Reply to 6: What is said in the passage to the effect that "the souls of
the dead do not see God as the angels do" is not to be understood as referring to an inequality of quantity, for even now some souls of the
Blessed are raised to the higher orders of the angels and so see God more
clearly than lower angels. It is to be understood as referring to an inequality of proportion because the angels, even the lowest, have all the

---

[32] I, question 75, article 2.

perfection of happiness they will ever have, while the separated souls of the saints have not.

Sixth Article

IS A PERFECTION OF THE BODY REQUIRED FOR HAPPINESS?

It seems that a perfection of the body is not required for man's complete happiness.

1. Perfection of the body is one kind of corporeal good. But we have already shown that happiness does not consist in corporeal goods.[33] Therefore some perfect disposition of the body is not required for man's happiness.

2. Man's happiness consists in the vision of the divine essence, as we have shown.[34] But we have pointed out in the preceding article that the body supplies nothing for this activity. Therefore no disposing of the body is required for happiness.

3. The more the intellect is withdrawn from the body the more perfectly it understands. But happiness consists in the most perfect act of the intellect. Hence the soul must be withdrawn from the body in every way. Therefore in no way is a disposition of the body required for happiness.

On the contrary: The reward of virtue is happiness, and hence it is written, "blessed shall you be if you do these things" (*John 13:17*). But the saints are promised as a reward not only the vision and enjoyment of God but also that their bodies will be well disposed, for it is written, "You shall see and your heart shall rejoice, and your bones shall flourish like an herb" (*Isaias 66:14*). Therefore a good disposition of the body is required for happiness.

Response: If the question refers to man's happiness as it can be had in this life, it is clear that a good disposition of the body is necessary, for this happiness consists "in activity in accordance with complete virtue." [35] It is also evident that in all activity of virtue man can be hindered by indisposition of the body.

If the question refers to perfect happiness, some have held that a disposing of the body is not required for happiness, and that the soul in fact must be wholly separate from the body. Augustine thus quotes Porphyry as saying that "in order for the soul to be happy, it must shun anything corporeal." [36] But this is not reasonable. Since it is natural to the soul to be united to the body, the perfection of the soul cannot exclude the natural perfection of the body.

Hence we must say that for complete happiness in all respects, a perfect disposition of the body is required both antecedently and conse-

---

[33] Question 2.   [34] Question 3, article 8.
[35] Aristotle, *Nicomachean Ethics* I, 13 (1102a 5).
[36] *The City of God* XXII, 26.

quently. It is required *antecedently* because, as Augustine says, "If the body be such that the ruling of it is difficult and burdensome, for as flesh it is corruptible and weighs upon the soul, the mind is turned away from the vision of the highest heaven." Hence he concludes that "when this body will no longer be 'animal,' but 'spiritual,' then will man be made equal to the angels, and that will be his glory which before was his burden." [37] It is required *consequently* because there will be an overflow to the body from the happiness of the soul so that the body too will attain its perfection. Hence Augustine says, "God made the soul so powerful in nature that from its fullness of happiness the vigor of incorruption flows over into the lower nature." [38]

Reply to 1: Happiness does not consist in a corporeal good as its object, but a corporeal good can add a certain embellishment or perfection to happiness.

Reply to 2: Although the body supplies nothing to the operation of the intellect whereby God's essence is seen, yet it can be a hindrance to it. Hence perfection of the body is required so as not to hinder the elevation of the mind.

Reply to 3: The perfect activity of the intellect does require a certain withdrawal from this corruptible body which weighs upon the soul, but not from the spiritual body, which will be wholly subject to the spirit. We shall treat this point later.[39]

Seventh Article

ARE ANY EXTERNAL GOODS REQUIRED FOR HAPPINESS?

It seems that external goods are required for happiness.

1. Whatever is promised to the saints as a reward belongs to happiness. But external goods are promised to the saints, for example food and drink, wealth and a kingdom. Thus it is written: "That you may eat and drink at my table in my kingdom" (*Luke 22:30*); "Lay up for yourselves treasures in heaven" (*Matthew 6:20*); and "Come, blessed of my Father, take possession of the kingdom" (*Matthew 25:34*). Therefore external goods are required for happiness.

2. According to Boethius, happiness is "a state brought to completion by the aggregation of all goods." [40] But some of man's goods are external, though they are the least good, as Augustine says.[41] Therefore they are also required for happiness.

---

[37] *A Literal Commentary on "Genesis"* XII, chapter 35.
[38] *Epistle to Discorus* (Epistle 118, 3).
[39] This is treated in the *Supplement*, question 82 and following.
[40] *The Consolation of Philosophy* III, prose 2.
[41] *Free Choice of the Will* II, 19.

3. Our Lord says, "Your reward is great in heaven" (*Matthew 5:12*). But to be in heaven implies being in a place. Therefore at least exterior place is required for happiness.

On the contrary: "For what have I in heaven? And besides Thee what do I desire upon earth?" (*Psalms 72:25*). This is as though to say "I desire nothing but this—*It is good for me to adhere to my God*" (*72:28*). Therefore nothing else external is required for happiness.

Response: External goods are required for the imperfect happiness which can be had in this life, not as being of the essence of happiness but as serving instrumentally for happiness, which consists in the activity of virtue, as is said in the *Ethics.*[42] In this life man needs bodily necessities both for the exercise of contemplative virtue and also for the exercise of practical virtue, and for the latter he also needs many other things so as to perform the works of practical virtue.

But for the perfect happiness which consists in the vision of God, goods of this kind are in no way required. The reason is that all external goods are required either for sustaining the animal life of the body or for certain actions belonging to human life which we perform by means of the body. Now the perfect happiness which consists in the vision of God will be either in the soul without the body or in the soul united to a body no longer animal in nature but spiritual. Hence external goods in no way are required for such happiness, for they are ordered to animal life. And because in this life the happiness of contemplation comes closer to paralleling perfect happiness than does that of action, since it is more God-like, as we have said,[43] hence it stands in less need of goods of the body, as is said in the *Ethics.*[44]

Reply to 1: All these promises of material things contained in Scripture are to be understood metaphorically, inasmuch as Scripture customarily designates spiritual matters by means of material things, "so that from the things we know we are able to rise to a desire of what we do not know," as Gregory says.[45] Thus by food and drink we are to understand delight in happiness, by wealth the sufficiency of God for man, by a kingdom the raising up of man to union with God.

Reply to 2: External goods serve animal life and do not belong to the spiritual life in which perfect happiness consists. Nevertheless there will be in perfect happiness an aggregation of all goods, because whatever good is found in them will all be possessed in the supreme source of good.

Reply to 3: According to Augustine,[46] the reward of the saints is not said to be in a material heaven; rather, "heaven" is to be understood as the height of spiritual goods. Nonetheless, there will be a corporeal place,

---

[42] I, 13 (1102a 5).
[44] X, 8 (1178b 1).
[46] *The Lord's Sermon on the Mount* I, 5.

[43] Question 3, article 5, reply to *1*.
[45] *Homily 11.*

namely, the empyrean heaven, for the Blessed, not as necessary for happiness, but by reason of a certain fittingness and embellishment.

Eighth Article

ARE FRIENDS NECESSARY FOR HAPPINESS?

It seems that friends are necessary for happiness.

1. Future happiness is frequently signified in Scripture by the name "glory." But glory consists in a man's good being brought to the notice of others. Therefore friendship is required for happiness.

2. Boethius says, "There is no enjoyment in the possession of a good without someone to share it." [47] But enjoyment is necessary for happiness. Therefore friendship is also required.

3. In happiness, charity is perfected. But charity extends to the love of God and neighbor. Therefore it seems that friendship is required for happiness.

On the contrary: "All good things come to me together with her" (*Wisdom 7:11*), that is, with divine wisdom, which consists in the contemplation of God. Therefore nothing else is required for happiness.

Response: If the question refers to the happiness of the present life then, as the Philosopher says,[48] the happy man needs friends, not because they are useful, since he is able to get along without help, nor for enjoyment, since the activity of virtue furnishes him with complete joy, but for good activity, that is, so that he may do good to them and delight in seeing them do good and be helped by them in doing his own good deeds. For, in order to do well, whether in the works of the active life or in the activity of the contemplative life, man needs the help of friends.

But if the question refers to the perfect happiness we will have in heaven, friendship is not a necessary requirement for happiness since man has in God all the fullness of his perfection. But friendship makes for the well-being of happiness. Hence Augustine says, "Spiritual creatures receive no other intrinsic aid to happiness than the eternity, truth, and charity of the Creator. But if they can be said to be helped extrinsically perhaps it is only by their seeing each other and rejoicing in their fellowship of God." [49]

Reply to 1: The glory which is essential to happiness is the glory man has, not in the sight of man, but in the sight of God.

Reply to 2: The quoted passage is to be understood of the possession of a good which does not fully satisfy, and hence is not relevant to the point at issue, since man possesses in God a sufficiency of every good.

---

[47] The words are taken from Seneca, *Epistle 6.*

[48] *Nicomachean Ethics* IX, 9. Chapter 9 discusses at length whether the happy man needs friends.

[49] *A Literal Commentary on "Genesis"* VIII, chapter 25.

Reply to 3: The perfection of charity is essential to happiness as regards love of God but not love of neighbor. Consequently if there were only one soul loving God, that soul would be happy, though not having a neighbor to love. But supposing the neighbor to be there, love of him follows from perfect love of God. Hence friendship is related in a concomitant way to perfect happiness.

The Attainment of Happiness

(In Eight Articles)

CAN MAN ATTAIN HAPPINESS?

It seems that man cannot attain happiness.

1. As the rational nature is above sense nature so the intellectual nature is above the rational, as Dionysius points out.[1] But brute animals, which have only sensation, cannot attain the end of the rational nature. Therefore man, who has a rational nature, cannot attain the end of the intellectual nature, which is happiness.

2. True happiness consists in the vision of God, Who is pure truth. But it is connatural to man to discern truth in material things, and hence "he understands the intelligible species in phantasms."[2] Therefore man cannot attain happiness.

3. Happiness consists in attaining the highest good. But one cannot arrive at what is highest without going through the middle. Since the angelic nature is midway between God and human nature, and man cannot transcend the angelic nature, it seems that man cannot attain happiness.

On the contrary: "Blessed is the man whom Thou shalt instruct, O Lord" *(Psalms 93:12).*

Response: Happiness means the attainment of the perfect good. Accordingly, whoever has a capacity for[3] the perfect good can attain happiness. That man has a capacity for the perfect good is evident from the fact that his intellect apprehends the universal and perfect good, and his will seeks it. Hence man can attain happiness. It is also evident from the fact that man has a capacity for seeing the divine essence, as we have explained.[4] We have also pointed out that the perfect or complete happiness of man consists in this vision.[5]

Reply to 1: The way rational nature exceeds sense nature differs from

---

[1] *The Divine Names* IV, 1-2; VI, 1; VII, 2.

[2] Aristotle, *On the Soul* III, 7 (431b 2).

[3] The Latin word here is "capax," translated as "has a capacity for." This is not to be understood in the sense that a created intellect can see the essence of God by its own unaided natural power, but only that God by His grace unites Himself to the created intellect as an object made intelligible to it. See I, question 12, article 4.

[4] I, question 12, article 1.   [5] Question 3, article 8.

the way the intellectual nature surpasses the rational.[6] The rational nature exceeds sense nature with respect to the object of knowledge because sense in no way can know what is universal, whereas reason has knowledge of this. The intellectual nature surpasses the rational with respect to the way in which it knows the same intelligible truth, for the intellectual nature grasps truth at once while the rational nature reaches it by means of investigation, as we have said.[7] Consequently what an intellect grasps at once reason arrives at by a certain discourse. Hence the rational nature can arrive at the happiness which is the perfection of the intellectual nature, yet in a way other than the angel does. The angels attained it right after the beginning of their creation while man arrives at it after a time. But the sense nature in no way can reach this end.

Reply to 2: According to his present state of life, man's connatural way of knowing intelligible truth is by means of phantasms. But after this state of life, he has another way of knowing connatural to him, as has been explained.[8]

Reply to 3: Man cannot go beyond the angels in grade of nature so as to be superior by nature to them. However, he can go beyond them by an act of the intellect when he understands that there is something above the angels which makes men happy, and that when he perfectly attains it he will be perfectly happy.

Second Article

CAN ONE MAN BE HAPPIER THAN ANOTHER?

It seems that one man cannot be happier than another.

1. Happiness is the reward of virtue, as Aristotle says.[9] But equal reward is given for all works of virtue, for, as is said, of all who worked in the vineyard "each received his denarius" (*Matthew 20:10*) because, as Gregory says, "each was equally rewarded with eternal life."[10] Therefore one man will not be happier than another.

2. Happiness is the supreme good. But there cannot be anything greater than what is supreme. Therefore the happiness of one man cannot be greater than that of another.

3. Happiness, since it is the "complete and sufficient good,"[11] brings man's desire to rest. But this desire is not at rest if some good is lacking which could be fulfilled. Now if nothing is lacking which could be ful-

---

[6] In this contrast, "intellectual nature" is taken as proper to the angel, "rational nature" as proper to man.

[7] I, question 58, article 3; question 79, article 8.

[8] I, question 84, article 7; question 89, article 1.

[9] *Nicomachean Ethics* I, 9 (1099b 16).   [10] *Homily 19.*

[11] Aristotle, *op. cit.* I, 7 (1097a 29).

filled, there cannot be any other greater good. Therefore either man is not happy, or if he is happy, there cannot be any happiness greater.

On the contrary: "In my Father's house there are many mansions" (*John 14:2*), which mansions, as Augustine says, "signify varying degrees of merit in eternal life." [12] But worthiness of eternal life, which is given for merit, is happiness itself. Therefore there are varying degrees of happiness, and the happiness of everyone is not equal.

Response: As we have said above,[13] two things are included in the notion of happiness: one, the ultimate end itself which is the supreme good; the other, the attainment or enjoyment of this good. With respect to the good itself, which is the object and cause of happiness, the happiness of one man cannot be greater than another, for there is only one supreme good, God, and by the enjoyment of Him men are happy. But with respect to the attainment or enjoyment of this good, one man can be happier than another, because the more one enjoys this good the happier he is. Now one man can enjoy God more completely than another because he is better disposed or ordered to the enjoyment of God. In this way one man can be happier than another.

Reply to 1: The uniformity of payment signifies a unity of happiness on the part of the object. But the diversity of mansions signifies a diversity of happiness according to varying degrees of enjoyment.

Reply to 2: Happiness is said to be the supreme good insofar as it is the perfect possession or enjoyment of the supreme good.

Reply to 3: None of the blessed lacks any good that should be desired, since each possesses the infinite good itself, which is "the good of all good," as Augustine says.[14] But one is said to be happier than another by a differing participation in the same good. However, the adding of other goods does not increase happiness. Hence Augustine says, "He who knows Thee, and others as well, is not happier for knowing them but is happy for knowing Thee alone." [15]

Third Article

CAN ONE BE HAPPY IN THIS LIFE?

It seems that happiness can be had in this life.

1. The Scriptures say, "Blessed are the undefiled in the way, who walk in the law of the Lord" (*Psalms 118:1*). Now this can take place in this life. Therefore one can be happy in this life.

2. Imperfect participation in the supreme good does not detract from the nature of happiness, otherwise one person would not be happier than another. But in this life men can participate in the supreme good by

---

[12] *Tract 67* in *Commentary on John.*
[13] Question I, article 8; question 2, article 7.
[14] *The Trinity* XIII, 7.   [15] *Confessions* V, 4.

knowing and loving God, though imperfectly. Therefore man can be happy in this life.

3. What is said by many cannot be wholly false, for what is in many seems to be natural, and nature does not wholly fail. But many hold that there is happiness in this life, as is evident from Scripture: "They have called the people happy that hath these things" (*Psalms 143:15*), namely, the good things of the present life. Therefore one can be happy in this life.

On the contrary: "Man born of a woman, living for a short time, is filled with many miseries" (*Job 14:1*). But happiness excludes misery. Therefore man cannot be happy in this life.

Response: Some participation in happiness can be had in this life, but true and perfect happiness cannot be had in this life. This can be shown in two ways. The first way is taken from the common notion of happiness, for happiness, since it is "the complete and sufficient good," [16] excludes all evil and fulfills all desire. Now in this life all evil cannot be excluded. The present life is subject to many evils which cannot be avoided: the evil of ignorance on the part of the intellect, the evil of inordinate affection on the part of desire, and the evil of much suffering on the part of the body, as Augustine carefully sets forth.[17] Likewise, the desire for good cannot be fully satisfied in this life, for man naturally desires the good he has to be permanent. Now what is good in the present life is transitory; for life itself, which we naturally desire, passes away, and we would like to hold on to it for ever, since man naturally shrinks from death. Hence it is impossible for true happiness to be had in this life.

The second way is taken from what happiness specifically consists in, the vision of the divine essence, which man cannot attain in this life, as has been shown.[18] It is thus clearly evident that no one can attain true and perfect happiness in this life.

Reply to 1. Some are said to be happy in this life either because of the hope of attaining happiness in the future life, as written in Scripture, "For in hope were we saved" (*Romans 8:24*), or because of some participation in happiness by reason of a certain enjoyment of the supreme good.

Reply to 2: Participation in happiness can be imperfect in two ways. One is on the part of the object itself of happiness, which is not seen according to its essence, and such imperfection does detract from the nature of true happiness. The other way is on the part of the one participating, who indeed attains the object of happiness in itself, namely, God, but imperfectly in comparison to the way God enjoys Himself. Such imperfection does nót detract from the true nature of happiness because,

---

[16] Aristotle, *Nicomachean Ethics* I, 7 (1097a 29).
[17] *The City of God* XIX, 4.   [18] I, question 12, article 2.

since happiness is a certain activity, as we have said,[19] the true nature of happiness is taken from the object which specifies the act, and not from the subject.

Reply to 3: Men think there is some happiness in this life because of a similarity of it to true happiness. They are not altogether wrong in so thinking.

Fourth Article

CAN HAPPINESS ONCE HAD BE LOST?

It seems that happiness can be lost.

1. Happiness is a perfection. But any perfection is in the perfectible according to that thing's mode of being. Since man is changeable by nature it seems that happiness is participated in by man in a changeable way. Thus it seems that man can lose happiness.

2. Happiness consists in an activity of the intellect, which is subject to the will. But the will is related to opposites. Therefore it seems that the will can discontinue the activity whereby man is happy, and thus man can cease to be happy.

3. The end corresponds to the beginning. But man's happiness has a beginning, for man was not always happy. Therefore it seems to have an end.

On the contrary: The just "will go into everlasting life" (*Matthew 25:46*), which, as we have said,[20] is the happiness of the saints. Now what is everlasting does not cease. Therefore happiness cannot be lost.

Response: If the question refers to the imperfect happiness which can be had in this life, it can be lost. This is evident in contemplative happiness, which is lost either through oblivion, as when knowledge deteriorates through some sickness, or by certain occupations which totally withdraw one from contemplation. The same is evident in the happiness of the active life, for a man's will can change so as to fall into vice from virtue, in the act of which happiness principally consists. Even if the virtue remains untouched, external changes can disturb such happiness insofar as they hinder many acts of virtue; yet they cannot wholly take away virtue, so long as there still remains that act of virtue whereby man bears such adversities nobly. Now because the happiness of this life can be lost—which seems to be contrary to the notion of happiness—hence the Philosopher says that some are happy in this life, not absolutely, but *as men,* whose nature is subject to change.[21]

If the question refers to the perfect happiness which we hope for after this life, it should be noted that Origen, following the error of certain

---

[19] Question 3, article 2.   [20] Article 2, *On the contrary.*
[21] *Nicomachean Ethics* I, 10 (1101a 19).

Platonists, held that man can fall into misery after this ultimate happiness.[22] This is clearly false for two reasons.

The first reason is drawn from the common notion of happiness. Since happiness is the complete and sufficient good, the desire of man must be brought to rest and all evil excluded. Now man naturally desires to hold on to the good which he has and to have the assurance of keeping it, otherwise he will be distressed by the fear of losing it or by sorrow in the certainty of losing it. Hence it is necessary for true happiness that man have an assured belief that he will never lose the good which he has. Now if this belief is true, the consequence is that happiness will never be lost. But if it is false, it is evil to have a false belief, for what is false is an evil for the intellect just as what is true is a good for it.[28] Hence he will no longer be truly happy if some evil exists in him.

The second reason is taken from the notion of what happiness is in particular. We have shown above that the perfect happiness of man consists in the vision of the divine essence.[24] Now it is impossible for one seeing the divine essence to wish not to see it. For any good which one has and still could wish to be without, either is insufficient and then something more sufficient is sought in its place, or it has something unfitting connected with it by reason of which it becomes distasteful. But the vision of the divine essence supplies the soul with every good, since the soul is united with the source of all goodness. Hence Scripture says, "I shall be satisfied when Thy glory shall appear" (*Psalms 16:15*), and "All good things came to me together with her" (*Wisdom 7:11*), namely, with the contemplation of wisdom. Likewise, it has nothing distasteful connected with it, for it is said of the contemplation of wisdom, "Her conversation hath no bitterness, nor her company any tediousness" (*Wisdom 8:16*). It is thus clear that one who is happy cannot give up happiness of his own accord.

Moreover, he cannot lose it by God taking it away because, since withdrawal of happiness is a punishment, it cannot be done by God, the just judge, except for some fault, and one who sees the essence of God cannot fall into fault, since rectitude of the will is a necessary consequence of this vision, as we have shown.[25] Nor can it be taken away by any other agent, for the mind united to God is raised above all other things, and hence no other agent can separate the mind from that union. Therefore it does not seem reasonable that, with the passing of time, man should be alternately happy and miserable, for such temporal changes can only be in things subject to time and motion.

Reply to 1: Happiness is an accomplished perfection which excludes every defect from the one who is happy. Hence one who has it, has it

[22] *On the Principles* II, 3. Cf. Augustine, *The City of God* X, 30.
[23] Cf. Aristotle, *op. cit.* VI, 3 (1139a 28).   [24] Question 3, article 8.
[25] Question 4, article 4.

without any possibility of change, this being accomplished by divine power, which raises man to a participation in eternity, transcending all change.

Reply to 2: The will is related to opposites with respect to means, but is ordered to the ultimate end by natural necessity. This is evident from the fact that man cannot not will to be happy.

Reply to 3: Happiness has a beginning because of the condition of the one participating in it, but it has no end in terms of the good, participation in which makes man happy. Hence the beginning of happiness is owing to one thing, its lacking an end to another.

Fifth Article

CAN MAN ATTAIN HAPPINESS BY HIS NATURAL POWERS? [26]

It seems that man can attain happiness by his natural powers.

1. Nature is not lacking in what is necessary. But nothing is as necessary as that by which the ultimate end is attained. Therefore this is not lacking to human nature. Hence man can attain happiness by his natural powers.

2. Since man is more noble than irrational creatures, it seems that he is more self-sufficient. But irrational creatures can attain their ends by their natural powers. Therefore much more so can man attain happiness by his natural powers.

3. Happiness is "perfect activity," according to the Philosopher.[27] Now it belongs to the same principle to begin a thing and to complete it. Accordingly, since imperfect activity, which is a sort of beginning of man's activity, is subject to that natural power whereby man is master of his own actions, it seems man can arrive at perfect activity, which is happiness, by his natural powers.

On the contrary: Man is the principle of his actions by intellect and will, which are natural powers. But the ultimate happiness which is prepared for the saints surpasses the intellect and will of man, for the Apostle says, "Eye has not seen nor ear heard, nor has it entered into the heart of man, what things God has prepared for those who love him" (*I Corinthians 2:9*). Therefore man cannot attain happiness by his natural powers.

Response: The imperfect happiness which man can have in this life can be acquired by his natural powers, as can virtue, which is the activity happiness consists in, as we shall see later on.[28] But, as we have already

---

[26] The question of whether man can *merit* happiness by his natural power is treated later: Question 109, article 5 and question 114, article 2. The question here is whether the activity in which ultimate happiness consists can be *attained* by man's natural power.

[27] *Nicomachean Ethics* VII, 13 (1153b 16).   [28] Question 63.

said,[29] man's perfect happiness consists in the vision of the divine essence. Now to see the essence of God is beyond the nature not only of man but of every creature, as we have shown.[30] For the natural knowledge of any creature is in accordance with the type of substance it is; thus it is said of a purely intellectual being that "it knows what is above it and what is below it in a way corresponding to its substance." [31] But all knowledge which is according to the mode of created substance falls short of the vision of the divine essence, which infinitely exceeds all created substance. Hence neither man, nor any other creature, can attain ultimate happiness by his own natural powers.

Reply to 1: Just as nature does not fail with respect to what is necessary for man although it has not provided him with weapons and clothing as it has in the case of other animals—providing reason and hands instead, by which he can acquire these things for himself—so nature does not fail with respect to what is necessary even if it does not give him a principle whereby he can attain happiness, because this would be beyond it. But nature did give him free judgment whereby he can turn to God Who can make him happy. "For what we can do through our friends we can in a sense do by ourselves." [32]

Reply to 2: A nature which can attain the perfect good, though it needs external help to attain it, is of a more noble condition than a nature which cannot attain the perfect good, but only some imperfect good, even though it does not need external help, as Aristotle says.[33] Thus a person is more disposed to health who can attain complete health, though he needs the assistance of medicine, than is one who can attain only imperfect health without the aid of medicine. Accordingly, the rational creature, who can attain the perfect good of happiness but needs divine help for this, is more perfect than the irrational creature who is not capable of attaining this good but attains some imperfect good by its own natural powers.

Reply to 3: When that which is imperfect and perfect are of the same kind, they can be caused by the same power. But this is not necessary if they are of different kinds, for not everything that can cause the disposition of matter can confer the ultimate perfection. Now the imperfect activity which is subject to man's natural power is not of the same kind as that perfect activity which is man's happiness, for an activity is specified by its object. Hence the argument given is not conclusive.

---

[29] Question 3, article 8. [30] I, question 12, article 4.
[31] *On the Causes,* prop. 8. [32] Aristotle, *op. cit.* III, 3 (1112b 27).
[33] *On the Heavens* II, 12 (292a 22).

Sixth Article

CAN MAN ATTAIN HAPPINESS THROUGH THE ACTION
OF SOME HIGHER CREATURE?

It seems that man can be made happy through the action of some
higher creature, namely, an angel.

1. A twofold order is found in things. One is the order of the parts of
the universe to each other, the other is the order of the whole universe
to a good outside the universe. The first is ordered to the second as to an
end,[34] as, in a parallel way, the ordering of the parts of an army to each
other is because of the order of the whole army to its leader. But the
order of the parts of the universe to each other is in terms of higher
creatures acting on lower, as we have said.[35] Now happiness consists in
man's being ordered to a good outside the universe, which is God. Therefore man is made happy through a higher creature, the angel, acting on
him.

2. That which is potentially such or such can be made actually so by
what is already such or such; thus, what can be hot is made actually hot
by something that is already hot. But man is potentially happy. Therefore man can be made happy by an angel who is actually happy.

3. Happiness consists in an activity of the intellect, as we have said.[36]
But an angel can enlighten man's intellect, as we have also said.[37] Therefore an angel can make man happy.

On the contrary: "The Lord will give grace and glory" (*Psalms 83:12*).

Response: Every creature is subject to the laws of nature, since each
has limited power and action; therefore, whatever exceeds created nature
cannot be brought about by the power of a creature. Hence if anything
needs to be accomplished that is beyond nature, it is done directly by
God, such as raising the dead, restoring sight to the blind, and things of
this kind. Now we have shown that happiness is a good which exceeds
created nature.[38] Consequently it cannot be bestowed through the action
of any creature; on the contrary, man is made happy by God alone, if we
are speaking of perfect happiness. But if it is a question of imperfect
happiness, the same thing will be said of it as is said of virtue, in whose
act it consists.[39]

Reply to 1: It often happens in the case of active powers ordered to
each other that the highest power is the one that directs to the ultimate

---

[34] Cf. Aristotle, *Metaphysics* XII, 10 (1075a 12).

[35] I, question 19, article 5, reply to 2; question 48, article 1, reply to 5; question 109,
article 2.

[36] Question 3, article 4.   [37] I, question 111, article 1.   [38] Article 5.

[39] Namely, natural virtue to a degree can be acquired by man and so can imperfect
happiness.

end while the lower powers assist in attaining the ultimate end by disposing things to that end; or, to take an example in another order, it belongs to the art of navigation, which governs the art of shipbuilding, to use a ship for the end for which it was made. In the order of the universe, accordingly, man is helped by angels in the attaining of his ultimate end with respect to dispositions leading to the attainment of it, but man attains the ultimate end through the first agent Himself, Who is God.

Reply to 2: When a form in act exists in something perfectly and according to its natural being, it can be a principle of acting on another; for instance, a hot thing heats through heat. But if a form exists in something imperfectly, and not according to its natural being,[40] it cannot be a principle of its communication to another; thus the likeness of a color in the pupil of the eye cannot make a thing white, nor can all the things that are illuminated or heated, light or heat other things, otherwise lighting and heating would go on endlessly. But the light of glory,[41] by which God is seen, is in God perfectly and naturally, whereas it is in any creature imperfectly and by likeness or participation. Hence no creature can communicate its happiness to another.

Reply to 3: An angel who is happy can enlighten the intellect of man, or even a lower angel, with respect to certain aspects of the divine works, but not with respect to the vision of the divine essence, as we have said.[42] In order to see the divine essence, all are directly enlightened by God.

Seventh Article

DOES MAN HAVE TO DO GOOD DEEDS IN ORDER
TO RECEIVE HAPPINESS FROM GOD?

It seems that no deeds are required of men in order to receive happiness from God.

1. Since God is an agent of infinite power, He requires, before acting, neither matter nor any disposing of matter, but can produce the whole effect instantly. Now man's works, since they are not required for happiness as the efficient cause, as we have said,[43] can only be required by way of disposition. Therefore God, Who does not need things disposed beforehand, bestows happiness without any previous deeds.

2. As God is the immediate author of happiness, so He is the immediate founder of nature. But when God first established nature, He produced creatures without any preceding disposition or action on the

---

[40] "Natural being" here is being opposed to "intentional being," that is, existence in a mind.
[41] This phrase signifies a supernatural strengthening of the intellect by God enabling the intellect to see the essence of God. Cf. I, question 12, articles 2 and 5.
[42] I, question 106, article 1.   [43] Article 6.

part of the creature, making each creature complete according to its kind immediately. Therefore it seems that He bestows happiness on man without any preceding deeds.

3. The Apostle says that happiness belongs to the man "to whom God credits justice without works" (*Romans 4:6*). Therefore no deeds of men are necessary for attaining happiness.

On the contrary: "If you know these things, blessed shall you be if you do them" (*John 13:17*). Therefore happiness is obtained through action.

Response: As we have said above,[44] rectitude of will is necessary for happiness, since it is simply the due ordering of the will to the ultimate end; and this is necessary for obtaining the ultimate end just as a right disposition of matter is necessary for receiving form. But we cannot show from this that an activity of man must precede his happiness, for God could make a will tend rightly to the end and at the same time attain the end, just as He sometimes disposes matter and induces form simultaneously. But the order of divine wisdom does not require that this be done, and so it is stated that "of those things which naturally have a capacity for the complete good, one has it without action, some with one action, and some with many actions." [45]

Now to possess the perfect good without any movement belongs to one who has it by nature, and to possess happiness by nature belongs to God alone. Not to be moved to happiness by any preceding operation therefore belongs to God alone. Since happiness surpasses all created nature, it is not appropriate that a mere creature attain happiness without some activity by which he tends to it. The angel, who is higher than man in the natural order, attained it, according to the order of divine wisdom, by one operation of meritorious activity, as we have explained.[46] Men attain it by many operations, which are called merits. Hence even according to the Philosopher, happiness is the reward of virtuous activity.[47]

Reply to 1: Deeds on the part of man are required for happiness not because of an inadequacy of the divine power that bestows happiness, but for preserving the order in things.

Reply to 2: God brought the first creature into being perfect from the start, without any preceding disposition or activity on the part of a creature, thus establishing the first individuals of the species so that through them the nature could be propagated to those coming after. In a similar way, because happiness was to be bestowed on others through Christ, Who is God and man, and "brought many sons into glory" (*Hebrews 2:10*), immediately from the beginning of His conception His soul was happy without any preceding meritorious work. But this is exclusive to Him, for in the case of baptized children, it is Christ's merit

---

[44] Question 4, article 4.
[45] Aristotle, *On the Heavens* II, 12 (292a 22).
[46] I, question 62, article 5   [47] *Nicomachean Ethics* I, 9 (1099b 16).

that makes it possible for them to attain happiness though they have no merits of their own, since by baptism they are made members of Christ.

Reply to 3: The Apostle is speaking of the happiness of hope, which we possess through sanctifying grace, which indeed is not given because of preceding works. For grace does not have the notion of a term of motion as happiness has; it is, rather, a principle of the motion by which we tend to happiness.

Eighth Article

DOES EVERY MAN DESIRE HAPPINESS?

It seems that not all desire happiness.

1. No one can desire what he does not know, for it is the good as known that is the object of desire.[48] But many do not know what happiness is, for as Augustine says, "Some have maintained happiness consists in pleasures of the body, some thought it consisted in virtue of the soul, and some in other things." [49] Therefore not all desire happiness.

2. The essence of happiness is the vision of the divine essence, as we have stated.[50] But some consider it impossible for man to see God in His essence, and hence do not desire it. Therefore not all desire happiness.

3. Augustine says, "Happy is the man who has all that he wills, and wills nothing evil." [51] But not all will in this way, for some have wrong desires and will to so desire. Therefore not all desire happiness.

On the contrary: Augustine says, "If that actor had said, 'You all wish to be happy, you do not wish to be miserable,' he would have said what none could fail to recognize as what he wills." [52] Therefore anyone desires to be happy.

Response: Happiness can be considered in two ways. First, from the point of view of the common notion of happiness, and as regards this, every man necessarily desires happiness. The common notion of happiness is that it is a perfect or complete good, as we have said.[53] Now since the object of the will is the good, the perfect good for a man is whatever wholly satisfies his will. Hence to desire happiness is simply to desire that one's will be wholly satisfied, and this everyone desires.

Secondly, we may speak of happiness from the point of view of what it is in particular, as regards the object in which happiness consists. Not all know happiness in this way because not all know the reality in which the common notion of happiness is found; and consequently, in this respect, not all desire happiness.

Reply to 1: The reply is clear from what is said above.

Reply to 2: The will follows the apprehension of the intellect or rea-

---

[48] Cf. Aristotle, *On the Soul* III, 10 (433a 27).
[49] *The Trinity* XIII, 4.   [50] Question 3, article 8.   [51] *Op. cit.* XIII, 5.
[52] *Op. cit.* XIII, 3.   [53] Articles 3 and 4.

son. Now just as it is possible that something is the same in reality which is diverse as considered by reason,[54] so also it is possible that what is the same in reality is desired in one way, and not in another. Accordingly, happiness can be considered as the ultimate and perfect good, which is the common notion of happiness, and thus considered, the will tends to happiness naturally and necessarily, as we have said.[55] Happiness can also be viewed with regard to certain special considerations: from the point of view of the activity itself, of the power of operation, and of the object; and thus considered, the will does not of necessity tend to happiness.

Reply to 3: The definition which some give of happiness—"Happy is he who has all he wills," or "whose every wish is fulfilled"—is a good and sufficient definition if it is understood in one way, but is imperfect if understood in another way. For if we understand it absolutely, as meaning all man desires by nature, then it is true that he who has all he wills is happy, for nothing fully satisfies man's natural appetite except the perfect good which is happiness. But if we take it to mean the things man desires according to the apprehension of his reason, there are certain things man desires which do not lead to happiness but rather to unhappiness, inasmuch as the possession of them hinders man from having all he naturally desires, as in a similar way reason may sometimes accept as true something that hinders it from arriving at knowledge of truth. Augustine took this into consideration when he added "and desires nothing evil," so as to include perfect happiness. However, the first part of the definition—"Happy is he who has all he wills"—is sufficient if it is correctly understood.

---

[54] For example, we make a distinction by reason between mercy and justice in God, though they are not really distinct in God.

[55] In this article, and also article 4, reply to 2.

The Voluntary and the Involuntary

(In Eight Articles)

Since happiness is to be gained through acts of some kind, we must now consider human acts in order to know which are the acts by which we shall achieve happiness and which will prevent us from achieving it. Because operations and acts are concerned with singulars, any practical science would be incomplete without a consideration of actions in their particularity. Hence a treatment of moral matters, since it deals with human acts, must first consider them universally and then in particular.[1]

In treating of what is universal in human acts, the first thing to be considered is human acts themselves; then we must consider the principles of human acts.[2] Now some acts which men do are proper to man, while others are common to men and animals. And since happiness is man's proper good, acts that are properly human are more closely related to happiness than are acts common to man and the other animals. Accordingly we must first consider the acts which are proper to man; then the acts common to man and the other animals.[3]

Apropos of human acts, there are two points to consider. The first is the condition for a human act [that is, what makes an act human]. The second is the distinction of human acts.[4] Now since those acts are properly called human which are voluntary—for the will is a rational appetite proper to man—we must consider acts insofar as they are voluntary. Hence first we will consider the voluntary and the involuntary in general; second, those voluntary acts which belong to the will itself immediately, as being elicited by the will;[5] third, the voluntary acts which belong to the will through the other powers being commanded by the will.[6]

Moreover, because voluntary acts have certain circumstances, according to which we form judgments about the acts, after treating the voluntary and involuntary in general, we will consider the circumstances of voluntary and involuntary acts.[7]

We therefore begin with the voluntary and involuntary in general.

---

[1] This treatment is taken up in II-II of the *Summa Theologiae*.
[2] Question 49 and thereafter, the treatises on habit, virtue, law, and grace.
[3] The treatise on the passions, questions 22-48.
[4] Questions 18-21.   [5] Questions 8-16.   [6] Question 17.
[7] Question 7.

First Article

IS THERE ANYTHING VOLUNTARY ABOUT HUMAN ACTS?

It seems that there is nothing voluntary about human acts.

1. That is voluntary "whose principle is within itself," as noted by Gregory of Nyssa,[8] Damascene,[9] and Aristotle.[10] However, the principle of human acts is not in man himself, but outside of him, for man's desire is moved to act by a desirable object outside of him, and is like "a mover that is not itself in motion." [11] Therefore there is not anything voluntary about human acts.

2. The Philosopher proves that in animals there is no new motion which did not come from another exterior motion.[12] But every human act is new, for no human act is eternal. Therefore the principle of every human act is outside of it. Hence there is nothing voluntary about a human act.

3. Whoever acts voluntarily can act of himself. But this does not belong to man, for "Without Me you can do nothing" (*John 15:5*). Therefore nothing voluntary is found in human acts.

On the contrary: Damascene says, "The act which is a rational operation is voluntary." [13] But human acts are of this kind. Therefore there is something voluntary in human acts.

Response: There must be something voluntary in human acts. To make this evident, we must note that the principle of certain acts or movements is within the agent, that is, in that which is moved, while the principle of other movements or acts is outside. Thus when a stone is thrown up, the principle of this movement is outside the stone, but when it falls downward the principle of the movement is in the stone. Now of those things moved by an intrinsic principle, some move themselves, others do not. And since every agent or thing moved acts or is moved for an end, as we have said,[14] those which are perfectly moved by an intrinsic principle are the ones in which there is an intrinsic principle not only of their movement, but of their movement to an end. Now in order that something be done for an end, some knowledge of the end is required. Hence whatever so acts or is moved by an intrinsic principle that it has some knowledge of the end, has within itself a principle of its acts, so that it not only acts, but acts for the sake of an end.

Now if a thing has no knowledge of an end, even though a principle of action or motion is within it, then the principle of acting or moving

---

[8] Cf. Nemesius, *On the Nature of Man,* 32.
[9] *On the Orthodox Faith* II, 24.   [10] *Nicomachean Ethics* III, 1 (111a 23).
[11] Aristotle, *On the Soul* III, 10 (433b 11).
[12] *Physics* VIII, 2 (253a 11).   [13] *On the Orthodox Faith* II, 24.
[14] Question 1, article 2.

for an end is not within it but in something else, from which the principle of its motion to an end is impressed upon it. Hence things of this kind are not said to move themselves but to be moved by others. But things which have knowledge of an end are said to move themselves, because there is in them a principle by which they not only act but act also for an end. And consequently, since both of these—to act and to act for an end—are from an intrinsic principle, the movements and acts of such things are called voluntary, for the name "voluntary" implies a motion or an act from one's own inclination. Hence, the definitions of Aristotle, Gregory of Nyssa, and Damascene[15] say not only that the voluntary is that "whose principle is within itself," but include "knowledge" as well. Hence since man most of all knows the end of his action and moves himself, the voluntary is found most of all in his actions.

Reply to 1: Not every principle is a first principle. Therefore, although it is of the nature of the voluntary that its principle be intrinsic, still it is not contrary to the nature of the voluntary that the intrinsic principle be caused or moved by an extrinsic principle, for it is not of the nature of the voluntary that its intrinsic principle be a first principle. On the other hand, it should be noted that a principle of movement can be first in a genus without being first absolutely. For example, in the genus of things subject to alteration, the first principle of alteration is a heavenly body, which is not, however, a first mover absolutely, but is moved according to place by a higher mover.[16] So, too, the intrinsic principle of the voluntary act, the cognitive and appetitive powers, is the first principle in the genus of appetitive movement, although it is moved by an extrinsic principle according to other kinds of motion.

Reply to 2: A new movement of an animal is preceded by an exterior motion in two respects. First, insofar as something to be sensed is presented to an animal's senses by an exterior motion which, being apprehended, moves desire. Thus a lion, seeing an approaching stag by reason of its movement, begins to be moved toward it. Second, insofar as some physical change is brought about in an animal's body by an exterior movement, for example, by cold or heat. Now when the body is thus changed by an exterior movement so also is sense desire accidentally, which is the power of a bodily organ; thus with a change in the body the desire is moved to seek something. This, however, is not contrary to the notion of the voluntary, for such movements from an exterior principle belong to another genus.

Reply to 3: God moves man to act, not only by offering to the senses what is desirable, or by bringing about some change in the body, but also

---

[15] Cf. notes 9-11 above.

[16] The illustration is taken from ancient Greek astronomy. Both Aristotle and St. Thomas held the basis for the "incorruptible celestial body" theory to be no more than likely (cf. *On the Heavens* I, 3 [270b 10]; St. Thomas Commentary, Lesson 7, n. 6). If taken as a fictive example, it can be used in argument.

by moving the will itself, for all motion, voluntary and physical, proceeds from God as from the first mover. Just as it is not contrary to nature that the movement of nature be from God as the first mover insofar as nature is a kind of instrument moved by God, so it is not contrary to the nature of a voluntary act that it be from God inasmuch as the will is moved by God. Nevertheless, it is common to physical and voluntary motion that they be from an intrinsic principle.

Second Article

ARE IRRATIONAL ANIMALS VOLUNTARY IN ANY WAY?

It seems that there is nothing voluntary in irrational animals.

1. The name "voluntary" is derived from the name "will." [17] Since the will is in reason,[18] it cannot be in irrational animals. Therefore nothing voluntary is found in them.

2. Insofar as human acts are voluntary, man is said to be master of his acts. But irrational animals do not have dominion over their acts, "for they do not act, but rather are acted upon," as Damascene says.[19] Therefore there is no voluntary act in irrational animals.

3. Damascene says that "praise and blame follow upon voluntary acts." [20] But the acts of irrational animals are not subject to praise or blame. Therefore their acts are not voluntary.

On the contrary: Aristotle says that "children and irrational animals share in voluntary action." [21] Damescene says the same,[22] and so does Gregory of Nyssa.[23]

Response: As we have said,[24] to be voluntary, the principle of the act must be within the agent, together with some knowledge of an end. Now knowledge of an end is twofold, perfect and imperfect. In perfect knowledge, not only is there apprehension of the thing which is an end, but there is knowledge of what an end is and of the comparative relation between the means and that end. Such knowledge of an end belongs only to a rational nature. Imperfect knowledge of an end consists only in apprehending it without knowing it as an end or knowing the comparative relation between the act and the end. This is the kind of knowledge of the end irrational animals have through sense and the estimative power.

Hence an act that is perfectly voluntary follows upon a perfect knowl-

---

[17] The derivation is clear in Latin: "Voluntarium a voluntate dicitur."

[18] Aristotle, *On the Soul* III, 9 (432b 5).   [19] *On the Orthodox Faith* II, 27.

[20] *Op. cit.* II, 24.   [21] *Nicomachean Ethics* III, 2 (1111b 8).

[22] *Op. cit.* II, 24.

[23] Cf. Nemesius, *On the Nature of Man,* 32.

[24] Article 1.

edge of the end; for, after grasping the end, a man, by deliberating about the end and the means to it, can be moved to attain the end or not. An imperfect kind of voluntariness results from an imperfect knowledge of of the end inasmuch as the one apprehending the end does not deliberate but is moved at once to the end. Hence the voluntary that is perfect in kind belongs only to a rational nature; the imperfect kind belongs also to irrational animals.

Reply to 1: "Will" is the name for rational appetite and hence it cannot be in beings lacking reason. But "voluntary" comes by way of denomination from "will" [25] and can be extended to those things in which there is some participation of will by way of likeness. It is thus that "voluntary" is attributed to irrational animals inasmuch as they are moved to an end through some kind of knowledge.

Reply to 2: Man is master of his own acts because he can deliberate about them, for when deliberating, reason is related to opposite alternatives, and the will can tend to either. But the voluntary in this sense is not in irrational animals.

Reply to 3: Praise and blame follow upon the voluntary act which is perfect in kind; there is not this kind in irrational animals.

Third Article

CAN THERE BE VOLUNTARINESS WITHOUT ANY ACT?

It seems that there cannot be voluntariness without any act.

1. That which is from the will is called voluntary. But nothing can proceed from the will except through an act, at least of the will itself. Therefore there cannot be voluntariness without some act.

2. Just as one is said to will by an act of the will, so when the act of the will ceases one is said not to will. But not to will causes involuntariness, which is opposed to voluntariness. Therefore there is not any voluntariness when the act of the will ceases.

3. Knowledge pertains to the notion of the voluntary, as we have pointed out.[26] But knowledge occurs through some act. Therefore there cannot be any voluntariness without an act.

On the contrary: "Voluntary" is said of the acts of which we are masters. We are masters with respect to willing and not willing, acting and not acting. Therefore just as willing and acting are voluntary, so also are not willing and not acting.

Response: That which is from the will is called voluntary. Now a thing is said to be from another in two ways. In one way directly, as one thing proceeds from another inasmuch as it is acting, as heating from heat. In

---

[25] See note 17 above. [26] Articles 1 and 2.

another way indirectly, as proceeding from something not acting; thus the sinking of a ship is attributed to a pilot by his failing to steer. Yet it should be noted that what follows from a defect in acting is not always to be attributed as a cause to an agent as not acting, but only when the agent can and should act. For if the pilot were unable to steer the ship, or the steering of the ship was not entrusted to him, the sinking of the ship could not be imputed to him, though happening by his absence.

Accordingly, by willing and acting, the will can prevent not willing and not acting, and sometimes should; and thus not to will and not to act can be imputed to the will as though coming from it. In this way there can be voluntariness without some act: sometimes without an exterior act though with an interior act, as when one wills not to act; sometimes without even an interior act, as when one does not will to act.

Reply to 1: The voluntary means not only what proceeds directly from the will, as from its acting, but also what proceeds indirectly from it by its not acting.

Reply to 2: "Not to will" is said in two ways. In one way, as though it were one word, and the infinitive of "I do not will." [27] Thus when I say "I do not will to read," the meaning is "I will not to read," and in this sense "not to will to read" signifies "to will not to read." And in this way "not to will" causes the involuntary. In another way, "not to will" is taken as a composite expression, and then no act of the will is affirmed. In this sense, "not to will" does not cause the involuntary.

Reply to 3: Just as an act of knowledge is required for voluntariness so also is an act of the will, that is, it must be within one's power to consider, to will, and to act. Then just as not to will and not to act are voluntary, when it is time to will or act, so also not to consider is voluntary.

Fourth Article

CAN VIOLENCE BE DONE TO THE WILL?

It seems that violence can be done to the will.

1. Anything can be compelled by what is more powerful. But God is more powerful than the human will. Therefore at least God can force the human will.

2. Everything passive is compelled by what acts upon it and changes it. But the will is a passive power, for it is "a moved mover." [28] Since therefore it is sometimes moved by its active principle, it seems that sometimes it is compelled.

3. A violent movement is one that is contrary to nature. But the movement of the will is sometimes contrary to nature, as is evident in the will's

---

[27] "Nolo" in Latin.
[28] Aristotle, *On the Soul* III, 10 (433b 16).

movement to sin, which is contrary to nature, as Damascene says.[29] Therefore the movement of the will can be compelled.

On the contrary: Augustine says that what is done voluntarily is not done by necessity.[30] Now everything done under compulsion is done by necessity. Hence what is done voluntarily cannot be under compulsion. Therefore the will cannot be forced to act.

Response: There is a twofold act of the will. One is its immediate act, the one that is elicited from it, namely, willing itself. The other act of the will is one commanded by the will and put into execution by means of some other power, as walking and speaking, which are commanded by the will to be executed by a motive power. The will can undergo violence with respect to these commanded acts insofar as violence can prevent exterior members from executing the will's command. But no violence can be done to the proper act of the will.

The reason for this is that the act of the will is simply a kind of inclination proceeding from the interior knowing principle, just as the natural appetite is a kind of inclination proceeding from an interior principle without knowledge. Now what is forced or violent comes from an exterior principle. Hence to be forced or compelled to will is contrary to the very nature of the will's own act, just as any forced or violent movement is contrary to the natural inclination or movement of natural things. For a stone can be moved upward by force, but it is impossible for this violent movement to be from its natural inclination. Similarly a man can be dragged by force, but that this happen by his own will conflicts with the notion of violence.

Reply to 1: God, being more powerful than the human will, can move the human will, as is said in Scripture: "The heart of the king is in the hand of the Lord; whithersoever He will He shall turn it" (*Proverbs 21:1*). But if this were done by violence it would not then be by an act of the will, nor would the will itself be moved, but it would be something contrary to the will.

Reply to 2: There is not always a movement of violence when what is passive is changed by its active principle, but only when this is done against the interior inclination of what is passive. Otherwise all alterations and generations would be unnatural and violent. They are natural, however, because of the natural interior aptitude of the matter or of the subject to such a disposition. In like manner, when the will is moved to what is desirable by its own inclination, the movement is not violent, but voluntary.

Reply to 3: What the will tends to in sinning, though evil and contrary to a rational nature, is nevertheless apprehended as good and suitable to nature insofar as it is suitable to man by reason of some pleasurable sensation or some bad habit.

---

[29] *On the Orthodox Faith* IV, 20.   [30] *The City of God* V, 10.

Fifth Article

DOES VIOLENCE CAUSE INVOLUNTARINESS?

It seems that violence does not cause involuntariness.
1. We say "voluntary" and "involuntary" in reference to the will. But violence cannot be done to the will, as we have shown.[31] Therefore violence cannot cause involuntariness.
2. What is done involuntarily is done with sorrow, as Damascene[32] and Aristotle[33] say. But sometimes one undergoes violence without being saddened by it. Therefore violence does not cause involuntariness.
3. What is willed cannot be involuntary. But some violent movements are voluntary; for instance, when a man with a heavy body moves upward or when a man bends his bodily members in a way contrary to their natural flexibility. Therefore violence does not cause involuntariness.
On the contrary: Aristotle[34] and Damascene[35] say that "things done under compulsion are involuntary."
Response: Violence is directly opposed to the voluntary and to what is natural. For what is common to the voluntary and to the natural is that both are from an intrinsic principle, whereas violence is from an extrinsic principle. Accordingly, just as in things lacking knowledge violence brings about something against nature, so in beings that know, violence brings about something against the will. Now whatever is done against nature is said to be unnatural, and likewise whatever is done against the will is said to be involuntary. Hence violence causes involuntariness.
Reply to 1: The involuntary is opposed to the voluntary. We have noted above[36] that "voluntary" is said not only of the immediate act of the will itself, but also of an act commanded by the will. With respect to the act which is immediately of the will, violence cannot be done to the will, as we have also said.[37] Hence violence cannot make such an act involuntary. But with respect to the commanded act, the will can undergo violence. In this respect violence can cause involuntariness.
Reply to 2: Just as what is according to the tendency of nature is said to be natural, so what is according to the inclination of the will is said to be voluntary. Now something is said to be natural in two ways. In one way, because it is from nature as from an active principle, as heating is natural to fire. In another way in reference to a passive principle, for there is in nature a tendency to receive action from an extrinsic principle; thus the movement of the heavens is said to be natural because of the natural tendency of a heavenly body to such a movement, though the

---

[31] Article 4.
[33] *Nicomachean Ethics* III, 1 (1111a 20).
[35] *Op. cit.* II, 25.
[36] Article 4.
[32] *On the Orthodox Faith* II, 25.
[34] *Op. cit.* (1109b 35).
[37] *Ibid.*

mover is a voluntary agent.[38] Similarly something is said to be voluntary in two ways. In one way, with reference to action, for example when one wills to do something; in another, with reference to undergoing an action, as when one wills to receive action from another. Hence when action is undergone from some exterior agent, so long as there remains in the one undergoing it a willingness to undergo it, this is not violent absolutely, for although the one acted upon contributes nothing to the action, nevertheless he contributes something by being willing to undergo it. Hence it cannot be called involuntary.

Reply to 3: As the Philosopher says,[39] a movement of an animal, which at times is against the natural tendency of the body, is still in some way natural to the animal, even though not natural to the body, since it is natural for an animal to be moved according to desire. Hence it is not absolutely violent, but only relatively so. The same is to be said when one flexes bodily members in a way contrary to their natural disposition. This is relatively violent—with respect to this or that member—but not violent absolutely with respect to man himself.

Sixth Article

DOES FEAR CAUSE COMPLETE INVOLUNTARINESS?

It seems that fear causes complete involuntariness.

1. Just as violence is in regard to what is at present contrary to the will, so fear is in regard to an impending evil which is abhorrent to the will. But violence causes complete involuntariness; therefore fear also causes complete involuntariness.

2. What is of itself so remains so no matter what is added; for instance, what is of itself hot, as long as it remains so regardless of what is added, is still hot. But whatever is done through fear is of itself involuntary. Therefore even when the fear is present, what is done is involuntary.

3. Whatever is so conditionally is so qualifiedly, whereas what is so unconditionally is so unqualifiedly. Thus what is necessary conditionally is necessary qualifiedly and what is necessary absolutely is necessary unqualifiedly. But that which is done through fear is involuntary absolutely, and is only voluntary conditionally, namely, in order to avoid some evil which is feared. Therefore that which is done out of fear is completely involuntary.

---

[38] See note 16 above. But two points are involved here that are independent of ancient astronomy. The first is that nature is said both of active and passive principles, so that a thing may have an active cause outside the thing and yet be natural in becoming and motion; for example, that water be heated by the sun is as natural as the sun shining upon it. The second point is that every work of nature is at the same time the work of intellect and will. Cf. I, question 104, article 1.

[39] *Physics* VIII, 4 (254b 14).

On the contrary: Gregory of Nyssa says,[40] and also Aristotle,[41] that what is done out of fear is "more voluntary than involuntary."

Response: As the Philosopher says,[42] and also Gregory of Nyssa,[43] actions done out of fear are "mixed in character, being partly voluntary and partly involuntary." For that which is done through fear, considered in itself, is not voluntary; but it becomes voluntary in the event that something is done to avoid an evil feared.

But if one considers this matter rightly, such acts are more voluntary than involuntary, for they are voluntary absolutely and involuntary in a certain respect. For a thing is said to be absolutely according as it is in act, but according as it is only in apprehension it is not said to be absolutely, but in a certain respect. Now that which is done out of fear is in act to the extent that it is done. For acts are in the order of singulars, and the singular as such takes place here and now; hence that which is actually done is that which takes place here and now and under these individual conditions. Accordingly that which is done out of fear is voluntary, inasmuch as it occurs here and now; that is, according as, in **this** instance, it prevents a greater evil which was feared. For example, the throwing of the cargo into the sea becomes voluntary at the time of a storm because of the fear of danger, and hence it is evident that it is voluntary absolutely. Accordingly voluntariness belongs to it because its. principle is intrinsic. But if we consider that which is done out of fear, as it is apart from this particular instance and as repugnant to the will, this exists only according to a consideration on the part of our mind. Hence it is involuntary in a certain respect, that is, apart from this or that particular instance.

Reply to 1: Things done out of fear and compulsion differ not only according to present and future but also in the following respect. With regard to what is done out of compulsion, the will does not consent, for compulsion is wholly against the inclination of the will, whereas what is done out of fear becomes voluntary in that the will is led to it, not because of itself, but on account of something else, namely, in order to avoid the evil which is feared. It suffices for the notion of the voluntary that something be willed for the sake of something else, for the voluntary is not only that which we will for its own sake as an end, but also what we will for the sake of something else, i.e., for an end. It is clear therefore that in what is done out of compulsion the will interiorly does nothing, whereas in what is done out of fear the will does do something. Hence Gregory of Nyssa in defining violence, in order to exclude things done out of fear, points out that not only should we say "violent action is one whose principle is extrinsic," but we should add, "with the one undergo-

---

[40] Cf. Nemesius, *On the Nature of Man*, 30.
[41] *Nicomachean Ethics* VI, 5 (1140b 12).   [42] *Ibid.*
[43] *Op. cit.*, 30.

ing violence contributing nothing," [44] for in what is done out of fear the will of the one fearing contributes something.

Reply to 2: Whatever is said absolutely remains so whatever is added to it, for example, what is cold or hot. But what is said in a relative way varies according to a comparison with different things. Thus what is large in comparison with one thing is small in comparison with another. Now something is said to be voluntary, not only because of itself as though absolutely, but also because of something else as though relatively. Consequently nothing prevents a thing which is not voluntary as compared to one thing from being voluntary as compared to another.

Reply to 3: That which is done out of fear is voluntary unconditionally, that is, when actually done, but is involuntary conditionally, that is, if such a fear were not threatening. Hence the argument given is more a proof of the opposite view.

Seventh Article

DOES CONCUPISCENCE CAUSE INVOLUNTARINESS?

It seems that concupiscence causes involuntariness.

1. Just as fear is a passion, so is concupiscence. But fear causes involuntariness in a certain way, and therefore also concupiscence.

2. Just as the timid man through fear acts contrary to what he has proposed to do, so does the incontinent man through concupiscence. But fear causes involuntariness in a certain way, and therefore concupiscence does also.

3. Knowledge is required for voluntariness. But concupiscence causes a deterioration of knowledge, for the Philosopher says that "delight," or lustful delight, "destroys the judgment of prudence." [45] Therefore concupiscence causes involuntariness.

On the contrary: Damascene says, "An involuntary act deserves mercy or indulgence, and is done with regret." [46] But neither of these is appropriate to what is done out of concupiscence. Therefore concupiscence does not cause involuntariness.

Response: Concupiscence does not cause involuntariness, but rather makes an act voluntary. For something is said to be voluntary from the fact that the will is moved to it. Now concupiscence disposes the will to consent to the object of concupiscence. Hence concupiscence makes something to be voluntary rather than involuntary.

Reply to 1: Fear is in regard to an evil, concupiscence to a good. Now evil of itself is contrary to the will, while good is in harmony with the

---

[44] *Ibid.*
[46] *On the Orthodox Faith* II, 24.

[45] *Nicomachean Ethics* VI, 5 (1140b 12).

will. Hence fear is more apt to cause involuntariness than concupiscence.

Reply to 2: In the one who acts from fear there remains repugnance of the will for what he is doing, considered in itself. But one who acts from concupiscence, inasmuch as he is incontinent, does not retain in his will the previous repudiation of the object of concupiscence; rather, his will is changed so that he wills the object which he previously repudiated. Hence, while that which is done out of fear is involuntary in a certain way, that which is done from concupiscence in no way is involuntary. For an incontinent man in yielding to concupiscence acts contrary to what he formerly intended, but not contrary to what he now wishes to do, while the timid person acts contrary to what he would now wish to do.

Reply to 3: If concupiscence were to destroy knowledge entirely—as happens to those who become demented through concupiscence—then concupiscence would destroy voluntariness. Yet, strictly speaking, this would not make the act involuntary, for there is neither voluntariness nor involuntariness in those lacking the use of reason. But sometimes in acts done out of concupiscence knowledge is not wholly destroyed, for the power of knowing is not destroyed but only the actual consideration of reason in respect to a particular act. But this itself is voluntary according as the voluntary means that which is within the power of the will, which includes *not to act* and *not to will,* and in like manner *not to deliberate,* for the will can resist passion, as we shall say later on.[47]

Eighth Article

DOES IGNORANCE CAUSE INVOLUNTARINESS?

It seems that ignorance does not cause involuntariness.

1. "An involuntary act deserves pardon," as Damascene says.[48] But sometimes what is done through ignorance does not deserve pardon, for "if anyone is ignorant of this, he shall be ignored" (*I Corinthians 14:38*). Therefore ignorance does not cause involuntariness.

2. Every sin is committed with ignorance, for "they err, that work evil" (*Proverbs 14:22*). Hence if ignorance caused involuntariness, then every sin would be involuntary, which is contrary to the saying of Augustine that "every sin is voluntary." [49]

3. "The involuntary act is done with regret," as Damascene says.[50] But some things done out of ignorance are done without regret; for example, one may kill an enemy whom he wants to kill though thinking at the time that he is killing a deer. Therefore ignorance does not cause involuntariness.

---

[47] Question 10, article 3; question 77, article 7.
[48] *On the Orthodox Faith* II, 24.   [49] *The True Religion,* 14.
[50] *Op. cit.*

On the contrary: Damascene,[51] and the Philosopher[52] say that "what is done through ignorance is involuntary."

Response: Ignorance causes involuntariness insofar as it deprives one of knowledge, which is a necessary condition for voluntariness, as explained above.[53] But not all ignorance deprives one of such knowledge. Accordingly we must note that ignorance is related in three ways to the act of the will: concomitantly, consequently, and antecedently. It is related *concomitantly* when there is ignorance of what is done, but in such a way that had knowledge been present the act would have been done anyway. In this instance, ignorance does not lead one to will this act, but it just happens that something at the same time is done and not known; thus, in the example given above, a man did want to kill his enemy, yet he killed him in ignorance thinking he was killing a deer. Such ignorance does not make an act involuntary, as the Philosopher says,[54] because it does not cause anything contrary to the will; but it does make the act *non-voluntary,* since what is unknown cannot be actually willed.

Ignorance is *consequent* to the will to the extent that the ignorance itself is voluntary. This happens in two ways, in accordance with the two modes of the voluntary act stated above.[55] The first way occurs when the act of the will is brought to bear on the ignorance, as when one wills not to know in order to have an excuse for sin, or so as not to be turned away from sin, as is said in Scripture: "We desire not the knowledge of Thy ways" (*Job 21:14*). This is known as *affected ignorance.* In a second way, ignorance is voluntary when it concerns that which one can and ought to know, and in this sense not to act and not to will are said to be voluntary, as we have said.[56] Ignorance of this kind occurs either when one does not actually consider what he can and should consider (this is ignorance of evil choice, arising either from passion or habit) or when one does not take care to acquire the knowledge which he ought to have (this is ignorance of the general principles of law, and since one is bound to know this, it is voluntary as arising from negligence). Now if ignorance is voluntary in either of these two ways, it cannot cause involuntariness absolutely. Nevertheless it does cause involuntariness in a certain respect insofar as it precedes the movement of the will toward doing something which would not be done if knowledge were present.

Ignorance is *antecedent* to the will when it is not voluntary and yet is the cause of willing what otherwise one would not will. For example, a man may be ignorant of some circumstance of an act which he is not bound to know, such that he does what he would not do if he knew the circumstance. For example, a man, having taken proper precaution, not

---

[51] *Op. cit.*   [52] *Nicomachean Ethics* III, 1 (1110a 1).
[53] Article 1.   [54] *Op. cit.* (1110b 25).   [55] Article 3.
[56] *Ibid.*

knowing that someone is coming along a road, shoots an arrow and kills him. Such ignorance causes involuntariness absolutely.

The replies to the objections are clear from the foregoing. The first objection deals with ignorance of what one is bound to know. The second concerns ignorance of choice, which is voluntary to a certain extent, as we have just pointed out. The third is about ignorance which is related concomitantly to the will.

The Circumstances of Human Acts

(In Four Articles)

IS A CIRCUMSTANCE AN ACCIDENT [1] OF A HUMAN ACT?

It seems that a circumstance is not an accident of a human act.

1. Cicero says that a circumstance is "that from which an orator adds authority and strength to his argument." [2] But rhetorical speech derives force principally from what pertains to the substance of a thing, such as definition, genus, species, and the like, from which Cicero also maintains that an orator should draw his argument. [3] Therefore a circumstance is not an accident of the human act.

2. It is proper to an accident to exist in something else. But a circumstance is that which is not in something else but rather is outside it. Therefore circumstances are not accidents of human acts.

3. What belongs to an accident is not an accident. But human acts themselves are accidents. Therefore circumstances are not accidents of acts.

On the contrary: The particular conditions of any singular thing are called individuating accidents of it. But the Philosopher calls circumstances "particulars," that is, particular conditions of singular acts. [4] Therefore circumstances are individual accidents of human acts.

Response: Since names are signs of things as they are understood, according to the Philosopher, [5] the process of naming follows the progress of knowing. Now our intellectual knowledge proceeds from the more known to the less known. Hence with respect to our way of knowing, names of things more known to us are transferred to signify things less known to us. Thus Aristotle remarks that the notion of distance has been extended from things that are distant according to place to any distance between extremes. [6] In like manner, names pertaining to local motion are used to signify other motions, since bodies which are circumscribed by place are best known to us. Hence the name "circumstance" has been extended from things that are in a place to human acts.

---

[1] A characteristic added to an act already established as having a certain morality.
[2] *On Rhetoric* I, 24.   [3] *Topics,* 3.
[4] *Nicomachean Ethics* III, 1 (1110b 33).   [5] *On Interpretation* I, 1 (16a 3).
[6] Cf. *Metaphysics* X, 4 (1055a 9).

Now in things located in a place, that which is extrinsic to the thing yet touches it or is near it as to place is said to "surround" it.[7] Hence whatever conditions are outside the substance of an act, and yet in some way affect the act, are called circumstances. But that which is outside the substance of a thing and yet affects it is called an accident of it. Therefore circumstances of human acts should be called their accidents.

Reply to 1: Rhetorical speech does derive the force of an argument primarily from the substance of the act, but secondarily from circumstances affecting the act. Thus a man is first of all indicted because of murder, but secondarily because of trickery, or greed, or committing it in a sacred place or time, and so on. Hence in the passage quoted, Cicero significantly says that through circumstances "an orator adds strength to his argument," that is, this adds to his argument as something secondary.

Reply to 2: A thing is said to be an accident of something in two ways. In one way because it is present in something else, as white is said to be an accident of Socrates. In another way because it exists at once with that thing in the same subject, as white is an accident of musical inasmuch as they come together and in a certain way join each other in the same subject. It is in this sense that circumstances are said to be accidents of human acts.

Reply to 3: An accident is said to be an accident of an accident by reason of their being together in the same subject. This happens in two ways. In one way, as two accidents are related to one subject but without any relation to each other, as white and musical are related to Socrates. In another way, when there is some order; for example, when a subject receives one accident by means of another, as a body takes on color by means of its surface. In this way one accident is said to be in another, for we say color is in the surface. Now circumstances are related to acts in both ways. For some circumstances which are related to acts belong to an agent otherwise than by means of the act, for example the place and the kind of person; others are related to the agent by means of the act, for example the manner in which the act is done.

Second Article

SHOULD THE THEOLOGIAN CONSIDER CIRCUMSTANCES OF HUMAN ACTS?

It seems that the theologian need not consider the circumstances of human acts.

1. The theologian considers human acts only as they are good or evil. But circumstances do not so qualify human acts since, formally speaking, nothing is qualified by what is extrinsic but only by what is intrinsic. Therefore circumstances of acts need not be considered by the theologian.

---

[7] The Latin is "circumstare."

2. Circumstances are accidents of acts. But one thing may be subject to an infinity of accidents, and hence Aristotle says "No art or science except that of sophistics treats accidental being." [8] Therefore the theologian does not have to consider circumstances.

3. The consideration of circumstances belongs to the rhetorician. But rhetoric is not a part of theology. Therefore it is not the theologian's concern to consider circumstances.

On the contrary: Ignorance of circumstances causes involuntariness, as Damascene[9] and Gregory of Nyssa[10] say. But involuntariness excuses one from sin, the consideration of which belongs to the theologian. Therefore the theologian also should consider circumstances.

Response: The theologian needs to consider circumstances for three reasons. First, because the theologian considers human acts according as man is ordered to happiness through them. Now whatever is ordered to an end must be proportioned to the end. But acts are proportioned to the end according to a certain measure, which results from due circumstances. Hence the theologian needs to consider circumstances. Second, because the theologian investigates human acts as good and evil, better and worse, and this diversity results from circumstances, as we shall show later on.[11] Third, the theologian investigates human acts as having merit or demerit, which is proper to human acts; and for this it is necessary that acts be voluntary. Now human acts are judged to be voluntary or involuntary according to knowledge or ignorance of circumstances, as we have said.[12] Hence the theologian needs to consider circumstances.

Reply to 1: A good ordered to an end is called useful, and this implies some kind of relation; hence the Philosopher says that the useful good is "the good which is relative to something else." [13] Now as being referred to another, a thing is denominated not only from that which is intrinsic, but also from that which adjoins it extrinsically, as is evident with right and left, equal and unequal, and in other similar instances. Hence, since the goodness of acts consists in their being useful for arriving at the end, nothing prevents their being called good or bad according to a proportion to something that adjoins them extrinsically.

Reply to 2: Accidents which are wholly accidental are not taken into account by any art because of their uncertainty and infinity. But such accidents are not counted as circumstances because, as we have said,[14] though circumstances are extrinsic to the act, yet they have a part in the act as ordained to it. And proper accidents do fall under an art.

Reply to 3: The consideration of circumstances belongs to the moral

[8] *Metaphysics* VI, 2 (1026b 3).   [9] *On the Orthodox Faith* II, 24.
[10] Cf. Nemesius, *On the Nature of Man,* 31.
[11] Question 18, articles 10, 11; question 73, article 4.
[12] Question 6, article 8.   [13] *Nicomachean Ethics* I, 6 (1096a 26).
[14] Article 1.

philosopher, the statesman, and the rhetorician. It belongs to the moral philosopher insofar as the mean of virtue in human acts and passions is gained or not gained in terms of circumstances. It belongs to the statesman and the rhetorician insofar as circumstances render acts worthy of praise or blame, excuse or accusation. The consideration is different in that the rhetorician persuades while the statesman judges. All these considerations belong to the theologian since all the arts are of service to theology. Thus along with the moral philosopher, the theologian has to consider virtuous and vicious acts, and with the rhetorician and the statesman he considers acts insofar as they merit reward or punishment.

Third Article

ARE CIRCUMSTANCES APPROPRIATELY ENUMERATED
IN THE *ETHICS?*

It seems that circumstances are not appropriately enumerated in the *Ethics*.[15]

1. A circumstance of an act is said to be related exteriorly to the act. Time and place are so related to the act. Therefore there are only two circumstances, *when* and *where.*

2. We judge from circumstances whether something is done well or badly; but this belongs to the mode or manner of acting. Therefore all the circumstances are included under one, the *mode or manner of acting.*

3. Circumstances do not belong to the substance of the act. But the causes of an act seem to belong to the substance of the act. Therefore no circumstance ought to be taken from the cause of the act. Accordingly, *who, why,* and *about what* are not circumstances, for *who* refers to the efficient cause, *why* to the final cause, and *about what* to the material cause.

On the contrary: The authority of the Philosopher in the *Ethics* suffices.

Response: Cicero lists seven circumstances, which are contained in the following line: *Who, what, where, by what aids, why, how,* and *when.*[16] For we must consider in acts who did it, by what aids or instruments he did it, what he did, where he did it, why he did it, how he did it, and when he did it. But in the passage in the *Ethics,* Aristotle adds another one, *about what,* which Cicero included under *what.*

The reason for this enumeration can be shown in the following way. A circumstance is said to exist outside the substance of the act though affecting it in some way. This happens in three ways: first, as the circumstance touches the act itself; second, as it affects the cause of the act; and third, as it touches the effect. A circumstance affects the act itself either

---

[15] *Nicomachean Ethics* III, 1 (1111a 3-7).   [16] *On Rhetoric* I, 24.

by way of a measure, as *time* and *place,* or by qualifying the act, as does the *manner of acting.* It touches the effect of the act when we consider *what* someone has done. It affects the cause of the act insofar as the circumstance *why* is referred to the final cause, *about what* to the material cause or object, *who* to the principal efficient cause, and *by what aids* to the instrumental efficient cause.

Reply to 1: Time and place surround an act by way of a measure, but the other circumstances surround an act inasmuch as they affect it in any other way as extrinsic to the substance of the act.

Reply to 2: The mode that concerns an act as well or badly done is not a circumstance, but a result of all the circumstances. But the mode which concerns the quality of the act is a special circumstance, for example, that one walks fast or slowly or strikes hard or gently, and so on.

Reply to 3: The condition of the cause on which the substance of the act depends is not called a circumstance; the circumstance has to be an adjoined condition. Thus, with respect to the object, it is not a circumstance of theft that the object is another's property, for this pertains to the substance of theft; the circumstance is whether the object is large or small. The same is to be said about the other circumstances taken on the part of the other causes. For the end which makes an act to be the kind of act it is, is not a circumstance; it is an adjoined end which is a circumstance.[17] For example, it is not a circumstance that a brave man acts valiantly to attain the good of the virtue of fortitude, but it is if he acts bravely in order to set a country free or for the freedom of Christian people, or for purposes like these. The same is to be said with respect to the *what;* it is not a circumstance when a man in pouring water on someone washes him; the circumstance would consist in making him cold or hot, in healing or injuring him.

Fourth Article

ARE THE CIRCUMSTANCE *WHY* AND THE CIRCUMSTANCE *WHAT IS DONE* [18] THE MOST IMPORTANT?

It seems that the circumstance *why* and the circumstance *what is done* are not the most important, as stated in the *Ethics.*[19]

1. Place and time seem to be circumstances of the act itself, but these do not seem to be the most important circumstances, since of all the circumstances they are most extrinsic to the act. Therefore the circum-

---

[17] The distinction is between the end of the act and the end of the agent.

[18] By this expression (in Latin, "et ea in quibus est operatio") is understood the circumstance *what is done,* a circumstance relating to the act itself and the material object of the act, which touches the substance of the act, particularly as implying its quantity.

[19] *Nicomachean Ethics* III, 1 (1111a 18).

stance relating to what is done [i.e., a circumstance relating to the act itself] is not the most important circumstance.

2. The end of a thing is extrinsic to it. It does not therefore seem to be the most important circumstance.

3. What is most important in anything is its cause and its form. But the cause of the act is the person who acts, and the form of the act is the manner in which it is being done. Therefore these two circumstances seem to be the most important.

On the contrary: Gregory of Nyssa says that "the two most important circumstances are why an act is done and what is done." [20]

Response: Acts are properly called human inasmuch as they are voluntary, as we have said.[21] Now the end is the object and motive of the will. Hence the most important of all circumstances is that which effects the act as to its end, namely the *why;* secondarily, that which affects the substance of the act, that is, *what is done.* The other circumstances are more or less important according as they more or less approach these.

Reply to 1: By the circumstance of what is done [i.e., what relates to the act itself], the Philosopher does not understand time and place, but what is adjoined to the act itself. Hence Gregory of Nyssa, in the passage cited, as if explaining the remarks of the Philosopher, substitutes *what is done* for what relates to the act itself.

Reply to 2: Although the end does not belong to the substance of the act, nevertheless it is the most important cause of the act insofar as it moves the agent to act. Hence the moral act is most of all specified by the end.

Reply to 3: The person who acts is the cause of the act insofar as he is moved to act by the end, and it is especially in terms of this that he is disposed to act. The other conditions affecting a person are not as principally related to the act. Nor is the manner in which the act is done the substantial form of the act, for the form of the act depends upon the object and the term or end of the act; the manner is, rather, a certain accidental quality of the act.

---

[20] Cf. Nemesius, *On the Nature of Man,* 31.
[21] Question 1, article 1.

What the Will Wills

(*In Three Articles*)

We must now consider the acts of the will in particular. First we shall treat the acts that are the will's immediately, as elicited from the will itself; then the acts which are commanded by the will.[1]

Now the will is moved to the end and to the means. Accordingly, we shall treat first the acts by which the will is moved to the end; then the acts by which it is moved to the means.[2]

There seem to be three acts of the will in reference to the end: willing it, enjoying it,[3] and intending it,[4] and we shall take them up in that order. With respect to willing itself, we must consider first what the will wills; second, what moves the will to will;[5] and third, how it is moved.[6]

First Article

DOES THE WILL WILL ONLY THE GOOD?[7]

It seems that the will does not will only what is good.

1. One and the same power is related to opposites, as sight is to white and black. But good and evil are opposites. Therefore not only good but evil is willed.

2. Rational powers can pursue opposite things, according to the Philosopher.[8] But the will is a rational power, for it is "in reason," as Aristotle says.[9] Therefore the will can be directed to opposite things. Hence the will can will evil as well as good.

3. Good and being are convertible. But the will can not only will the being of something but also its non-being, for sometimes we will not to walk or not to speak. And we also sometimes will future things which do not actually yet exist. Therefore we do not will only the good.

---

[1] Question 17.   [2] Question 13.   [3] Question 11.
[4] Question 12.   [5] Question 9.   [6] Question 10.

[7] It should be noted that throughout question 8 as a whole, as well as this article, we are considering a specific act of the will, distinct not only from the power itself, also called "will," but also from other specific acts of the will, such as enjoyment or choice. The specific act now treated is a simple willing, that is, the willing of something as an end.

[8] *Metaphysics* IX, 2 (1046b 8).   [9] *On the Soul* III, 9 (432b 5).

On the contrary: Dionysius says that "evil is outside the power of the will," [10] and that "all desire the good." [11]

Response: The will is a rational appetite.[12] Now appetite is only for the good. The reason for this is that appetite is simply an inclination for something on the part of the one who desires it. Now nothing is favorably disposed to something unless it is like or suitable to it. Hence, since everything, insofar as it is a being and a substance, is a good, every inclination is to a good. Therefore the Philosopher says that the good is "that which all desire." [13]

But it must be noted that since every inclination arises from some form, natural appetite[14] arises from the form that is present in the natural thing, whereas sense appetite as well as rational appetite—the will—arises from a form as known. Hence just as natural appetite tends to a good that is in fact good, so sense appetite as well as the will tend to the good as known. Consequently, for the will to tend to something, it is not required that it be in truth good, but that it be apprehended as good. This is why the Philosopher says that "the end is the good or the apparent good." [15]

Reply to 1: One and the same power is related to opposites but not in the same way to each. Accordingly, the will is related to good and evil, but to the good as seeking it and to evil as avoiding it. Hence the actual appetite for good is called *will* as meaning the will's act, for it is in this sense that we are now speaking of will. But avoidance of evil is better named *unwillingness.* Hence just as the will is of the good so unwillingness is of the evil.

Reply to 2: A rational power is not directed to all opposites, but to those which are contained under its proper object, for a power pursues only what is appropriate to it. Now the object of the will is the good. Hence the will seeks such opposites as are contained under the good, for example being moved and being at rest, speaking or being silent, and things of this kind, for the will can be directed to either under the aspect of good.

Reply to 3: That which is not something in the real order is taken as something existing in reason, and thus negations and privations are called beings of reason. In this way, also, future events, inasmuch as they are apprehended, are beings. Hence insofar as they are beings in this way, they are grasped under the aspect of good, and it is thus that the will

---

[10] *The Divine Names* IV, 32.   [11] *Op. cit.,* 10.

[12] The Latin is "appetitus," which sometimes can be translated as "desire."

[13] *Nicomachean Ethics* I, 1 (1094a 3).

[14] "Natural desire" or "natural appetite" refers to an inclination each and every thing of its own nature has for something suitable to it. It is a desire which does not presuppose knowledge, and thus is distinguished from sense desire and rational desire. See I, question 78, article 1, reply to 3; question 80, article 1.

[15] *Physics* II, 3 (195a 26).

tends to them. Therefore the Philosopher says that "the lack of evil is accounted as good." [16]

Second Article

DO WE WILL THE END ONLY OR ALSO THE MEANS? [17]

It seems that we do not will the means but only the end.

1. Aristotle says, "We will the end but choose the means." [18]

2. "For objects differing in kind, different powers of the soul correspond to them." [19] But ends and means are different kinds of good, for the end, which is either an unqualified good [20] or a pleasurable good, is in the genus of quality or of action or of passion. On the other hand, the good which is called useful, and is a means, is in the genus of relation.[21] Therefore if the volition is of the end, it will not be of the means.

3. Habits are proportioned to powers, since they are the perfections of powers. But in the habits which are called practical arts, the end belongs to one art and the means to another; for example, the use of a ship, which is its end, belongs to the art of the navigator, while the building of the ship, which is a means to the end, belongs to the art of the shipbuilder. Therefore, since volition is of the end, it will not be of the means.

On the contrary: In natural things, it is by the same power that a thing passes through intermediate stages and arrives at the term. Therefore, if the willing is of the end, it is also of the means.

Response: Sometimes by "will" we mean the power itself by which we will and sometimes we mean the will's act. If in speaking of the will we mean the power, then it extends both to the end and to the means. For any power extends to those things in which its kind of object can be found in any way; for example, sight extends to all things whatsoever which in any way share color. But the aspect of good, which is the object of the power of the will, is found not only in the end but also in the means.

However, if we are speaking of the will as it means particularly the act, then it relates to the end only. For every act denominated from a power designates the simple act of that power; for example, "understanding" designates the simple act of the intellect. Now the simple act of a power is referred to that which is in itself the object of that power. But that which is good and willed for itself is the end. Hence, strictly speaking, the simple act of willing is of the end itself. The means, on the other hand, are good or willed, not in themselves, but only as referred to the end. Hence the will is directed to the means only as it is directed to an end,

---

[16] *Nicomachean Ethics* V, 1 (1129b 8).   [17] See note 7 above.

[18] *Nicomachean Ethics* III, 2 (1111b 26).   [19] Aristotle, *op. cit.* VI, 1 (1139a 11).

[20] The Latin is "bonum honestum."

[21] Cf. Aristotle, *Nicomachean Ethics* I, 6 (1096a 26).

so that what is willed in the means is the end. Thus, too, understanding pertains properly to things known in themselves, namely, the first principles; we do not speak of what is known by means of principles as "understanding" except insofar as we see in such knowledge the principles themselves. Hence the end is to appetite as principles are to knowledge.[22]

Reply to 1: The Philosopher is speaking of the will as signifying the simple act of the will, not as signifying the power of the will.

Reply to 2: There are different powers for objects which differ generically on the same level; for example, sound and color are the different genera of sensed objects to which hearing and sight are referred. However, the useful good and the unqualified good are not on the same level for one is good in itself and the other in relation to another. Now objects related in this way are always referred to the same power. The power of sight, for example, senses both color and the light by which color is seen.

Reply to 3: Not everything which diversifies a habit diversifies a power, for habits are determinations of the powers to certain special acts. Nonetheless any practical art considers both the end and the means. For the art of the navigator considers the end, as something to be realized, and directs the means to bringing this about. On the other hand, the art of the shipbuilder considers what the means are for the end it produces, and considers the end as that to which its production is ordered. Furthermore, in any practical art there is an end which is proper to it and a means which properly pertains to that art.

Third Article

IS THE WILL MOVED BY THE SAME ACT TO THE END AND TO THE MEANS?

It seems that the will is moved by the same act to the end and to the means.

1. According to the Philosopher, "where something is for the sake of another, only one thing is involved." [23] But we will a means only because of the end. Therefore the will is moved to both by the same act.

2. The end is the reason for willing the means, just as light is the reason we see colors. But light and color are seen in the same act. Therefore the movement by which we will the end and the means is the same.

3. It is one and numerically the same natural movement which reaches an end through a middle. But means is related to end in willing, as middle is to end in movement. Therefore the movement by which we will the end and the means is the same.

On the contrary: Acts are diversified according to their objects. But the

---

[22] Cf. Aristotle, *op. cit.* VII, 8 (1151a 16).   [23] *Topics* III, 2 (117a 18).

end is a different kind of good from the means, which is called a useful good. Therefore the will does not tend to both by the same act.

Response: Since an end is willed for itself while a means as such is willed only because of an end, it is clear that we can will an end without willing a means, whereas we cannot will a means as such unless we have an end in mind. Accordingly the will is moved to an end in two ways: first, absolutely and of itself; second, as the reason for willing the means. Now it is clear that the will is moved by one and the same movement to the end, as the reason for willing the means, and to the means themselves. But it is another act by which the will is moved to the end absolutely. Sometimes this act precedes in time; for example, a man first wills health and then, after deliberating about how he can be made healthy, wills to send for a doctor to cure him. This is parallel to what happens in relation to the intellect. First we understand the principles by themselves; afterward we understand them in the conclusions inasmuch as we assent to conclusions because of the principles.

Reply to 1: The argument given holds with respect to the willing of the end being the reason for willing the means.

Reply to 2: Whenever a color is seen, light is seen in the same act, but light can be seen without that color being seen. Likewise, whenever one wills a means the end is willed in the same act, but not conversely.

Reply to 3: In the carrying out of a work, the means are like a middle and the end like a term. Hence, just as a natural movement sometimes stops midway and does not reach the term, so sometimes one occupies himself with the means and does not attain the end. But in willing, it is the reverse, for it is through willing the end that one goes on to will the means, as in a parallel way the intellect arrives at conclusions through the principles, which are called means. Hence sometimes the intellect understands the means without going on to the conclusion. In a similar way, we sometimes will an end without going on to will the means to the end.

With respect to what is stated in *On the contrary,* the solution is evident from what we have said above.[24] For a useful good and an absolute good are not species equally dividing the good, but are related as that which is for the sake of another and that which is for its own sake. Hence an act of the will can be moved to the latter without being moved to the former, but not conversely.

---

[24] Article 2, reply to 2.

What Moves the Will

(In Six Articles)

IS THE WILL MOVED BY THE INTELLECT?

It seems that the will is not moved by the intellect.

1. In commenting on *Psalms 118:20,* "My soul hath coveted too long for thy justifications," Augustine says, "The intellect flies on ahead, the desire follows sluggishly or not at all; we know what is good, but we do not delight in the doing of it." [1] This would not be the case if the will were moved by the intellect, for the movement of the movable follows upon the motion of the mover. Therefore the intellect does not move the will.

2. The intellect as representing what is desirable is related to the will as the imagination in representing what is desirable is to sense appetite. But in representing what is desirable, the imagination does not move the sense appetite; in fact, sometimes what we imagine affects us no more than what is seen in a painting, and does not move us at all. [2] Therefore the intellect also does not move the will.

3. One and the same thing is not the same with respect to both mover and moved. But the will moves the intellect, for we understand when we want to understand. Therefore the intellect does not move the will.

On the contrary: The Philosopher says that "what is understood as desirable moves without being moved, whereas the will is both mover and moved." [3]

Response: Insofar as a thing needs to be moved by something else, it is in potency to several things, for whatever is potential needs to be brought to act by what is actual, and to do this is to move. Now a power of the soul is in potency to different things in two ways: in one way, with respect to acting and not acting; in another way, with respect to this act or that act. For example, sometimes sight sees actually and sometimes not; and sometimes it sees white and other times black. Hence a mover is needed in two respects, for the exercise or use of the act, and for determining the act. The first is on the part of the subject, which is sometimes

---

[1] *Commentary on the Psalms 118:20,* sermon 8.
[2] Cf. Aristotle, *On the Soul* III, 3 (427b 23).
[3] *Op. cit.,* 10 (433b 16).

acting and sometimes not; the other is on the part of the object, in conformity with which the act is specified.

Now the motion of the subject is due to some agent, and since every agent acts because of an end, as we have shown above,[4] the principle of this movement is the end. Thus an art which is concerned with an end directs an art which is concerned with the means, "as the art of navigation directs the art of shipbuilding." [5] Now the good in general, which has the nature of an end, is the object of the will. Hence in this respect, the will moves the other powers of the soul to their acts, for we use the other powers when we wish to. For the ends and perfections of all other powers are included under the object of the will as particular goods, and the art or power to which the universal end belongs always moves to act the arts or powers to which belong the particular ends included in the universal end. Thus the general of an army, who intends a common good—the ordering of the whole army—moves by his command an officer who intends the ordering of a company.

The object, on the other hand, moves by determining the act after the manner of a formal principle, like the form by which action is specified in natural things, for instance heating by heat. Now the first formal principle is universal being and truth, which is the object of the intellect. Hence the intellect moves the will in this way, as presenting its object to it.

Reply to 1: This view does not establish that the intellect does not move, but that it does not move by necessity.

Reply to 2: Just as the imagining of something without estimating its fittingness or harmfulness does not arouse sense desire, so neither does the apprehension of what is true without the aspect of goodness and desirability. Hence the speculative intellect is not a mover, but the practical intellect is.

Reply to 3: The will moves the intellect as to the exercise of its act, since the true, which is the perfection of the intellect, is included as a particular good under the universal good. But with respect to the determination of the act, which is in terms of the object, the intellect moves the will, for even the good itself is apprehended as a particular notion included under the universal notion of the true. Thus it is clear that the mover and the moved are not the same with respect to the same thing.

Second Article

IS THE WILL MOVED BY THE SENSE APPETITE?

It seems that the will cannot be moved by the sense appetite.

1. "The mover and agent is superior to the thing acted upon," as Augustine says.[6] But the sense appetite is inferior to the will, which is

---

[4] Question 1, article 2.   [5] Aristotle, *Physics* II, 2 (194b 5).
[6] *A Literal Commentary on "Genesis"* XII, chapter 16.

the intellectual appetite, just as sense is inferior to intellect. Therefore the sense appetite does not move the will.

2. No particular power can produce a universal effect. But the sense appetite is a particular power, for it follows the particular perception of sense. Therefore it cannot cause the movement of the will, which is concerned with the universal, as following the universal apprehension of the intellect.

3. The mover is not moved by that which it moves so that there is reciprocal motion.[7] But the will moves the sense appetite inasmuch as the sense appetite obeys reason. Therefore the sense appetite does not move the will.

On the contrary: "But everyone is tempted by being drawn away and enticed by his own concupiscence" (*James 1:14*). Now no one is drawn away by concupiscence unless his will is moved by sense desire, wherein concupiscence is found. Therefore the sense appetite does move the will.

Response: As we have said above,[8] that which is apprehended as being good and fitting is what moves the will as an object. Now something may seem to be good and fitting in two ways, either from the condition of the thing proposed or of the one to whom it is proposed. Since fittingness is based upon a relation, it depends upon each extreme of the relation. Thus taste, as it is differently disposed, reacts differently to what is fitting or unfitting. Hence the Philosopher says that "according as a man is, such does the end seem to him." [9]

Now it is clear that man is changed as to his disposition according to the passions of the sense appetite. Hence something seems fitting to a man when experiencing a certain passion which would not seem so with the passion absent; for example, something seems good to a man when angry which does not seem so when he is calm. In this way, on the part of the object, the sense appetite moves the will.

Reply to 1: Nothing prevents that which is absolutely and in itself superior from being relatively inferior. The will is absolutely superior to the sense appetite, but in the one in whom passion prevails, insofar as he is subject to the passion, sense appetite is dominant.

Reply to 2: Human acts and choices are about singular matters. Hence, from the fact that sense appetite is a particular power, it has great effect in disposing man so that something appears to him as such or otherwise in singular matters.

Reply to 3: As the Philosopher says,[10] reason, in which the will resides, moves the irascible and concupiscible powers by its command—not by a despotic rule, as a slave is ruled by a master—but by a royal or political rule, as free men are ruled by a governor and yet can act against his com-

---

[7] Cf. Aristotle, *Physics* VIII, 5 (257b 23).   [8] Article 1.
[9] *Nicomachean Ethics* III, 5 (1114a 32).   [10] *Politics* I, 2 (1254b 5).

mands. Hence the irascible and concupiscible powers can move contrary
to the will, and so nothing prevents the will from being moved by them
at times.

Third Article

DOES THE WILL MOVE ITSELF?

It seems that the will does not move itself.

1. Every mover, as a mover, is as such in act, while that which is moved
is in potency, for "motion is the act of that which is in potency insofar as
it is in potency." [11] But the same thing is not in potency and in act in
the same respect. Therefore nothing moves itself, and hence neither can
the will move itself.

2. What is movable is moved by the mover being present to it. But
the will is always present to itself. If therefore it moved itself, it would
always be moved, which is clearly false.

3. The will is moved by the intellect, as we have said.[12] Accordingly,
if the will moved itself, it would follow that the same thing is moved immediately by two movers, which seems unreasonable. Therefore the will
does not move itself.

On the contrary: Because the will has dominion over its own acts, it is
possible for it to will and not to will. But this would not be the case if
it did not have the power to move itself to will. Therefore it moves itself.

Response: As we have said,[13] it belongs to the will to move the other
powers by reason of an end, which is the object of the will. But as we
have also said,[14] the end in relation to what is desirable is like a principle
in relation to what is intelligible. But clearly the intellect through its
knowledge of a principle brings itself from potency to act with regard to
knowledge of conclusions, and in this way moves itself. Similarly the
will, through willing the end, moves itself to will the means to the end.

Reply to 1: The will is not mover and moved in the same respect.
Hence it is not in act and in potency in the same respect. But insofar as
it actually wills the end, it brings itself from potency to act with respect
to the means, so as to will them actually.

Reply to 2: The power of the will is always actually present to it, but
the act of the will, by which it wills an end, is not always present in the
will. But it is by this act that the will moves itself. Hence it does not follow that the will is always moving itself.

Reply to 3: The will is not moved by the intellect and by itself in the
same way. It is moved by the intellect with regard to its object, but is
moved by itself as to the exercise of its act in respect to the end.

---

[11] Aristotle, Physics III, 1 (201a 10).   [12] Article 1.
[13] *Ibid.*   [14] Question 8, article 2.

Fourth Article

IS THE WILL MOVED BY AN EXTERIOR PRINCIPLE?

It seems that the will is not moved by anything exterior.

1. The movement of the will is voluntary. But what is voluntary is from an intrinsic principle just as what is natural is. Therefore the movement of the will is not from anything exterior.

2. The will cannot undergo violence, as we have shown.[15] But a violent act is one "whose principle is extrinsic." [16] Therefore the will cannot be moved by anything external.

3. That which is adequately moved by one mover does not need to be moved by another. But the will adequately moves itself. Therefore it is not moved by something external.

On the contrary: The will is moved by an object, as we have said.[17] But an object of the will can be some external thing presented to the senses. Therefore the will can be moved by something external.

Response: Insofar as the will is moved by an object, it is clear that it can be moved by something external. But even with respect to its being moved to exercise its act, it is necessary to maintain that the will is moved by some external principle. For every agent which is sometimes in act and sometimes in potency needs to be moved by some mover. Now it is evident that the will begins to will something which it did not will before. Therefore it must be moved by something to will it. It indeed moves itself, as we have said,[18] in that by willing an end it is led to will the means. Now this cannot be done without deliberating about the means. For example, when someone wills to be cured, he begins to cogitate about how this can be realized, and through such reflection he concludes that he can be cured by a doctor, and so he wills it. But since he did not always actually will to have health, he must begin to will to have health by something moving him. And if he moved himself to will this, he must have done this by means of deliberation following upon a previous willing. Now this cannot go on endlessly. Hence it is necessary to hold that it is due to the impulse of some external mover that the will is roused to its first movement, as Aristotle concludes.[19]

Reply to 1: It belongs to the notion of the voluntary that its principle be intrinsic, but not that this intrinsic principle be a first principle not moved by something else. Hence voluntary movement, though having a proximate intrinsic principle, comes from an external first principle, just

---

[15] Question 6, article 4.
[16] Aristotle, *Nicomachean Ethics* III, 1 (1110a 1).
[17] Article 1.   [18] Article 3.
[19] *Eudemian Ethics* VII, 14 (1248a 14).

as the first principle of natural movement, the one that moves nature, is something external.

Reply to 2: For a movement to be violent, it is not enough that its principle be external; we have to add "without anything contributed by the one undergoing the action." [20] This does not occur when the will is moved by an exterior principle, for it is the will that wills, though moved by another. This movement would be violent if it were contrary to the movement of the will, which is impossible in the question at issue, for then the will would will and not will the same thing.

Reply to 3: The will adequately moves itself with respect to something in its own order, as a proximate agent, but it cannot move itself with respect to everything. Hence it needs to be moved by another as a first mover.

Fifth Article

IS THE WILL MOVED BY A HEAVENLY BODY?

It seems that the will is moved by a heavenly body.

1. All the varying and multiple forms of motion are reduced as to their cause to a uniform motion, which is the motion of the heavens, as is proved by Aristotle.[21] But human movements are varied and of multiple forms, for they begin to be after they were not. Therefore they are reduced as to their cause to the movement of the heavens, which is the uniform movement in nature.

2. According to Augustine, "the lower bodies are moved by the higher." [22] But movements of the human body, which are caused by the will, cannot be referred back to the movement of the heavens as to their cause unless the will too is moved by the heavens. Therefore the heavens move the human will.

3. By observing the heavenly bodies, astrologers truly foresee the outcome of future human acts, which come from the will. This could not be so if heavenly bodies could not move the human will. Therefore the human will is moved by a heavenly body.

On the contrary: Damascene says that "the heavenly bodies are not the cause of our acts." [23] But they would be if the will, which is the principle of human acts, were moved by the heavenly bodies. Therefore the will is not moved by the heavenly bodies.

Response: According as the will is moved by an exterior object, it can

---

[20] Aristotle, *Nicomachean Ethics* III, 1 (1110a 3).

[21] *Physics* VIII, 9 (265a 27). See also IV, 14 (223b 18). This position is still tenable inasmuch as time is a constant of nature, but time is itself a motion which by reason of its regularity and speed is the measure of all motions. Cf. the articles in *Encyclopaedia Britannica* on *Time, Measure.*

[22] *The Trinity* III, 4.   [23] *On the Orthodox Faith* II, 7.

be moved by the heavenly bodies, that is, insofar as exterior bodies, which are presented to sense, move the will and insofar as the organs of the sense powers also are subject to the movements of the heavenly bodies.

But some have held that the heavenly bodies can make a direct impression on the human will by way of an external agent moving the will with respect to the exercise of its act. This, however, is impossible, for the will is in reason.[24] Now reason is a power of the soul that is not bound by a bodily organ, and hence is a wholly immaterial and incorporeal power. Now clearly no body can act upon an incorporeal thing, but rather the reverse, for incorporeal and immaterial things are more formal and more universal in power than any corporeal things whatsoever. Hence it is impossible for the heavenly bodies to make a direct impression on the intellect or the will. Because of this Aristotle attributes to those who held that the intellect does not differ from sense the opinion that "such is the will of men, as is the day which the father of men and of gods brings on" [25] (namely, Jupiter, by whom they understand the whole heavens). For all sense powers, being acts of corporeal organs, can be moved accidentally by the heavenly bodies, namely, when they move the bodies with which their acts are concerned.

But since the intellectual appetite is moved in a certain way by the sense appetite, the movement of the heavenly bodies can indirectly influence the will, namely, insofar as the will is moved through the passions of the sense appetite.

Reply to 1: The varied forms of the motion of the human will are reducible to a uniform cause which, however, is superior to the intellect and the will. This cannot be said of a body but only of a higher immaterial substance. Hence there is no need to reduce the movement of the will to the movement of the heavens as to its cause.

Reply to 2: Human bodily movements are referred to the movement of a heavenly body, as to a cause, insofar as the suitable disposition of the organs for movement is somehow due to the influence of the heavenly bodies; insofar, also, as the sense appetite is affected by the influence of the heavenly bodies; and insofar, finally, as external bodies are moved in accordance with the movement of heavenly bodies which, when it occurs, causes the will to begin to will or not will something—for example, when it gets cold we want to make a fire. But this movement of the will is in respect to an object presented externally, not in respect to an interior prompting.

Reply to 3: As we have pointed out before,[26] sense desire is the act of a corporeal organ. Hence nothing prevents one from being inclined to anger or concupiscence, or some other passion, by influence of the heav-

---

[24] Cf. Aristotle, *On the Soul* III, 9 (432b 5).
[25] *Op. cit.*, 3 (427a 25). Cf. Homer, *Odyssey* XVIII, 136.
[26] I, question 84, articles 6 and 7.

enly bodies, as we also are by our natural temperament. Now most men follow their passions, which only those who are wise resist. Hence it is that, for the most part, predictions about human acts based upon observation of the heavenly bodies are verified. Nevertheless, as Ptolemy says, "the wise man dominates the stars," [27] meaning thereby that the one who resists the passions, prevents through the will which is free and in no way subject to the movement of the heavens such effects of the heavenly bodies.

Or, as Augustine says, "We must acknowledge that when the truth is foretold by astrologers, this happens because of some hidden inspiration which the human mind is subject to without knowing it. And since this is done in order to deceive men, it is the work of deceiving spirits." [28]

Sixth Article

IS THE WILL MOVED BY GOD ALONE AS AN EXTERIOR PRINCIPLE?

It seems that the will is not moved by God alone as an exterior principle.

1. It is natural for what is inferior to be moved by its superior; thus the lower bodies are moved by the heavenly bodies. But in addition to God, there is something superior to the will of man, namely, the angels. Therefore the will of man can also be moved by the angel as an exterior principle.

2. The act of the will follows the act of the intellect. But the intellect of man is brought to act not only by God, but also by the angel through illumination, as Dionysius says.[29] For the same reason, therefore, the will is.

3. God is the cause of only what is good, for "God saw all the things that He had made, and they were very good" (*Genesis 1:31*). Accordingly, if the will of man were moved by God alone, it would never be moved to evil; yet the will is that by which "we sin or live rightly," as Augustine says.[30]

On the contrary: "For it is God Who of His good pleasure works in you both the will and the performance" (*Philippians 2:13*).

Response: The movement of the will is from an intrinsic principle, just as natural movement is. Now although something can move a natural thing which is not the cause of the nature of the thing, still it cannot cause a natural movement in it except as it is in some way the cause of the nature. For man can move a stone upward though he is not the cause of

---

[27] *Centiloquium,* prop. 5. Cf. Albertus Magnus, *Commentary on the Sentences* II, d. XV, article 4.
[28] *A Literal Commentary on "Genesis"* II, chapter 17.
[29] *On the Celestial Hierarchy* IV, 2.   [30] *Retractions* I, 9.

the nature of a stone, but this movement is not natural to a stone; its natural movement is caused only by that which causes the nature. Hence it is said that whatever brings things into existence moves light and heavy things according to place.[31] Therefore man, as having a will, can be moved by something which is not his cause, but it is impossible that his voluntary movement be from an extrinsic principle which is not the cause of the will.

Now the cause of the will can be none other than God. This is evident for two reasons. First, the will is a power of the rational soul, which is caused by God alone through creation, as we have said.[32] Second, the will is ordered to the universal good. Hence nothing else can be the cause of the will except God Himself, who is the universal good. For every other thing is called good by participation and is some kind of particular good, and a particular cause does not produce a universal inclination. Hence prime matter also, which is in potency to all forms, cannot be caused by a particular agent.

Reply to 1: The angel is not above man so as to be the cause of his will in the way that the heavenly bodies are the cause of natural forms, from which result the natural movements of natural bodies.

Reply to 2: The intellect of man is moved by the angel on the part of the object, which is proposed for him to know by the power of angelic light. Thus also the will can be moved by an external creature, as we have said.[33]

Reply to 3: God as the universal mover moves the will of man to the universal object of the will, which is the good. Without this universal motion, man cannot will anything. But man by his reason determines himself to will this or that thing, which is either a true good or an apparent good. However, sometimes God particularly moves some to will a determinate good; in this case He moves them by grace, as we shall show later.[34]

---

[31] Aristotle, *Physics* VIII, 4 (255b 35).

[33] Article 4.

[32] I, question 90, articles 2 and 3.

[34] Question 109, article 2.

QUESTION X

The Manner in Which the Will Is Moved

(In Four Articles)

First Article

IS THE WILL MOVED TO ANYTHING NATURALLY?

It seems that the will is not moved to anything naturally.

1. A natural agent is contradistinguished from a voluntary agent.[1] Therefore the will is not moved to something naturally.

2. That which is natural is in the thing always, as being hot is in fire. But no motion is always in the will. Therefore no motion is natural to the will.

3. Nature is determined to one thing whereas the will is related to opposites. Therefore the will wills nothing naturally.

On the contrary: The movement of the will follows upon the act of the intellect. But the intellect understands some things naturally. Therefore the will also wills some things naturally.

Response: As Boethius[2] and the Philosopher[3] say, "nature" is said in many ways. Sometimes it is said of the intrinsic principle of things which move; in this sense, nature is the matter or form of the material thing.[4] In another way, it is said of the substance or even of any being of the thing, and in this sense something is said to be natural to a thing which is proper to it according to its substance; this is what is essential to the thing. Now whatever is not essential to a thing is reducible to a principle that is essential to the thing. Hence, taking nature in this way, the principle of what belongs to a thing must always be a natural principle. This is clearly evident in the case of the intellect, for the principles of intellectual knowledge are naturally known. Similarly, the principle of voluntary movements must be something naturally willed.

Now this is the good in general, which the will naturally tends to as any power does to its object; it is also the ultimate end, which is related to all desirable things as the first principles of demonstration are to all intelligible things; and universally it is all the things which belong to the one who wills according to his nature. For we do not seek through the will only what belongs to the power of the will, but also what belongs to

---

[1] Cf. Aristotle, *Physics* II, 5 (196b 19).   [2] *On Person and the Two Natures* I.
[3] *Metaphysics* IV, 4 (1014b 16).   [4] Cf. Aristotle, *Physics* II, 1 (193a 28).

101

each of the other powers and to man as a whole. Hence man not only naturally wills the object of the will, but also whatever belongs to the other powers; for example, the knowledge of truth, which belongs to the intellect; to exist and to live, and other things like this which concern his natural well-being. All of these are included under the object of the will as various particular goods.

Reply to 1: The will is contradistinguished from nature as one cause is contradistinguished from another, for some things come to be naturally and some are done voluntarily. However, there is another way of causing, which is proper to the will as master of its own acts apart from the way which is proper to nature as determined to one thing. But because the will is established in a nature, the will necessarily shares to some extent in the movement proper to nature, just as a posterior cause shares in what belongs to a prior cause. For the very being of a thing, which is from nature, precedes an act of willing, which is from the will. Hence it is that the will wills something naturally.

Reply to 2: In the things of nature, that which is natural as following upon the form alone is always actual, as heat in fire. But that which is natural as following upon matter is not always actual, but is sometimes only potential; for form is act while matter is potency. Now motion is "the act of what is in potency." [5] Hence in the case of natural things, whatever belongs to or results from a movement is not always in them; thus fire does not always move upward, but only under certain conditions. Likewise it is not necessary that the will, which is brought from potency to act when it wills something, should always be in the act of willing, but only when it is in some determinate disposition. But the will of God, which is pure act, is always in the act of willing.

Reply to 3: There is always something one that corresponds to nature, yet proportionate to it. Thus something one in genus corresponds to nature generically, something one in species corresponds to nature taken specifically, and something individually one corresponds to nature as individuated. Consequently, since the will is an immaterial power, as is the intellect, something one that is common—the good—corresponds naturally to it, just as something one that is common also corresponds to the intellect—the true, or being or the *what it is* of something. And under the good that is common many particular goods are contained, to none of which the will is determined.

Second Article

IS THE WILL NECESSARILY MOVED BY ITS OBJECT?

It seems that the will is necessarily moved by its object.

1. The object of the will is compared to the will as the mover to the

---

[5] Aristotle, *op. cit.* III, 1 201a 10).

movable.[6] But a·mover, if it be adequate, necessarily moves the movable. Therefore the will can be moved necessarily by its object.

2. The will is an immaterial power, just as the intellect is, and each is ordered to a universal object, as we have said.[7] But the intellect is moved necessarily by its object. Therefore the will also is necessarily moved by its object.

3. Whatever one wills is either an end or a means. But it seems that one wills the end necessarily, because it is like a principle in speculative matters, which we assent to necessarily. Now the end is the reason for willing the means, and thus it seems we also will the means necessarily. Therefore the will is necessarily moved by its object.

On the contrary: Rational powers are related to opposites.[8] But the will is a rational power, for it is in reason.[9] Therefore the will is related to opposites. Therefore it is not necessarily moved to one of the opposites.

Response: The will is moved in two ways: in one way, with respect to the exercise of its act; in another way, with respect to the specification of its act, which is from the object. In the first way, no object moves the will necessarily, for no matter what the object may be, it is in man's power not to think of it, and hence not actually to will it.

But with respect to the second way, the will is moved necessarily by one object but not by another. For in the movement of any power by its object, we have to consider what it is about the object which moves that power. Thus the visible moves sight by reason of a color that is actually visible. Hence if color is offered to sight, it moves the sight necessarily unless one avoids seeing, which belongs to the exercise of the act. But if sight were offered something not actually colored in all respects, but only in certain respects and not in others, sight would not necessarily see such an object, for it might be looking at that part of the object which is not actually colored and so not see it. Now just as what is actually colored is the object of sight, so good is the object of the will. Hence if the will be offered an object that is good universally and from every point of view, the will tends to it necessarily, if it wills anything at all, for it cannot will the opposite. But if the will be offered an object which is not good from every point of view, the will will not necessarily tend to it.

Now because the lack of any good whatsoever has the aspect of a non-good, consequently only that good which is perfect and lacking in nothing is such a good that the will cannot not will it, and such a good is happiness. Any other particular good, insofar as it lacks some good, can

---

[6] Cf. Aristotle, *On the Soul* III, 10 (433b 10; b 16).
[7] Article 1, reply to 3.
[8] Cf. Aristotle, *Metaphysics* VIII, 2 (1046b 8).
[9] Cf. Aristotle, *On the Soul* III, 9 (432b 5).

be regarded as non-good, and in this respect can be refused or accepted by the will, which can tend to one and the same thing from different points of view.

Reply to 1: The adequate mover of a power is simply the object which in every respect is of the kind to move that power. But if it is deficient in any respect, it will not necessarily move it, as we have just said.

Reply to 2: The intellect is necessarily moved by an object which is such as to be always and necessarily true, but not by that which could be true or false, that is, by that which is contingent, as we have indicated with respect to the good.

Reply to 3: The ultimate end necessarily moves the will because it is the complete good; so also whatever is ordered to such an end without which the end cannot be attained, such as to exist and to live, and things of this kind. But other things, without which the end can be had, are not willed necessarily by one who wills the end, just as one who assents to the principles does not necessarily assent to the conclusions, without which the principles can be true.

Third Article

IS THE WILL MOVED WITH NECESSITY BY THE LOWER APPETITE? [10]

It seems that the will is moved with necessity by a passion of the lower appetite.

1. The Apostle says, "For I do not do the good that I wish, but the evil that I do not wish, that I perform" (*Romans 7:19*). This is said because of concupiscence, which is a passion. Therefore the will is moved with necessity by passion.

2. "According as a man is, such does the end seem to him." [11] But it is not within the power of the will to throw off a passion at once. Therefore it is not within the power of the will not to will what passion inclines it to.

3. A universal cause is not applied to a particular effect except through an intermediate particular cause; thus universal reason moves only by means of a particular judgment. [12] But universal reason is related to the particular judgment as the will is related to the sense appetite. Consequently, the will is not moved to will some particular thing except by means of the sense appetite. Therefore, if the sense appetite is disposed toward something by a passion, the will could not be moved contrary to it.

On the contrary: "Thy lust shall be under thee, and thou shalt have

---

[10] "Lower appetite" signifies sense desire as distinguished from "intellectual appetite," the will.

[11] Aristotle, *Nicomachean Ethics* III, 5 (1114a 32).

[12] Cf. Aristotle, *On the Soul* III, 11 (434a 19).

dominion over it" (*Genesis 4:7*). Therefore the will of man is not moved with necessity by the lower appetite.

Response: As we have said above,[13] the passion of the sense appetite moves the will in the respect in which the will is moved by the object; thus man, as disposed in a certain way by a passion, judges something to be good and fitting which he would not so judge apart from such a passion. Now man can be influenced by passion in two ways. First, in such a way that his reason is wholly bound by the passion so that he does not have the use of reason, as happens with those who, through violent anger or lust, become mad or insane; this may also happen because of some other bodily disorder, for such passions do not occur without a change in the body. Such men are considered to be like irrational animals who follow with necessity the impulse of passion, for in animals there is no movement of reason, nor consequently of will either.

Sometimes, however, reason is not wholly enmeshed in passion, so that the judgment of reason retains its freedom to a certain extent. Accordingly, some movement of the will remains. Insofar, therefore, as reason remains free and not subject to passion, the movement of the will which remains, does not of necessity tend to what the passion inclines it to. Accordingly, either there is no movement of the will in man, and only passion dominates, or, if there is movement of the will, it does not follow passion with necessity.

Reply to 1: Although the will cannot prevent the movement of concupiscence from arising—and it is this the Apostle is speaking about when he says, "but the evil that I do not wish, that I perform," that is, I desire—nonetheless it is within the power of the will not to will to desire or not to consent to concupiscence. Hence it does not follow the movement of concupiscence with necessity.

Reply to 2: Since there is a twofold nature in man, intellectual and sensitive, sometimes man is totally disposed to one of the two, either because sense is wholly subject to reason, as with those who are virtuous, or, conversely, because reason is wholly enmeshed in passion, as with those who are deranged. But sometimes, though reason is clouded by passion, still something of reason remains free. One can then repel the passion entirely or at least restrain oneself from following the passion. For in such a circumstance, since man is disposed in different ways according to different parts of the soul, a thing appears to him otherwise according to his reason than it does according to the passion.

Reply to 3: The will is moved not only by the universal good grasped through reason but also by the good perceived by sense. Consequently the will can be moved to a particular good without the passion of sense desire. For we will and do many things by choice alone, without passion, as is evident most of all in those instances wherein reason resists passion.

---

[13] Question 9, article 2.

Fourth Article

IS THE WILL MOVED WITH NECESSITY BY AN EXTERNAL
MOVER, WHICH IS GOD?

It seems that the will is moved with necessity by God.

1. Every agent that cannot be resisted necessarily moves what it moves.
But God cannot be resisted since His power is infinite, for "who resists
His will?" (*Romans 9:19*). Therefore God moves the will with necessity.

2. The will is moved with necessity in regard to what it wills naturally,
as we have said.[14] But "whatever God does in a thing is what is natural
to it," as Augustine says.[15] Therefore the will wills with necessity everything to which God moves it.

3. A thing is possible if when it is posited, nothing impossible follows.
But what is impossible follows if it is posited that the will does not will
that to which God moves it, for in such a case the operation of God
would be inefficacious. It is not possible, therefore, for the will not to
will that to which God moves it. Therefore it wills it with necessity.

On the contrary: "God made man from the beginning, and left him in
the hand of his own counsel" (*Ecclesiasticus 15:14*). Therefore God does
not move man's will with necessity.

Response: As Dionysius says, "It belongs to divine providence not to
destroy the nature of things, but to conserve them." [16] Hence it moves
all things in accordance with their condition, so that from necessary
causes, by divine motion, effects follow with necessity, and from contingent causes effects follow contingently. Since, then, the will is an active
principle which is not determined to one thing, but is related indifferently to many, God so moves it that He does not determine it to one
thing with necessity, but leaves its movement contingent and not necessary, except in regard to what it is moved to naturally.

Reply to 1: The divine will extends not only to the doing of something
by the thing which the divine will moves, but also to its being done in
the way which is consistent with its nature. Hence it would be more repugnant to divine motion if the will were moved with necessity, which
is not proper to its nature, than if it were moved freely as is proper to
its nature.

Reply to 2: That is natural to a thing which God works in it so that
it may be natural to it, for something belongs to a thing in the way God
wills that it belong to it. But He does not will that whatever He works
in things be natural to them, for example resurrecting the dead. However, this He does will to be natural to each thing, that it be subject to
divine power.

---

[14] Article 2, reply to 3.   [15] *Against Faustus* XXVI, 3.
[16] *The Divine Names* IV, 33.

Reply to 3: If God does move the will to something, it is not possible, given this supposition, that the will not be moved to it. But it is not impossible absolutely. Hence it does not follow that the will is moved by God with necessity.

Enjoyment, an Act of the Will

(*In Four Articles*)

IS ENJOYMENT AN ACT OF THE APPETITIVE POWER?

It seems that enjoyment does not belong only to an appetitive power.

1. Fruition [i.e., enjoyment] seems to be nothing other than to experience the fruit. But it is the intellect which experiences the fruit of human life, which is happiness, as we have shown.[1] Therefore enjoyment is not an act of the appetitive power, but of the intellect.

2. Any power has its proper end, which is its fulfillment; thus the end of sight is to know the visible and the end of hearing is to perceive sounds, and so of the other powers. But the end of a thing is its fruit. Therefore enjoyment belongs to any power and not only to the appetitive power.

3. Enjoyment implies a certain delight. But a sense delight belongs to sense, which delights in its object, and for the same reason intellectual delight belongs to the intellect. Therefore enjoyment belongs to a knowing power and not to an appetitive power.

On the contrary: Augustine says that "enjoyment is to adhere lovingly to something for itself." [2] But love belongs to an appetitive power. Therefore enjoyment is also the act of an appetitive power.

Response: Fruition [i.e., enjoyment] and the fruit seem to refer to the same thing, one being derived from the other. Which one derives from which is not relevant to our present inquiry, though it seems probable that the one which is more readily known was first named. Now the things we know first are those which are more evident to sense, and thus it seems that the name "fruition" is derived from fruits that are enjoyable to the senses.

Now a fruit enjoyable to sense is what we expect a tree to produce ultimately, and which is savored with a certain delight. Hence fruition, that is, enjoyment, seems to relate to the love or delight which one has from the thing that is ultimately expected, which is the end. But the end and the good is the object of the appetitive power. Hence it is clear that enjoyment is the act of an appetitive power.

---

[1] Question 3, article 4.
[2] *On Christian Doctrine* I, 4; *The Trinity* X, 10, 11.

Reply to 1: Nothing prevents one and the same thing belonging to different powers for different reasons. Thus the vision of God, as vision, is the act of the intellect, but as a good and an end it is the object of the will. It is in the latter sense that it is the will's fruition. And thus the intellect attains this end as an agent power while the will attains it as a power moving to the end and enjoying the end once it is attained.

Reply to 2: The fulfillment and end of any other power is contained under the object of the appetitive power as what is proper is contained under what is common, as we have said.[3] Hence the fulfillment and end of each power, insofar as it is a good, belongs to the appetitive power. Therefore the appetitive power moves other powers to their ends, and itself reaches its end when any other power reaches its end.

Reply to 3: Two things are involved in delight. One is the perception of what is appropriate, which belongs to the knowing power; the other is the satisfaction with what is offered as appropriate. The latter belongs to the appetitive power in which the aspect of delight is fulfilled.

Second Article

DOES ENJOYMENT BELONG ONLY TO THE RATIONAL CREATURE OR ALSO TO IRRATIONAL ANIMALS?

It seems that enjoyment belongs only to human beings.

1. Augustine says that "it is given to us men to enjoy things and make use of them."[4] Therefore other animals do not have enjoyment.

2. Fruition, or enjoyment, relates to the ultimate end. But the irrational animals cannot attain an ultimate end. Therefore fruition, or enjoyment, does not belong to them.

3. As the sense appetite is below the intellectual, so natural appetite is below the sense appetite. Accordingly, if enjoyment belongs to the sense appetite, it would seem with equal reason to belong to natural appetite. This is clearly false since the natural appetite cannot delight in anything. Therefore enjoyment does not belong to the sense appetite and accordingly does not belong to animals.

On the contrary: Augustine says, "It is not absurd to suppose that even animals enjoy food and any bodily pleasure."[5]

Response: As we have said above,[6] enjoyment is not the act of the power that attains the end by achieving it, but of the power that commands the achievement of it, for it has been pointed out that enjoyment belongs to the appetitive power. Now in things that have no knowledge, there is a power which attains an end by way of execution; for

---

[3] Question 9, article 1.   [4] *On Christian Doctrine* I, 22.
[5] *Book of Eighty-three Questions,* question 30.
[6] Article 1, reply to 2.

example, that by which a heavy body tends downward and a light one upward. But a power to which the end belongs by way of command is not found in such things, but in a higher nature[7] which moves all nature by its command, just as the appetite, in beings having knowledge, moves the other powers to their acts. Hence in things that have no knowledge, it is clear that although a power attains an end, there is no enjoyment in the possession of the end; this is reserved to beings having knowledge.

However, knowledge of the end is twofold, perfect and imperfect. When there is perfect knowledge, one knows not only that which is an end and a good, but also the universal nature of an end and a good, and such knowledge belongs only to a rational nature. With an imperfect knowledge, a particular end and good is known, and such knowledge is found in animals. Furthermore, their appetitive powers do not command with freedom, but are moved by natural instinct to what they apprehend. Hence enjoyment of a perfect kind belongs to a rational nature, enjoyment of an imperfect kind to animals, and to other things in no way at all.

Reply to 1: Augustine is speaking of perfect enjoyment.

Reply to 2: It is not necessary that enjoyment be of the last end absolutely; it can be of that which each thing has as its ultimate end.

Reply to 3: Sense appetite results from some knowledge, but not natural appetite, especially in things that have no knowledge.

Reply to "On the Contrary": Augustine is speaking there of imperfect enjoyment. This is clear from his manner of speaking, for he says that "it is not so absurd to suppose that even animals enjoy things," but it would be most absurd to say that they have the enjoyment obtained by using or possessing something.

Third Article

IS ENJOYMENT ONLY OF THE ULTIMATE END?

It seems that enjoyment is not only of the ultimate end.

1. The Apostle says, "Yea, indeed, brother! May I enjoy Thee in the Lord" (*Philemon 1:20*). But it is clear that Paul had not regarded man as his ultimate end. Therefore enjoyment is not only of the ultimate end.

2. The fruit of something is what one enjoys. But the Apostle says, "The fruit of the Spirit is charity, joy, peace" (*Galatians 5:22*), and other similar things which are not accounted as the ultimate end. Therefore enjoyment is not only of the ultimate end.

3. Acts of the will are reflexive, for I will to will and I love to love. But enjoyment is an act of the will, for "it is the will by which we enjoy," as Augustine says.[8] Therefore one enjoys his enjoyment. However, the

---

[7] The reference is to the divine nature which alone moves all things by its command.
[8] *The Trinity* X, 10.

ultimate end of man is not enjoyment, but the uncreated good alone, which is God. Therefore enjoyment is not only of the ultimate end.

On the contrary: Augustine says, "One does not enjoy that which he desires for the sake of something else." [9] But it is only the ultimate end which one does not desire for the sake of something else. Therefore enjoyment is only of the ultimate end.

Response: As we have said above,[10] two things belong to the notion of fruit or enjoyment: first, that it is something ultimate and, second, that desire should be quieted by a certain sweetness or delight. Now a thing is ultimate either absolutely or relatively. It is ultimate absolutely if it is not referred to something else; it is ultimate relatively if it is ultimate in a particular order.[11] That which is ultimate absolutely and in which one delights as in the ultimate end is properly called the fruit, and this is what one is properly said to enjoy. But that which is in itself not delightful, but is only desired as ordered to something else, as bitter medicine for health, in no way can be called the fruit.

Now that which in itself has a certain delight, to which other preceding things are referred, in a certain way can be called the fruit, but we cannot properly and in the complete sense of the term be said to enjoy it. Hence Augustine says that "we enjoy what we know when the delighted will rests in it." [12] But the will rests absolutely only in what is ultimate, because so long as one expects something else the will remains in suspense even though one has now arrived at some end. Similarly in motion according to place, although the midway point between the extremes is a beginning and an end, it is not taken actually as an end unless there is a resting in it.

Reply to 1: As Augustine says, "if he had said, 'may I enjoy thee,' without adding 'in the Lord,' he would seem to have placed the end of his love in his brother. But because he added 'in the Lord,' he has signified that he regarded the Lord as his end and also that his enjoyment was in him." [13] Hence he has spoken in such a way as to imply that he enjoyed his brother not as an end, but as intermediate.

Reply to 2: The fruit is related otherwise to a tree that produces it and to a man who enjoys it. With respect to a tree that produces it, it is compared as effect to cause; to the man who enjoys it, it is like something ultimately hoped for and delighted in. Hence the fruits enumerated by the Apostle in the place cited are so called because they are certain effects of the Holy Spirit in us—and hence called *fruits of the Spirit* —but this does not mean that we enjoy them as the ultimate end. Or, according to Ambrose, we can say they are called fruits "because we

---

[9] *Op. cit.* X, 11.   [10] Article 1.

[11] Thus happiness would be ultimate absolutely while the good of virtue would be ultimate in the order of moral action.

[12] *The Trinity* X, 10.   [13] *On Christian Doctrine* I, 33.

should desire them for their own sake," [14] not as though they were not referred to happiness, but because they are such that we should find pleasure in them.

Reply to 3: As we have said above,[15] an end is understood in two ways: first, as the thing itself; second, as the possession of the thing. This does not mean that there are two ends, but one end, considered in itself, and in relation to something else. Hence God is the ultimate end as the object ultimately sought, while enjoyment consists in the possession of this ultimate end. Consequently, just as God is not one end and the enjoyment of God another, so it is the same enjoyment whereby we enjoy God and enjoy our enjoyment of God. This also applies to created happiness, which consists in enjoyment.

Fourth Article

IS ENJOYMENT ONLY OF THE END POSSESSED?

It seems that enjoyment is only of the end possessed.

1. Augustine says, "to enjoy is to use joyfully, not with the joy of hope, but of possession." [16] But as long as something is not possessed, there is not the joy of possession but of hope. Therefore enjoyment is only of the end possessed.

2. As we have stated above,[17] there is enjoyment properly only of the ultimate end, because only the ultimate end brings desire to rest. But desire is brought to rest only by the end being possessed. Therefore enjoyment, properly speaking, is only of the end possessed.

3. To enjoy is to experience the fruit. But one does not experience the fruit unless one already possesses the end. Therefore enjoyment is only of the end possessed.

On the contrary: "To enjoy is to adhere lovingly to something for its own sake," as Augustine says.[18] But this we can do even in regard to a thing which is not possessed. Therefore enjoyment can also be of an end not possessed.

Response: Enjoyment implies some kind of relation of the will with the ultimate end inasmuch as the will does possess something as an ultimate end. Now an end can be possessed in two ways, perfectly and imperfectly. It is possessed perfectly when it is had not only in intention but also in fact; it is possessed imperfectly when it is had only in intention. Therefore there is perfect enjoyment of an end already really possessed. Imperfect enjoyment is also enjoyment of an end, but of one possessed not really but in intention only.

---

[14] *Gloss on Galatians* 5:22; cf. Peter Lombard, *Sentences* I, d. 1, 3.

[15] Question 1, article 8; question 2, article 7.

[16] *The Trinity* X, 11.   [17] Article 3.

[18] *On Christian Doctrine* I, 4.

Reply to 1: Augustine is speaking at this point of perfect enjoyment.

Reply to 2: The bringing to rest of the will is prevented in two ways: first, on the part of the object, when the object is not the ultimate end but is ordered to something else; secondly, on the part of the one who desires the end but who is not yet in possession of it. Now it is the object which specifies the act, but the manner of acting depends upon the agent, and hence is perfect or imperfect according to the condition of the agent. Therefore the enjoyment of anything that is not the ultimate end is not enjoyment properly speaking since it falls short of the full nature of enjoyment. But enjoyment of the ultimate end not yet possessed is enjoyment properly speaking, though imperfect because of the imperfect way in which it is possessed.

Reply to 3: One is said to attain or to possess an end, not only in fact, but also in intention, as we have just said above.

Intention

(In Five Articles)

IS INTENTION AN ACT OF THE INTELLECT
OR OF THE WILL?

It seems that intention is an act of the intellect and not of the will.

1. "If thy eye be sound, thy whole body will be full of light" (*Matthew 6:22*). In this passage the eye signifies intention, according to Augustine.[1] But the eye, since it is an organ of sight, signifies a power of knowing. Therefore intention is not an act of an appetitive power but of a knowing power.

2. Augustine says in the same place that Our Lord spoke of intention as a light when He said "If the light that is in thee is darkness . . ." (*Matthew 6:23*). But light pertains to knowledge. Therefore intention also does.

3. Intention denotes a certain order to an end. But order belongs to reason. Therefore intention does not pertain to the will but to reason.

4. An act of the will is either about an end or a means. But the act of the will with respect to an end is called a volition or an enjoyment, while with respect to a means it is called choice. Intention differs from both of these. Therefore intention is not an act of the will.

On the contrary: Augustine says that "the intention of the will unites the body seen to sight, and likewise it unites the image in the memory to the power of the soul thinking within itself." [2] Intention is therefore an act of the will.

Response: Intention, as the name indicates, signifies a tending to something. Now both the action of a mover and the movement of the movable tend to something. But it is due to the action of the mover that the movement of the movable tends to something. Hence intention primarily and principally belongs to the one that is the mover to an end, and thus we say that an architect, or anyone who is in charge, moves others by his command to that which he intends. Now the will moves every other power of the soul to an end, as we have said.[3] Hence it is clear that intention is properly an act of the will.

Reply to 1: The eye stands for intention metaphorically, not because

---

[1] *The Lord's Sermon on the Mount* II, 13.
[2] *The Trinity* XI, 4.   [3] Question 9, article 1.

intention refers to knowledge, but because it presupposes the knowledge which presents to the will the end for which it moves. So, too, with the eye we foresee where we should move in place.

Reply to 2: Intention is called a light because it is evident to the one who intends. And hence our deeds are called "darkness" because, though man knows what he intends, he does not know what may follow from what he does, as Augustine explains in the same place.

Reply to 3: The will does not order, but it does tend to something according to the order of reason. Hence the word "intention" denominates an act of the will, but presupposes the role of reason ordering something to an end.

Reply to 4: Intention is an act of the will regarding an end. But the will is concerned with an end in three ways. First, simply, and thus we speak of *volition* according as we will simply to have health or something of this kind. Secondly, an end is considered as that which the will rests in, and thus *enjoyment* regards the end. Thirdly, an end is considered as a term toward which something is ordered, and thus *intention* regards the end. For we are said to intend health not only because we will it but because we will to attain it by means of something else.

Second Article

IS INTENTION ONLY OF THE ULTIMATE END?

It seems that intention is only of the ultimate end.

1. "The intention of the heart is a cry for God."[4] But God is the ultimate end of the human heart. Therefore intention is always in regard to the ultimate end.

2. Intention regards the end as a terminus, as we have said.[5] But a terminus is conceived as something ultimate. Therefore intention is always in regard to the ultimate end.

3. Just as intention regards the end, so does enjoyment. But enjoyment is always of the ultimate end. Therefore also intention.

On the contrary: There is one ultimate end of human willing, happiness, as we have said.[6] If intention were only of the ultimate end, there would not be different intentions among men. This is clearly false.

Response: As we have stated above,[7] intention regards the end as the term of the movement of the will. Now the term of movement can be taken in two ways. It may mean the ultimate term wherein movement ceases, which is the term of a whole movement; or it may mean a midway point which is the principle of one part of a movement and the end or term of another part. Thus in going from A to C through B, C is the ultimate term while B is a term but is not ultimate. Now intention can be

---

[4] Prosper of Aquitaine, *Sentences,* 100.   [5] Article 1, reply to *4.*
[6] Question 1, article 7.   [7] Article 1, reply to *4.*

of both. Hence, although intention is always of the end, it need not always be of the ultimate end.

Reply to 1: The intention of the heart is called a cry for God not because God is always the object of the intention, but because He sees our
intention; or because, when we pray, we direct our intention to God,
which intention has the force of a cry.

Reply to 2: A term is conceived as something ultimate, not always
ultimate in respect to a whole, but sometimes in respect to some part.

Reply to 3: Enjoyment implies a resting in the end, which belongs
only to the ultimate end. But intention implies a movement toward an
end, not a resting in it. Hence the comparison does not hold.

Third Article

CAN ONE INTEND TWO THINGS AT THE SAME TIME?

It seems that one cannot intend several things at the same time.

1. Augustine says that man cannot intend God and bodily goods at the
same time.[8] With equal reason, therefore, he cannot intend any other two
things at the same time.

2. Intention denominates a movement of the will toward a term. But
in any one movement in the same direction there cannot be several terms.
Therefore the will cannot intend several things at the same time.

3. Intention presupposes an act of reason or intellect. But "it is not
possible to understand many things at the same time." [9] Therefore neither
can several things be intended at the same time.

On the contrary: Art imitates nature. But nature intends two uses for
one instrument; for example, "the tongue is ordered to taste and
speech." [10] Therefore, with equal reason, art or reason can order one
thing to two ends at the same time. Thus one can intend several things
at the same time.

Response: We can consider two things in two ways, either as ordered
to one another or not. If they are ordered to one another, it is clear from
what has been said that man can intend several things at the same time.
For intention is not only of the ultimate end, but of an intermediate end,
as we have said.[11] Thus one intends at the same time a proximate end,
the preparation of medicine, and an ultimate end, health.

Now if two things are not ordered to one another, man can still intend several things at the same time. This is evident from the fact that
a man prefers one thing to another because it is better than the other.
Now one of the conditions for a thing's being better than another is that
it can serve for several ends, and thus one thing is preferred to another

---

* *The Lord's Sermon on the Mount* II, 14; 17.
* Aristotle, *Topics* II, 10 (114b 35).   [10] Aristotle, *On the Soul* II, 8 (420b 18).
[11] Article 2.

because it has more uses. It is evident, then, that a man can intend several things at once.

Reply to 1. What Augustine means is that man cannot intend God and temporal goods as ultimate ends at the same time because, as we have shown,[12] a man cannot have many ultimate ends.

Reply to 2: There can be several terms of one motion in the same direction if one is ordered to another, but not if the two terms are not ordered to one another. Nevertheless, it must be noted that what is not one in reality can be considered as one by reason. Now intention is a movement of the will to something already ordained by reason, as we have said.[13] Hence, things that are many in reality can be taken as one term of intention in proportion as reason takes them as one. This happens either because two things concur to constitute something one, as heat and cold in due proportion bring about health, or because two things are contained under one common thing which may be intended; for example, the acquiring of wine and clothing is included under wealth as under something common, and thus nothing prevents one who intends wealth from intending at the same time wine and clothing.

Reply to 3: As we have said before,[14] many things can be understood at once inasmuch as they are one in some way.

Fourth Article

IS INTENTION OF THE END THE SAME ACT AS WILLING THE MEANS TO THE END?

It seems that intention of the end and willing the means to the end are not one and the same movement.

1. Augustine says that "to will to see the window has as its end the seeing of the window, and is a distinct act from the will to see passers-by through the window." [15] But to will to see passers-by through the window pertains to intention, while to will to see the window pertains to willing the means. Therefore intending the end and willing the means to the end are distinct movements of the will.

2. Acts are distinguished by their objects. But the end and the means are distinct objects. Therefore intending the end and willing the means to the end are distinct movements of the will.

3. The willing of the means is called choice. But choice and intention are not the same. Therefore intending the end and willing the means to the end are not the same movement of the will.

On the contrary: A means is related to an end as a midway point is to a terminus. But in natural things the movement is the same which goes

---

[12] Question 1, article 5.   [13] Article 1, reply to 3.
[14] I, question 12, article 10; question 58, article 2; question 85, article 4.
[15] *The Trinity* XI, 6.

through the midway point to the terminus. Therefore, in voluntary acts, intending the end and willing the means to the end is also the same movement.

Response: The movement of the will to the end and to the means to the end can be considered in two ways. First, according as the will is moved to each absolutely and in itself; and thus there are two movements of the will simply. Secondarily, according as the will is moved to the means because of the end; in this way, willing the end and willing the means to the end are one and the same movement. For example, when I say "I want to take medicine for my health," I designate only one movement of the will, and this is because the end is the reason for willing the means. Now the object and the reason it is an object fall within the same act, just as it is the same act of sight that sees color and light, as we have said.[16] The same holds for the intellect. If the intellect considers principles and conclusions absolutely, it considers each by a distinct act, but when it assents to the conclusion because of the principles there is only one act of the intellect.

Reply to 1: Augustine is speaking of seeing the window and seeing passers-by through the window as the will is moved to each absolutely.

Reply to 2: The end, as something real, and the means to that end, are distinct objects of the will. But insofar as the end is the reason for willing the means, they are one and the same object.

Reply to 3: A movement in one subject can be distinguished by reason according to its beginning and end, as in the case of ascent and descent.[17] Now insofar as the movement of the will is to the means as ordered to the end, it is called choice, but the movement of the will to the end as acquired by the means is called intention. A sign of this is that we can intend the end without having determined the means, which relates to choice.

Fifth Article

IS THERE INTENTION IN IRRATIONAL ANIMALS?

It seems that irrational animals intend an end.

1. Nature, in those things that have no knowledge, differs more from rational nature than does the sense nature of irrational animals. But in things having no knowledge, nature intends an end.[18] Therefore much more so do animals intend an end.

---

[16] Question 8, article 3, reply to 2.

[17] Just as one to two and two to one are the same interval, so ascent and descent are the same and yet can be distinguished in terms of a beginning and an end. Cf. Aristotle, *Physics* III, 3 (202a 16-22).

[18] Cf. Aristotle, *Physics* II, 8 (199b 30).

2. Just as intention is of the end, so also is enjoyment. But enjoyment is found in animals, as we have said.[19] Therefore intention also is.

3. To intend an end belongs to one who acts for an end, since to intend is nothing else than to tend to something. But animals act for an end, for an animal is moved to seek food or something of the kind. Therefore animals intend an end.

On the contrary: Intending an end implies the ordering of something to an end, which belongs to reason. Since animals do not have reason, it seems that they do not intend an end.

Response: As we have said,[20] to intend is to tend to something, and this belongs both to a mover and what is moved. Accordingly, as what is moved to an end by another is said to intend the end, so nature is said to intend an end as moved to its end by God, like the arrow directed by the archer. In this way too, animals intend an end as moved to something by natural instinct. Another way of intending the end belongs to a mover according as he orders the movement of himself or another to an end. This belongs only to reason. Hence, in this proper and principal sense of intending, an animal does not intend, as we have said.[21]

Reply to 1: The argument given takes intending as it belongs to what is moved to an end.

Reply to 2: Enjoyment does not imply an ordering of one thing to another, as intention does, but an absolute repose in the end.

Reply to 3: Animals are moved to an end, but not as though they reflect that they can attain the end through this movement, which is what is proper to one who intends. Through desiring the end by natural instinct, animals are moved to the end as though moved by another, in which respect they are like other things moved naturally.

---

[19] Question 11, article 2.   [20] Article 1.   [21] *Ibid.*

Choice, an Act of the Will in Relation to the Means

(In Six Articles)

We must now consider those acts of the will which are related to the means. There are three of them: choice, consent and use. Now choice is preceded by deliberation. We must therefore first of all consider choice; secondly, deliberation;[1] thirdly, consent;[2] and fourthly, use.[3]

First Article

IS CHOICE AN ACT OF THE WILL OR OF REASON?

It seems that choice is not an act of the will, but of reason.

1. Choice implies a kind of comparison whereby one thing is preferred to another. But to compare belongs to reason. Therefore choice is an act of reason.

2. It is the same power that forms a syllogism and draws the conclusion. But it is reason that forms syllogisms about actions. Hence, since choice is a sort of conclusion about practical affairs, as Aristotle says,[4] it seems that it is an act of reason.

3. Ignorance does not belong to the will but to a knowing power. Now there is a certain ignorance connected with choice, as is said in the *Ethics*.[5] Therefore it seems that choice does not belong to the will, but to reason.

On the contrary: The Philosopher says that choice is "the desire of things which are in our power." [6] Now desire is an act of the will. Therefore choice also is.

Response: The word "choice" implies something belonging to reason or intellect and something belonging to the will, and thus the Philosopher says that choice is "either reason influenced by desire or desire influenced by reason." [7] Now whenever two things concur to form something one, one of them is formal with respect to the other. Hence Gregory of Nyssa says that choice "is not desire simply, nor deliberation only, but a combination of the two. For just as we say that an animal is composed of soul

---

[1] Question 14.   [2] Question 15.   [3] Question 16.
[4] *Nicomachean Ethics* III, 3 (1113a 4).   [5] *Op. cit.,* 1 (1110b 31).
[6] *Op. cit.,* 3 (1113a 9).   [7] *Op. cit.* VI, 2 (1139b 4).

and body, and is not the body only nor the soul, but both, so it is with choice." [8]

Now with respect to the acts of the soul, we must note that an act belonging essentially to one power or habit receives its form and species from a superior power or habit, inasmuch as the lower is ordered by the higher. Thus, if an act of fortitude is done out of love for God, it is materially an act of fortitude but formally an act of charity. Now it is clear that reason precedes the will in a certain way and orders its act to the extent that the will tends to its object according to the order of reason, for the power of knowing presents the appetite with its object. Therefore, the act whereby the will tends to something proposed to it as good, from the fact that it is ordered to the end by reason, it is materially an act of the will and formally an act of reason. Now in matters of this kind, the substance of the act is related as matter to the order imposed by a superior power. Consequently, choice is substantially an act of the will, not an act of reason, for a choice is brought to completion in a kind of movement of the soul toward the good which is chosen. Hence the act clearly belongs to the appetitive power.

Reply to 1: Choice implies a previous comparison and is not essentially the comparison itself.

Reply to 2: The conclusion of a syllogism about actions does belong to reason. It is called a "decision" or a "judgment," and choice follows upon it. For this reason the conclusion seems to belong to choice, which follows upon it.[9]

Reply to 3: Ignorance is said to be connected with choice, not that choice itself is knowledge, but because one does not know what should be chosen.

Second Article

IS CHOICE FOUND IN IRRATIONAL ANIMALS?

It seems that choice is found in animals.

1. Choice is "the desire of something because of an end." [10] But animals seek something because of an end, since they act for an end, and from desire. Therefore choice is found in animals.

2. The word "choice" seems to signify the selecting of one thing rather than another. But animals select one thing rather than another, as is apparent when a sheep eats one plant and refuses another. Therefore choice is found in animals.

3. "It is by prudence that one makes a good choice of means." [11] But

---

[8] Cf. Nemesius, *On the Nature of Man*, 33.
[9] I.e., choice seems like a conclusion because it follows upon the decision reached.
[10] Aristotle, *Nicomachean Ethics* III, 2 (1111b 27); (1113a 11).
[11] Aristotle, *op. cit.* VI, 12 (1144a 8).

122   CHOICE, AN ACT OF THE WILL

prudence is found in animals, and so it is said, "Some animals, like bees, which cannot hear sounds, are prudent without acquiring it by learning." [12] This is apparent from the remarkable instances of sagacity in the activities of such animals as bees, spiders, and dogs. Thus, a dog in tracking a stag and coming to a crossroad, tries by scent to discover whether the stag has gone by the first or the second road; if he finds the stag has gone by neither of these, being thus assured, he follows the third road without testing the scent, as though reasoning by exclusion that the stag must have gone this way since he did not go the other two ways, and there are no others. Therefore it seems that choice can be found in animals.

On the contrary: Gregory of Nyssa says that "children and animals act voluntarily, but not from choice." [13] Therefore choice is not found in animals.

Response: Since choice is the selection of one thing rather than another, it must deal with a plurality of things which can be chosen. Consequently, if something is wholly determined to one thing, there is no place for choice. Now the difference between sense appetite and the will, as we have stated,[14] is that the sense appetite is determined to one particular thing according to the order of nature, while the will, though determined by nature to something one in general, the good, is undetermined with respect to particular goods. Hence, to choose belongs properly to the will and not to the sense appetite, which is all the animals have. For this reason, choice does not belong to irrational animals.

Reply to 1: Not every desire of something because of an end is called choice; it also requires a certain discrimination between one thing and another. There is no occasion for this unless the appetite can be moved to several things.

Reply to 2: The animal selects one thing rather than another because its desire is naturally determined to it. Hence as soon as something is presented to an animal by sense or imagination which its appetite naturally inclines to, it is moved to that alone without choice. So also fire moves upward and not downward, without choice.

Reply to 3: "Motion is the act of the movable caused by a mover." [15] Consequently, the power of the mover shows itself in the motion of that which it moves. Accordingly, in all things moved by reason, the order of reason which moves them is evident even though they are without reason. Thus, through the motion of the archer the arrow goes straight for the target as though there were reason in it directing it. The same is evident in the movements of clocks and all inventions devised by art. Now as works of art are compared to human art so all natural things are compared to divine art. Hence, an order is evident in things moved by nature

---

[12] Aristotle, *Metaphysics* I, 1 (980b 22).
[13] Cf. Nemesius, *On the Nature of Man*, 33.
[14] Question 1, article 2, reply to 3.   [15] Aristotle, *Physics* III, 3 (202a 13).

just as it is in things moved by reason, as is said in the *Physics.*[16] Hence a certain sagacity is evident in the activities of animals inasmuch as they have a natural inclination to certain kinds of well-ordered processes, which are ordained by a supreme art. This is why some animals are called prudent or sagacious; it is not because there is any reason or choice in them. This is clear from the fact that all things which are of one kind act in the same way.

Third Article

IS CHOICE ONLY ABOUT THE MEANS OR SOMETIMES ALSO ABOUT THE END?

It seems that choice is not only about the means.

1. The Philosopher says that "virtue makes us choose rightly, but it belongs not to virtue but to some other power to do those things which are to be done to carry out our choice." [17] But that for the sake of which something is done is the end. Therefore choice is about the end.

2. Choice implies selecting one thing rather than another. But just as one means can be selected rather than another, so also one end can be selected in preference to another. Therefore choice can be about ends as well as means.

On the contrary: The Philosopher says that "willing refers to the end, but choice to the means." [18]

Response: As we have said,[19] choice follows upon a decision or a judgment, which is like the conclusion of an operative syllogism.[20] Hence what the operative syllogism concludes to falls under choice. Now in the practical order, the end is like a principle, not a conclusion, as Aristotle remarks.[21] Therefore the end as such is not a matter of choice.

But just as in the speculative order nothing prevents the principle of one demonstration or of one science from being the conclusion of another demonstration or science—though a first indemonstrable principle cannot be the conclusion of any demonstration or science—so also what is the end of one action can be ordered to something else as an end. In this way, the end can be a matter of choice. For example, in the practice of medicine health is the end, and is not a matter of choice for the doctor, but is supposed as a principle. But the health of the body is ordered to the good of the soul; consequently, for one whose care is the well-being

---

[16] *Op. cit.* II, 5 (196b 17).   [17] *Nicomachean Ethics* VI, 12 (1144a 20).
[18] *Op. cit.* III, 2 (1111b 26).   [19] Article 1, reply to 2.
[20] An operative or practical syllogism is used in reasoning about proposed actions. The conclusion is a judgment of choice, and since actions are singular, the conclusion of the operative syllogism is singular; for example, the decision to pay this debt is arrived at by reasoning from the moral principle that debts should be paid. Cf. *Summa Theologiae* I-II, question 76, article 1.
[21] *Physics* II, 9 (200a 20).

of the soul, to be well or to be ill can be a matter of choice. Thus the Apostle says, "For when I am weak, then I am strong" (*II Corinthians 12:10*). But the ultimate end in no way is a matter of choice.

Reply to 1: The proper ends of the virtues are ordered to happiness as to the ultimate end. In this way ends can be a matter of choice.

Reply to 2: As we have said,[22] there is only one ultimate end. Hence, when there are a number of ends there can be choice among them inasmuch as they are ordered to an ultimate end.

Fourth Article

IS CHOICE ONLY ABOUT WHAT WE DO?

It seems that choice is not only about human acts.

1. Choice is about the means. However, not only acts but also tools are means.[23] Therefore choice is not only about human acts.

2. Action is distinguished from contemplation. But choice has its place even in contemplation insofar as one opinion is preferred to another. Therefore choice is not only about human acts.

3. Men who are chosen for an office, either secular or ecclesiastical, are not objects of action for the ones who choose them. Therefore choice is not only about human acts.

On the contrary: The Philosopher says that "no one chooses except what he thinks he can do himself." [24]

Response: Just as intention is about the end, so choice is about the means. Now the end is either an action or a thing. When the end is a thing, some action must intervene, either insofar as man produces that thing as an end, as the doctor brings about health as an end (and thus the producing of health is said to be the end of the doctor), or insofar as man in some way uses or enjoys the thing which is the end, as with the miser whose end is money or the possession of money. The same is to be said with respect to the means. For the means must necessarily be either an action or a thing, with some action intervening by which one either produces the means or makes use of the means. Thus choice always has to do with human actions.

Reply to 1: Tools are ordered to an end insofar as man uses them for an end.

Reply to 2: In the very contemplation itself, there is an act of the intellect assenting to this or that opinion. It is external action which is in contradistinction to contemplation.

Reply to 3: The one who chooses a bishop or a civic leader does choose to name him for that dignity. If the action in the establishment of a bishop or a civic leader were not his, the choice would not be his. Like-

---

[22] Question 1, article 5.   [23] Cf. Aristotle, *Physics* II, 3 (195a 1).
[24] *Nicomachean Ethics* III, 2 (1111b 25).

wise, whenever one thing is chosen in preference to another, some action of the one who chooses is involved.

Fifth Article

IS CHOICE ONLY ABOUT WHAT IS POSSIBLE?

It seems that choice is not only about what is possible.

1. Choice is an act of the will, as we have said.[25] But "one may wish even for what is impossible."[26] Therefore there is also a choice of what is impossible.

2. Choice concerns what can be done by us, as we have pointed out.[27] Therefore it does not matter, as far as choice is concerned, whether one chooses what is impossible absolutely or impossible with respect to the one choosing. But frequently we choose what we cannot accomplish, and so these are impossible for us. Therefore choice may be of what is impossible.

3. Man does not try to do something except by choice. But St. Benedict says that if a superior commands what is impossible, it should be attempted.[28] Therefore choice can be about what is impossible.

On the contrary: The Philosopher says that "choice cannot relate to what is impossible."[29]

Response: As we have said,[30] our choice always refers to our acts. Now whatever is done by us is possible for us. Hence it must be said that choice is only about what is possible.

Further, the reason for choosing something is that it leads us to an end. Now that which is impossible cannot lead us to some end. A sign that this is the case is that when men, taking counsel together, arrive at what is impossible for them, they give up as though there were nothing further that could be done about the matter.

This is evident also by examining the preceding argument. For the means, with which choice is concerned, is related to the end as a conclusion to a principle. Now it is clear that an impossible conclusion does not follow from a possible principle. Hence an end cannot be possible unless the means is possible. But no one can be moved toward what is impossible. Hence no one would tend to an end unless it appeared that a means were possible. Consequently, the impossible does not fall within choice.

Reply to 1: The will is midway between the intellect and external activity, for the intellect presents the will with its object and the will causes external action. Consequently, the intellect, which apprehends something as good in general, is regarded as being the principle of the will's move-

---

[25] Article 1.
[26] Aristotle, *Nicomachean Ethics* III, 2 (1111b 22).
[27] Article 4.   [28] *Rule of St. Benedict,* Chapter 68.
[29] *Nicomachean Ethics* III, 2 (1111b 20).   [30] Article 4.

ment, but the action by which one tends to the attainment of a thing is regarded as being the term or perfection of the will's act, for the movement of the will is from the mind to the thing. Consequently, the perfection of the will's act is reckoned in terms of its being something good for one to do. Now this is something that is possible. Hence a complete willing relates only to what is possible, which is a good for the one who wills, but an incomplete willing relates to what is impossible, which is called by some a *velleity*,[31] in the sense that one would will this if it were possible. But choice implies an act of the will already determined to what is now to be done. Hence choice relates only to what is possible.

Reply to 2: Since the object of the will is the good as apprehended, we must judge of the object of the will as it is subject to being apprehended. Accordingly, just as sometimes the will inclines to what is apprehended as good without really being good, so choice is sometimes about what is apprehended as possible to the one who chooses, yet is not possible for him.

Reply to 3: The reason this is said is that the subject should not determine by his own judgment whether something is possible or not but in each instance should abide by the judgment of his superior.

Sixth Article

DOES MAN CHOOSE WITH NECESSITY OR FREELY?

It seems that man chooses with necessity.[32]

1. The end is related to the objects of choice as principles are to what follows from them.[33] But conclusions follow with necessity from their principles. Therefore the end necessarily moves one to choose.

2. As we have said,[34] choice follows reason's judgment of what is to be done. But reason judges about some things with necessity because of the necessity of the premises. Therefore it seems that choice also follows with necessity.

3. If two things are wholly equal, a man is not moved to one more than another. For example, if a starving man is faced with two portions of food equally appetizing at equal distances, he is not moved to one more than another, and the reason for this, as Plato says, is the immobility of the earth in the center of the world.[35] But even less can one choose what is considered as less than what is considered as equal. Hence if two or more things are given, and one appears better, it is impossible to choose any of the others. Therefore one chooses necessarily that which appears best. But

---

[31] I.e., a wishing for something without expectation.
[32] See I, question 83, for the extent to which this question has already been treated.
[33] Cf. Aristotle, *Nicomachean Ethics* VII, 8 (1151a 16).
[34] Article 1, reply to 2.
[35] Cf. Aristotle, *On the Heavens* II, 13 (295b 25).

every act of choice is in regard to something that seems in some way better. Therefore every choice is made with necessity.

On the contrary: Choice is an act of a rational power, and this power is related to opposites, according to the Philosopher.[36]

Response: Man does not choose with necessity. The reason for this is that what is possible not to be is not necessary to be. Now the possibility of not choosing or choosing arises from a twofold power in man. For a man can will and not will, or act and not act; he can also will this or that, or do this or that. The reason for this lies in the very power of reason. For whatever reason can apprehend as good, the will can tend to. Now reason can grasp that it is good to will or to act and also that it is good not to will or not to act. Further, in all particular goods, reason can consider the good that is in something and the lack of good in it, that is, which is accounted as evil, and thus it can apprehend any one of these goods as something to be chosen or avoided. It is only the perfect good, which is happiness, that reason cannot apprehend as evil or as lacking anything. Accordingly, man wills happiness necessarily, and he cannot will not to be happy, that is, to be miserable. But choice, since it is not about the end but the means, as we have said,[37] is not about the perfect good which is happiness, but about particular goods. Consequently man chooses freely and not with necessity.

Reply to 1: A conclusion does not always follow necessarily from principles, but only when the principles cannot be true if the conclusion is not true. Similarly, the end a man has does not always necessitate the choosing of the means to the end, since not every means is such that the end cannot be attained without it, or if it is such, it is not always considered under that aspect.

Reply to 2: Reason's decision or judgment of what is to be done is about contingent matters which can be done by us. In these matters, conclusions do not necessarily follow from necessary principles with absolute necessity, but only conditionally, as in the following example; *If someone runs, he moves.*

Reply to 3: If two things are presented as equal according to one consideration, there is nothing to prevent our considering one of them as better from a particular point of view, and thus the will is inclined to one rather than to the other.

---

[36] Cf. *Metaphysics* VIII, 2 (1046b 8).   [37] Article 3.

Deliberation, Which Precedes Choice

(In Six Articles)

IS DELIBERATION AN INQUIRY?

It seems that deliberation or counsel is not an inquiry.

1. Damascene says that "deliberation is an [inquiring] of the appetite." [1] But inquiry is not an act of the appetite. Therefore deliberation is not an inquiry.

2. Inquiry is a discursive act of the intellect, and hence it is not found in God, whose knowledge is not discursive, as we have said.[2] But deliberation is attributed to God in Scripture: "He works all things according to the counsel [or deliberation] of His will" (*Ephesians 1:11*). Therefore deliberation is not an inquiry.

3. An inquiry is about doubtful matters. But counsel [which is the term of deliberation] is given about matters which are certainly good, and so the Apostle says, "Now concerning virgins I have no commandment of the Lord, yet I give counsel" (*I Corinthians 7:25*). Therefore deliberation is not an inquiry.

On the contrary: Gregory of Nyssa says, "All deliberation is an inquiry, but not all inquiry is deliberation." [3]

Response: As we have said,[4] choice follows upon a judgment of reason regarding things to be done. But there is much uncertainty about things to be done, for actions are about singular contingent things, which because of their variability are uncertain. Now in doubtful and uncertain matters, reason does not propose a judgment without previous inquiry. Hence an inquiry of reason is necessary before judging what is to be chosen, and this inquiry is called taking counsel or deliberating. For this reason, the Philosopher says that choice is "what is desired after deliberation." [5]

Reply to 1: When the acts of two powers are ordered to one another, there is something in each belonging to the other power, and hence each act can be denominated from either power. Now it is clear that an act of

---

[1] *On the Orthodox Faith* II, 22.   [2] I, question 14, article 7.
[3] Cf. Nemesius, *On the Nature of Man*, 34.
[4] Question 13, article 1, reply to 2; article 3.
[5] *Nicomachean Ethics* III, 3 (1113a 11).

reason directing in regard to the means, and an act of the will tending to the means according to reason's direction, are ordered to one another. Hence in choice, an act of the will, there is something of reason, namely, order; and in deliberation, an act of reason, there is something of the will, as matter, for deliberation concerns what man wishes to do, and also as mover, for from the fact that man wills an end he is moved to deliberate about the means. Hence the Philosopher says that "choice is reason influenced by desire," [6] thereby indicating that both concur in the act of choice. Damascene also says that deliberation is "desire based on inquiry," [7] thereby signifying that in a way deliberation belongs both to the will, in behalf of which and from which the inquiry is made, and to reason as making the inquiry.

Reply to 2: Things said about God are to be understood without any of the defect they have in us. For example, science, in us, is a knowledge of conclusions reached by reasoning from causes to effects, whereas science as said of God signifies certitude about all the effects in the first cause without any reasoning process. Similarly, deliberation is attributed to God in regard to the certitude of His decision or judgment, whereas it comes about in us through the inquiry of deliberation. But an inquiry of this kind has no place in God, and consequently deliberation is not attributed to God in this sense. In this context, Damascene says that "God does not deliberate, for only those who are lacking in knowledge deliberate." [8]

Reply to 3: Things which are most certainly good according to the opinion of wise and spiritually minded men may not be certainly good according to the opinion of the multitude, or of sensually minded men. Consequently, counsel can be given about such matters.

Second Article

DOES DELIBERATION CONCERN THE END
OR ONLY THE MEANS?

It seems that deliberation is not only about the means, but also about the end.

1. Whatever is doubtful can be the subject of an inquiry. But in human actions there can be doubt about the end and not only about the means. Consequently, since deliberation is an inquiry about what is to be done, it seems that there can be deliberation in regard to the end.

2. Human acts constitute the matter of deliberation. But some human actions are ends, as is said in the *Ethics.*[9] Therefore there is deliberation in regard to the end.

---

[6] *Op. cit.* VI, 2 (1139b 4).   [7] *On the Orthodox Faith* II, 22.
[8] *Ibid.*
[9] Aristotle, *Nicomachean Ethics* I, 1 (1094a 4).

On the contrary: Gregory of Nyssa says that "deliberation is not about the end, but about the means." [10]

Response: The end in actions is considered as a principle in that the reason for the means is taken from the end. Now a principle cannot be called into question, for principles must be presupposed in any inquiry. Accordingly, since deliberation is an inquiry, it is not about the end, but only about the means. Nevertheless, it can happen that what is an end with respect to some things is ordered to a further end, just as the principle of one demonstration is the conclusion of another. Hence, that which is taken as the end in one inquiry can be taken as a means in another. In this way, there will be deliberation about an end.

Reply to 1: That which is taken as an end is already determined. Hence, as long as there is any doubt about it, it is not regarded as an end. Therefore, if there is deliberation about it, it will not be deliberation about it as an end but as a means.

Reply to 2: Deliberation is about acts, inasmuch as they are ordered to some end. Hence, if any human action is an end, to that extent there is not deliberation in regard to it.

Third Article

IS DELIBERATION ONLY ABOUT WHAT WE DO?

It seems that deliberation is not only about the things we do.

1. Deliberation implies a conferring together. But several can confer with each other, even about immobile things, which are not subject to our actions, for example about the natures of things. Therefore deliberation is not only about the things we do.

2. Sometimes men seek counsel about what is laid down by law, and hence there are men who are called counselors-at-law. Yet those who seek counsel in this way do not make laws. Therefore counsel or deliberation is not only about the things we do.

3. There are some who are said to take counsel about future events, which nevertheless are not within our power. Therefore deliberation is not only about the things we do.

4. If deliberation were only about the things we do, no one would take counsel regarding what another does. But this is clearly false. Therefore deliberation is not only about the things we do.

On the contrary: Gregory of Nyssa says that "we deliberate about things which are within our power and which we are able to do." [11]

Response: Taking counsel implies strictly a conferring together by several persons. The name itself designates this, for "counsel" means a sitting down together,[12] inasmuch as many sit down together in order to

---

[10] Cf. Nemesius, *On the Nature of Man,* 34.

[11] *Ibid.*

[12] From *considium,* and as related to *consilium,* a counsel or deliberation.

confer with each other. Now we must note in regard to singular contingent matters that various conditions or circumstances have to be taken into account in order for something to be known with a certainty; these cannot be considered easily by one person alone, but they are taken into account with greater certainty by several, for what one notices escapes the attention of another. In necessary and universal matters, however, the consideration is more simple and more absolute, in which respect one man by himself can be sufficient. Consequently, the inquiry of counsel properly concerns singular contingent matters. Now the knowledge of truth in these matters is not so great as to be desirable of itself, as the knowledge is of universal and necessary truths, but it is desirable as useful for action, for actions concern singular contingent events. Hence it must be said that deliberation properly is about the things we do.

Reply to 1: Deliberation implies not any sort of conferring but a conferring about things to be done, for the reason given above.[13]

Reply to 2: That which is laid down by law, though not due to the action of one who seeks counsel, nevertheless is directive of one's action, for the mandate of law is one reason for doing something.

Reply to 3: Counsel refers not only to what is to be done but also about whatever is ordered to action. For this reason, we can speak about taking counsel in regard to future events inasmuch as one is led to do or omit something through knowledge of future events.

Reply to 4: We seek counsel about the acts of others to the extent they are in some way one with us, either by a union of affection, as a man is concerned about what affects his friend as though it concerned himself; or by way of an instrument; for a principal agent and an instrument are as though one cause, since one acts through another, and thus a master deliberates about what should be done through his servant.

Fourth Article

DO WE DELIBERATE ABOUT EVERYTHING WE DO?

It seems that we deliberate about whatever we are to do.

1. Choice is the desire of what has been deliberated about, as we have said.[14] But choice is about everything we do. Therefore deliberation also is.

2. Deliberation implies an inquiry by reason. But except for acting through the impulse of passion, we proceed by an inquiry of reason. Therefore we deliberate about everything we do.

3. The Philosopher says that "if something can be done by several means, we deliberate by inquiring by which one it can be done most easily and best; but if by one, how it can be done by this."[15] But whatever is

---

[13] In the body of this article.   [14] Article 1.
[15] *Nicomachean Ethics* III, 3 (1112b 16).

done, is done by one means or by several. Therefore we deliberate about everything we do.

On the contrary: Gregory of Nyssa says that "there is no deliberation about what is done by science or art." [16]

Response: Deliberation is a kind of inquiry, as we have said.[17] Now we usually inquire about matters admitting of doubt, and hence the investigation of reason, which is called an argument, "makes one go from doubt to conviction." [18] Now it can happen in two ways that there is not something doubtful about human acts. In the first, it is because one proceeds in determinate ways to determinate ends, as occurs in the arts which have certain rules of procedure; thus a person who writes does not seek counsel on how to form letters, since this is determined by art. In the second, it is because it does not matter whether something is done this way or that, and this refers to small matters which do not help or hinder much with respect to an end that is sought, and which reason regards as though of no account. Hence we do not deliberate about these two, although something is being ordered to an end, as the Philosopher says,[19] namely, about small matters, or about what should be done in a determinate way, as in producing works of art "except in those arts which involve conjecture, such as medicine, commerce, and the like," as Gregory of Nyssa says.[20]

Reply to 1: Choice presupposes deliberation because of its judgment or decision. Hence, when a judgment or decision is evident without inquiry, there is no need for the inquiry of deliberation.

Reply to 2: In matters that are evident, reason makes no inquiry but judges at once. Consequently, it is not necessary that there should be an inquiry of deliberation in everything done by reason.

Reply to 3: When a thing can be done by one means but in different ways, doubt can arise, just as it can when done by several means; hence the need of deliberation. But when not only the means, but also the way of doing it, is determined, then there is no need for deliberation.

Fifth Article

DOES DELIBERATION PROCEED BY WAY OF RESOLUTION?

It seems that deliberation does not proceed by way of resolution.[21]

1. Deliberation is about the things we do. However, our acts do not

---

[16] Cf. Nemesius, *On the Nature of Man,* 34.

[17] Article 1.   [18] Cicero, *On Invention* I, 34.

[19] Cf. *Nicomachean Ethics* III, 3 (1112b 9).

[20] Cf. Nemesius, *op. cit.*

[21] "By way of resolution" means the resolving of a whole into its parts or the reducing of what is complex to something more simple, i.e., the reducing of an effect as more complex to a cause as more simple. This method is opposed to "by way of composition," which means the composing of a whole from its parts, i.e., by applying causes to effects or by proceeding from the more simple to the more complex.

proceed in a resolutory manner, but rather in a compositive manner, that is, by proceeding from the simple to the composite. Therefore deliberation does not always proceed by way of resolution.

2. Deliberation is an inquiry of reason. But reason begins from what is prior and arrives at what is posterior, according to the more fitting order. Since, therefore, the past precedes the present and the present the future, in deliberating one should go from the present and the past to the future, which is not by way of resolution. Therefore the resolutory mode is not observed in deliberation.

3. Deliberation is only about matters which are possible for us.[22] But whether something is possible for us depends on what we can do or not do in order to attain a certain end. Therefore the inquiry of deliberation should start from the present state of affairs.

On the contrary: The Philosopher says that "he who deliberates seems to inquire and resolve."[23]

Response: In every inquiry, one must begin from some principle. Now if a principle is prior in knowledge and also in being, the process is not one of resolution but rather of composition, for to proceed from cause to effect is to proceed by way of composition, since causes are more simple than effects. But if what is prior in knowledge is posterior in being, the process is one of resolution, as when we judge about effects which are manifest to us by resolving them back to their simple causes. Now the principle in the inquiry of deliberation is the end which, though prior in intention, is nevertheless posterior in being. Accordingly, the inquiry of deliberation must be by way of resolution, namely, by beginning from what is intended in the future and continuing until one arrives at what must be done at once.

Reply to 1: Deliberation is about action. But the reason for an action is taken from the end, and hence the order of reasoning about action is contrary to the order of action itself.

Reply to 2: Reason begins with what is prior according to the order of reason, but not always with what is prior in time.

Reply to 3: If something is not suitable for attaining an end, we would not seek to know whether it is possible for attaining that end. Hence we must first inquire whether something is conducive to the end before we consider whether it is possible.

Sixth Article

DOES DELIBERATION PROCEED TO INFINITY?

It seems that the inquiry of deliberation proceeds to infinity.[24]

1. Deliberation is an inquiry about singular matters with which action

---

[22] Cf. Aristotle, *Nicomachean Ethics* III, 3 (1112b 26; b 32).
[23] *Op. cit.* (1112b 20).
[24] "Proceeds to infinity," i.e., goes on endlessly and hence without any resolution.

is concerned. But there is an infinity of such singulars. Therefore the inquiry of deliberation is endless.

2. It falls within the inquiry of deliberation not only to consider what should be done, but also how obstacles should be removed. But any human action can be hindered, and an obstacle can be removed by some human means. Therefore an inquiry about removing obstacles can go on endlessly.

3. The inquiry of demonstrative knowledge does not go on without end because one arrives at some self-evident principles which are altogether certain. But such certitude cannot be found in singular contingent matters, which are variable and uncertain. Therefore the inquiry of deliberation goes on endlessly.

On the contrary: "No one is moved to what is impossible to attain." [25] But it is impossible to traverse the infinite. Accordingly, if the inquiry of deliberation were infinite, no one could begin to deliberate. This is clearly false.

Response: The inquiry of deliberation is actually finite at both ends, on the part of the principle and on the part of the term. Now a twofold principle is taken with respect to the inquiry of deliberation. The first is a proper one, belonging to the very genus of actions, and this is the end, about which there is not deliberation but which is supposed as a principle, as we have said.[26] The other principle is taken as it were from another genus, just as in demonstrative sciences one science assumes something from another about which it does not inquire. Now the principles taken for granted in the inquiry of deliberation are facts of sense observation, for example, that this is bread or this is iron; also taken for granted are the general principles known in some speculative or practical science, for example, that adultery is prohibited by God or that man cannot live without sufficient nourishment. No one who deliberates inquires about such matters.

Now inquiry terminates in what we are able to do at once. For just as the end has the nature of a principle, so that which is done because of the end has the nature of a conclusion. Therefore, that which presents itself as first to be done stands like an ultimate conclusion, and with respect to this, inquiry comes to an end. However, nothing prevents deliberation from being potentially infinite inasmuch as there can be matters for deliberation to infinity.

Reply to 1: Singulars are not actually infinite, but only potentially so.

Reply to 2: Although human action can be hindered, nevertheless whatever hinders is not always present. Hence it is not always necessary to deliberate about removing an obstacle.

---

[25] Aristotle, *On the Heavens* I, 7 (274b 17).
[26] Article 2.

Reply to 3: In singular contingent matters, something may be taken as certain, not absolutely so, but for the time being and with respect to what is to be done. For example, that Socrates is sitting is not necessary, but that he is sitting while he sits is necessary. In this way a certitude can be had.

Consent, an Act of the Will in Relation to the Means

(In Four Articles)

IS CONSENT AN ACT OF AN APPETITIVE POWER OR A KNOWING POWER?

It seems that consent belongs only to an apprehending part of the soul.

1. Augustine says that consent is attributed to the superior part of reason.[1] But reason is named as the power of apprehending. Therefore to consent belongs to a power of apprehending.

2. To consent is *to sense along with.*[2] But to sense belongs to a knowing power. Therefore to consent also does.

3. Just as to assent is said to be the applying of the intellect to something so is to consent. But to assent belongs to the intellect, which is a power of apprehending. Therefore to consent also belongs to a power of apprehending.

On the contrary: Damascene says that "if one judges and his liking is not affected by that which he judges, there is not a decision,"[3] that is, a consent. But an act of liking belongs to an appetitive power. Therefore consent also does.

Response: To consent implies the application of sense to something. Now it is proper to sense to know things as present, for the imagination apprehends the likenesses of corporeal things even in the absence of the things whose likenesses they are, whereas the intellect apprehends universal notions, which it can grasp with no concern as to the presence or absence of the singulars. Now because the act of an appetitive power is a sort of inclination to the thing itself according to a certain likeness, the very application of the appetitive power to the thing, inasmuch as it adheres to it, takes on the name *sense* since it acquires, so to speak, an experience of the thing to which it adheres, inasmuch as it finds satisfaction in it. Hence it is said in Scripture, "Think of [*sentite*] the Lord in goodness" (*Wisdom 1:1*). Accordingly, to consent is an act of the appetitive power.

---

[1] *The Trinity* XII, 12. On meaning of "superior reason," see note 12 below.
[2] "Consentire est *simul sentire.*"   [3] *On the Orthodox Faith* II, 22.

Reply to 1: "The will is in reason." [4] Hence, when Augustine attributes consent to reason, he takes reason to include the will.

Reply to 2: Properly speaking, to sense belongs to a knowing power. But by way of likeness to a kind of experience, it belongs to an appetitive power, as we have stated. [5]

Reply to 3: To assent is, as it were, *to agree with something else,* and thus it implies some sort of distance from that to which assent is given. But to consent is *to sense along with,* and this implies a certain union with the object consented to. Hence the will, to which it belongs to tend to the thing itself, is more properly said to *consent* whereas the intellect, whose act does not consist in movement toward the thing, but rather the reverse, [6] is more properly said to *assent,* although the names are often used interchangeably. We could also say that the intellect assents, inasmuch as it is moved by the will.

Second Article

DOES CONSENT BELONG TO IRRATIONAL ANIMALS?

It seems that consent belongs to irrational animals.

1. Consent implies a determination of appetite to one thing. But the appetite of animals is determined to one thing. Therefore consent is found in animals.

2. If what is prior is removed, then what is posterior is removed. But consent precedes the carrying out of an action. Therefore, if there were not consent in animals, there would be no action accomplished. This is clearly false.

3. Men are sometimes said to consent to do something out of passion, for example out of concupiscence or anger. But animals act from passion. Therefore consent is found in them.

On the contrary: Damascene says that "after judging, man settles upon and likes what he has determined upon by deliberation, which is called a decision," [7] that is, a consent. But there is not deliberation in animals. Hence there is also not consent.

Response: Properly speaking, consent is not found in animals. The reason for this is that consent implies the application of the movement of appetite to something that is to be done. But to apply appetitive movement to the doing of something belongs to one in whose power appetitive movement is; for example, to touch a stone is something which a stick can do, but to apply the stick to touching the stone belongs to one who has the power of moving the stick. Now animals are not masters of

---

[4] Aristotle, *On the Soul* III, 9 (432b 5).   [5] In the body of this article.

[6] Cf. *Summa Theologiae* I, 16, article 1; 49, article 2.

[7] *On the Orthodox Faith* II, 22.

the movement of their appetite, for such movement in them is by natural instinct. Hence, in the animal there is movement of appetite but the animal does not apply appetitive movement to some particular thing. For this reason, the animal is not properly said to consent; this belongs only to a rational nature, which has control over appetitive movement, and can apply or not apply it to this or that thing.[8]

Reply to 1: In animals, the determination of appetite to something is passive only. Consent, however, implies active determination of the appetite, not just a passive determination.

Reply to 2: When what is prior is removed, the posterior is removed which properly follows only from that thing. But if something can follow from several things, it is not removed if one of the prior things is; for example, if hardening follows from both heat and cold (for bricks are hardened by fire and water by cold), then by removing heat it does not follow that there is no hardening. Now the carrying out of an action follows not only from consent, but also from immediate impulse of the appetite, and it is the latter which is found in animals.

Reply to 3: Men who act out of passion are also able not to follow passion, whereas animals are not. Hence the comparison does not hold.

Third Article

IS CONSENT ABOUT THE END OR THE MEANS?

It seems that consent is about the end.

1. That for the sake of which something is, is more than that thing is.[9] But we consent to the means because of the end. Therefore we consent more to the end.

2. The action of the intemperate man is his end, just as the action of the virtuous man is his end. But the intemperate man consents to his own action. Therefore consent can be about an end.

3. Choice is the desiring of the means, as we have said above.[10] Accordingly, if consent were only about the means, it would not seem to differ in any way from choice. This appears to be false, according to Damascene, who says that "after an approval," which he called a decision, "comes choice." [11] Therefore consent is not only about the means.

On the contrary: Damascene says in the same place that "there is a decision," or a consent, "when a man settles upon and likes what he has determined upon by deliberation." But deliberation is only about the means. Therefore consent also is.

---

[8] I.e., only man can exercise command over his desire.

[9] "Quia propter quod unumquodque, illud magis." Cf. Aristotle, *Posterior Analytics* I, 2 (72a 30), and *Commentary* of St. Thomas, I, Lesson 6, nn. 3 and 4, for an explanation of this principle. Cf. also *Summa Theologiae* I, question 87, article 2, reply to 3.

[10] Question 13, article 1.   [11] *On the Orthodox Faith* II, 22.

Response: Consent means the application of appetitive movement to something already in the power of the one making the application. In the order of things to be done, first there must be an apprehension of the end, then a desire for the end; following this, there is deliberation about the means, and then a desire of the means. Now desire tends to the ultimate end naturally, and hence we do not consider the application of appetitive movement to the end apprehended as consent but as simple volition. But the things we direct our attention to after the ultimate end, insofar as they are for the end, fall under deliberation, and so there can be consent about them inasmuch as the appetitive movement is applied to what has been decided upon by deliberation.

However, the movement of appetite to the end is not applied to deliberation; rather, deliberation is applied to it because deliberation presupposes desire for the end. On the other hand, the desire for the means presupposes a determination by deliberation. Hence, the application of appetitive movement to a determination of the deliberation is consent proper. Consequently, since deliberation is only about the means, consent, properly speaking, is only about the means.

Reply to 1: Just as in a science we know conclusions through principles, although the knowledge of the principles themselves is not science but something greater, namely, an intuitive understanding, so we consent to the means because of the end, although there is not a consent about the end but something greater, namely, a simple volition.

Reply to 2: The end of the intemperate man is the delight he finds in the act, and he consents to the action because of this delight rather than for the action itself.

Reply to 3: Choice adds to consent a certain relation to something which is preferred to something else; and hence, after consent is given, there still remains choice. For it may be that through deliberation several means are found that are conducive to the end; and as long as each of these is acceptable, consent is given to each one, but among those which are acceptable we give preference to one by making a choice. However, if we find that only one means is acceptable, then consent and choice do not differ in reality but only according to reason; hence we call it consent, inasmuch as doing that thing is acceptable, and choice according as we prefer it to whatever is not acceptable.

Fourth Article

DOES CONSENT TO THE ACT BELONG ONLY TO THE
SUPERIOR PART OF THE SOUL?

It seems that consent to the act does not always belong to the superior reason.[12]

---

[12] Superior and inferior reason, although one and the same power in man, are distinguished in the way conclusions are reached. What is called the superior reason

1. "Delight follows upon action and completes it, just as beauty complements youth." [13] But consent to delight belongs to the inferior reason, as Augustine says.[14] Therefore consent to the act does not belong only to the superior reason.

2. An act to which we consent is called voluntary. But many powers can produce voluntary acts. Therefore consent to the act is found not only in the superior reason.

3. "The superior reason is intent upon the contemplation and consideration of eternal things," as Augustine says.[15] But man often consents to an act, not for eternal reasons, but for temporal ones, or even because of a passion. Therefore consent to the act does not belong only to the superior reason.

On the contrary: Augustine says, "It is not possible for the mind effectively to resolve to commit a sin unless that intention of the mind within which is the supreme power of moving the members to or restraining them from an act, submits to and complies with the bad action." [16]

Response: A final decision always belongs to the one who is a superior and to whom it belongs to judge of the others, for as long as a judgment remains to be given there is not a final decision. Now it is clear that it belongs to the superior reason to judge of everything else, for we judge of sensible matters by reason and we judge of matters pertaining to human reason according to divine motives, which belongs to the superior reason. Consequently, as long as one is uncertain whether he should resist or not according to divine motives, no judgment of reason has the aspect of a final decision. Now the final decision for acting is the consent to the act. Therefore consent to the act belongs to the superior reason, yet in the sense in which reason includes the will, as we have said.[17]

Reply to 1: Consent to delight in the act belongs to the superior reason just as consent to the act itself does, but consent to delight in thinking about something belongs to the inferior reason just as it belongs to inferior reason to think. Nevertheless, the superior reason exercises judgment on thinking or not thinking considered as a sort of action, and likewise on the ensuing delight. But to the extent that the act of thinking is taken as ordered to another act, it belongs to the inferior reason. For that which is ordered to something else belongs to a lower art or power than does the end to which it is ordered. Hence an art which is concerned with the end is called the architectonic or principal art.

---

results in a judgment based on divine law; the inferior reason is based upon natural law and upon what reason can discern by its own power. The Ten Commandments, for instance, form the basis for conclusions of superior reason. Inferior reason is based upon motives gathered by reason alone. Cf. *Summa Theologiae* I, question 79, article 9; I-II, question 74, article 7.

[13] Aristotle, *Nicomachean Ethics* X, 4 (1174b 31).
[14] *The Trinity* XII, 12.   [15] *Op. cit.,* 7.   [16] *Op. cit.,* 12.
[17] Article 1, reply to *1*.

Reply to 2: Because actions are called voluntary from the fact that we consent to them, it does not follow that consent is the act of any power; consent is an act of the will, from which we name an act as voluntary, and which is in reason, as we have said.[18]

Reply to 3: The superior reason is said to consent, not only because it always moves to act from eternal motives, but also because it does not dissent for the same motives.

[18] *Ibid.*

Use, an Act of the Will in Relation to the Means

(*In Four Articles*)

IS USE AN ACT OF THE WILL?

It seems that use is not an act of the will.[1]

1. Augustine says, "to use is to refer that which is practicable to the obtaining of something else." [2] But to refer one thing to another is an act of reason, to which it belongs to compare and order. Therefore use is an act of reason and not of the will.

2. Damascene says that "man is aroused suddenly to activity, and this is called an impulse; he then makes use [of powers] and this is called use." [3] But activity belongs to the power of execution. Now an act of the will does not follow upon an act of the power of executing, for the carrying out of the act is last. Therefore use is not an act of the will.

3. Augustine says, "All things which were made, were made for the use of man, because reason which was given to men makes use of all things by its judgment." [4] But a judgment about things created by God belongs to speculative reason, which seems to be wholly distinct from the will, the principle of human acts. Therefore use is not an act of the will.

On the contrary: Augustine says, "To use is to put a means in the power of the will." [5]

Response: The use of something implies its application to some activity, and hence the activity to which we apply a thing is called its use, just as to go horseback riding is to make use of a horse, and to hit is to make use of a stick. Now we apply the interior principles of action to activity, namely, the powers of the soul or the members of the body, for example, the intellect to understanding and the eye to seeing, as well as external things, such as the stick for hitting. But it is clear that we apply

---

[1] Use is here considered as an act of the will whereby the will uses other powers to carry out the command dictated by reason. Thus, in deciding to buy a suit, one must still voluntarily exercise whatever powers are necessary actually to purchase the suit.

[2] *On Christian Doctrine* I, 4; cf. also *On the Trinity* X, 10.

[3] *On the Orthodox Faith* II, 22.

[4] *Book of Eighty-three Questions,* question 30.

[5] *On the Trinity* X, 10.

external things to action only by means of intrinsic principles, which are either powers of the soul, habits of the powers, or organs, which are members of the body.

Now it was shown above[6] that it is the will which moves the powers of the soul to their acts, and this is to apply them to operation. Hence it is clear that use primarily and principally belongs to the will as to a first mover, to reason as directing, and to other powers as executing, which powers are compared to the will which applies them as instruments to the principal agent. Now action is attributed properly, not to an instrument, but to the principal agent, just as building is attributed to the builder and not to his tools. Hence it is clear that use properly is an act of the will.

Reply to 1: Reason does refer one thing to another, but the will tends to that which is referred to something else by reason. In this way to use is to refer one thing to another.

Reply to 2: Damascene is speaking of use as it belongs to the powers of executing.

Reply to 3: Even the speculative reason is applied to the act of understanding or judging by the will. Hence speculative reason is said to be used, as moved by the will, in the same way as the other powers of executing.

Second Article

IS USE FOUND IN IRRATIONAL ANIMALS?

It seems that irrational animals make use of things.

1. It is more worthwhile to enjoy than to make use of something, since, as Augustine says, "we use things by referring them to something else which we shall enjoy." [7] But enjoyment belongs to irrational animals, as we have said.[8] Therefore even more so does use belong to them.

2. To apply members of the body to action is to make use of them. But irrational animals apply their members to doing things, for instance their feet for walking and their horns for striking. Therefore use belongs to irrational animals.

On the contrary: Augustine says, "Unless an animal participates in reason it cannot make use of a thing." [9]

Response: As we have said,[10] use is the application of some principle of action to an action; thus to consent is to apply the movement of appetite to a thing desired, as we have also said.[11] Now to apply one thing to another belongs only to one who has dominion over it, and this belongs only to one who knowingly refers one thing to something else, which per-

---

[6] Question 9, article 1.   [7] *On the Trinity* X, 11.   [8] Question 11, article 2.

[9] *Book of Eighty-three Questions,* question 30.

[10] Article 1.   [11] Question 15, articles 1-3.

tains to reason. Hence none but a rational animal consents and makes use of a thing.

Reply to 1: Enjoyment implies a complete movement of appetite to what is desirable whereas use implies a movement of appetite to one thing as ordered to another. Consequently, if use and enjoyment are compared with respect to their objects, enjoyment is more worthwhile than use, for that which is wholly desirable is better than that which is desirable only as ordered to something else. But if they are compared to the power of apprehending which precedes them, a greater excellence is required on the part of use; for to order one thing to another belongs to reason, while to apprehend something by itself can be attained even by sense.

Reply to 2: By means of their bodily members, animals do something by natural instinct, though not by knowing the ordering of their members to their operations. Hence they are not said properly to apply their members to action nor to make use of their members.

Third Article

CAN THERE BE USE EVEN OF THE ULTIMATE END?

It seems that there can be use even of the ultimate end.

1. Augustine says, "Whoever enjoys a thing uses it." [12] But man enjoys the ultimate end. Therefore he uses the ultimate end.

2. Augustine says, "To use is to put a means in the power of the will." [13] But more than anything else, the ultimate end is the object of the will's application. Therefore use can refer to the ultimate end.

3. Hilary says that "Eternity is in the Father, species is in the Image," that is, in the Son, "and use is in the Gift," that is, the Holy Spirit. [14] But the Holy Spirit, since He is God, is the ultimate end. Therefore the ultimate end can be used.

On the contrary: Augustine says, "No one rightly makes use of God, but enjoys Him." [15] But God alone is the ultimate end. Therefore we cannot use the ultimate end.

Response: Use, as we have said, [16] implies the application of one thing to another. Now that which is applied to another is regarded as a means, and hence use is always of a means. For this reason, things adapted to an end are said to be useful, and their very utility is sometimes called "use."

We must note, however, that the ultimate end can be taken in two ways, absolutely and in relation to someone. Now since the end, as we have said, [17] sometimes signifies the thing itself and sometimes the attainment or possession of the end—for example, the end of the miser is

---

[12] *On the Trinity* X, 11.   [13] *Ibid.*   [14] *On the Trinity* II.

[15] *Book of Eighty-three Questions,* question 30.

[16] Article 1.

[17] Question 1, article 8; question 2, article 7.

either money or the possession of it—it is clear that, absolutely speaking, the ultimate end is the thing itself, for the possession of money is good only because there is good in the money. But with respect to the individual, the attainment of the money is the ultimate end, for the miser would not seek money except to have it. Therefore, speaking absolutely and properly, a man enjoys money because he has set it up as his ultimate end, but insofar as he refers to possession, he is said to use it.

Reply to 1: Augustine speaks of use in general as implying an ordering of the end to the enjoyment which one seeks in that end.

Reply to 2: The end is the object of the will's application insofar as the will rests in it. Hence the very resting in the end, which is enjoyment, is called a use of the end in this sense. But the means is brought into the power of the will not only with respect to its use as a means, but with respect to something else in which the will rests.

Reply to 3. "Use," as Hilary speaks of it, refers to rest in the ultimate end just as, speaking generally, one who obtains the end is said to use the end, as we have said.[18] Hence Augustine says, "such love, delight, felicity, or happiness is called a use by him." [19]

Fourth Article

DOES USE PRECEDE CHOICE?

It seems that use precedes choice.

1. After choice nothing follows except execution. But use, since it belongs to the will, precedes execution. Therefore it also precedes choice.

2. What is absolute precedes what is relative. Hence what is less relative precedes what is more relative. But choice implies two relations, one of what is chosen in regard to the end, the other in regard to the thing it is preferred to. Now use only implies a relation to the end. Therefore use is prior to choice.

3. The will uses other powers inasmuch as it moves them. But the will also moves itself, as we have pointed out.[20]

Therefore it also makes use of itself by applying itself to act. But it does this when it consents. Therefore there is use in the consent itself. But consent precedes choice, as we have said.[21] Therefore use also precedes choice.

On the contrary: Damascene says that "the will, after choice, is impelled to action, and thereafter it uses [the powers]." [22] Therefore use follows upon choice.

Response: There is a twofold relationship of the will to what it wills. One comes from the willed thing's being in some way in the one who wills

---

[18] In the body of this article.
[19] *The Trinity* VI, 10.
[20] Question 9, article 3.
[21] Question 15, article 3, reply to 3.
[22] *On the Orthodox Faith* II, 22.

through some proportion or order to that willed thing. Hence things that are naturally proportioned to some end are said to desire it naturally. But to have an end in this way is to have it imperfectly. Now everything imperfect tends to what is perfect. Therefore both the natural and the voluntary appetite or desire[23] move to possess an end really, which is to possess it perfectly. This is the second relationship of the will to what is willed.

Now the will wills not only the end but also the means. And the last act belonging to the first relationship of the will in respect to the means is choice, for there the proportion of the will is completed so that it wills the means completely. But use belongs to the second relationship of the will wherein the will tends to the realization of what is willed. Clearly, then, use follows upon choice if we take use to mean that the will uses its power of execution in moving itself. However, since the will in a certain way also moves reason and uses it, use can be understood of the means as reason considers the means, that is, in reference to an end. In this sense use precedes choice.

Reply to 1: The movement of the will to the executing of a work precedes execution but follows choice. And thus, since use belongs to this movement of the will, it stands as midway between choice and execution.

Reply to 2: What is essentially relative is posterior to what is absolute, but the thing to which relations are attributed need not be posterior. In fact, the more a cause is prior, the more it has a relation to many effects.

Reply to 3: Choice precedes use if each is referred to the same thing. But nothing prevents the use of one thing from preceding the choice of another. And because the acts of the will can turn back on themselves, in any act of the will we can find consent, choice, and use, such that we can say that the will consents to choose and consents to consent, and uses itself in consenting and choosing. And those acts which are ordered to what is prior are always prior.

---

[23] Natural desire, as distinct from voluntary desire, is the inclination following upon the form of any thing toward the end to which it is ordered by nature.

Acts Commanded by the Will

(In Nine Articles)

IS COMMAND AN ACT OF REASON OR OF THE WILL?

It seems that command is not an act of reason but of the will.

1. To command is to move in a certain kind of way, for Avicenna says that there is a fourfold way of moving, namely, "as perfecting, disposing, commanding and deliberating." [1] But it is the will that moves all the other powers of the soul, as we have said.[2] Therefore command is an act of the will.

2. Just as to be commanded characterizes whoever is a subject, so to command seems to characterize whoever is most of all free. But the root of liberty is in the will principally. Therefore command belongs to the will.

3. Command is followed immediately by action. But action does not follow immediately an act of reason, for one who judges that something should be done does not at once do it. Therefore command is not an act of reason, but of the will.

On the contrary: Gregory of Nyssa says that "the appetite obeys reason." [3] The Philosopher says the same.[4] Therefore command belongs to reason.

Response: Command is an act of reason but it presupposes an act of the will. To make this evident, we must consider that since the act of the will and of reason can be brought to bear on each other, inasmuch as reason reasons about willing and the will wills to reason, an act of the will can precede an act of reason and conversely. And because the power of a prior act carries over into the act which follows, it sometimes happens that there is an act of the will which retains something from the power of the act of reason, as we noted above with respect to use[5] and choice,[6] and conversely, there can be an act of reason which retains something from the power of the will's act.

Now command is essentially an act of reason, for the one commanding,

---

[1] *On Sufficiency* I, 10; *On the Soul* I, 5.   [2] Question 9, article 1.
[3] Cf. Nemesius, *On the Nature of Man,* 16.
[4] *Nicomachean Ethics* I, 13 (1102b 26).   [5] Question 16, article 1.
[6] Question 13, article 1.

by enjoining or by declaring orders the one who is commanded to do something, and to order by way of enjoining or declaring belongs to reason. But reason can enjoin or declare something in two ways. In one way simply, and then the enjoining is expressed by a verb in the indicative mood, as when one says, "This is what you should do." Sometimes, however, reason orders someone to do something by way of impelling him to it, and then it is expressed by a verb in the imperative mood, as when one says, "Do this!"

Now among the powers of the soul, the first mover in regard to the doing of an act is the will, as we have pointed out above.[7] And since the second mover moves only in virtue of the first mover, it follows that it is due to the power of the will that reason moves by way of command. Hence to command is an act of reason, presupposing an act of the will[8] in virtue of which reason moves, by commanding, to the doing of the act.

Reply to 1: To command is to move, not in any way whatever, but by way of enjoining someone as to what he should do to another. This belongs to reason.

Reply to 2: The root of liberty is the will as to its subject, but as to its cause it is reason. For it is because reason can have different conceptions of what is good that the will can incline freely toward different things. Hence philosophers define free will as "a free judgment arising from reason," [9] implying that reason is the cause of liberty.

Reply to 3: The argument given proves that command is not an act of reason absolutely, but an act of reason together with a kind of motion, as we have said.[10]

Second Article

DOES COMMAND BELONG TO IRRATIONAL ANIMALS?

It seems that command belongs to irrational animals.

1. According to Avicenna, "the power commanding movement is the appetite, and the power executing movement is in the muscles and nerves." [11] But both powers are in animals. Therefore command is found in animals.

2. A servant is regarded as one to be commanded. But the body is related to the soul as servant to master, as the Philosopher says.[12] Therefore the body is commanded by the soul even in animals, since they are composed of soul and body.

---

[7] Question 9, article 1. Cf. I, question 82, article 4.
[8] The act of the will which is presupposed to command is choice, as is made clear below in article 3, reply to 1.
[9] Cf. Boethius, *Commentary on Aristotle's "On Interpretation"* III, Prologue.
[10] In the body of this article.   [11] *On the Soul* I, 5.
[12] Cf. *Politics* I, 2 (1254b 4).

3. Through command, man causes the impulse toward action. But an impulse toward action is found in animals, as Damascene says.[13] Therefore command is found in animals.

On the contrary: Command is an act of reason, as we have said.[14] But animals do not have reason, and therefore they do not have command.

Response: To command is nothing else than to order someone to do something by some enjoining motion. Now to bring about order is the characteristic act of reason. Hence it is impossible that animals should command in any way, since they are without reason.

Reply to 1: The appetitive power is said to command movement insofar as it moves reason as it commands. But this is found only in man. In animals, the appetitive power is not a power of commanding properly unless "command" be taken broadly for a moving power.

Reply to 2: The body of the animal is capable of obeying, but the soul is not capable of commanding because it does not have that whereby it could order. This is the reason that there is no account of commander and commanded as regards them, but only of mover and moved.

Reply to 3: Impulse to action is found differently in animals and in man. Man's impulse to act arises from the ordering of reason, and hence impulse in him has the nature of command. But in animals the impulse to action comes from natural instinct, for immediately upon apprehending what is agreeable or disagreeable, their appetite naturally moves to seek or avoid it. Hence they are ordered to act by another; they do not order themselves to act. Consequently there is impulse in them but not command.

Third Article

DOES USE PRECEDE COMMAND?

It seems that use precedes command.

1. Command is an act of reason presupposing an act of the will, as we have said.[15] But use is an act of the will, as we have also said.[16] Therefore use precedes command.

2. Command is something that is ordered to an end. But we use things that are for an end. Therefore it seems that use is prior to command.

3. Every act of a power moved by the will is called a use because the will uses other powers, as we have stated.[17] But command is an act of reason moved by the will, as we have noted.[18] Therefore command is a sort of use. Now what is common is prior to what is proper. Therefore use precedes command.

On the contrary: Damascene says that the impulse to act precedes use.[19]

---

[13] Cf. *On the Orthodox Faith* II, 22.   [14] Article 1.
[15] Article 1.   [16] Question 16, article 1.
[17] *Ibid.*   [18] Article 1.
[19] Cf. *On the Orthodox Faith* II, 22.

But an impulse to act comes about through command. Therefore command precedes use.

Response: The use of that which is ordered to an end, insofar as it is in reason as referring it to an end,[20] precedes choice, as we have said.[21] Therefore, much more does it precede command. However, the use of that which is ordered to an end, as it is subject to the power of executing, follows command in that use in the user is joined to the act of the thing used, for we do not use a stick until we do something with the stick. But command is not simultaneous with the act of that which is commanded, for the command is naturally prior to the obeying of the command, and sometimes even prior in time.[22] Hence it is clear that command is prior to use.

Reply to 1: Not every act of the will precedes the act of reason which is command, but an act of the will does precede it, namely, choice; and another follows, use. For after a determination by deliberation, which is a judgment of reason, the will chooses, and after choice reason commands that power by which what has been chosen is to be done. Finally, the will begins the act of use by executing the command of reason; sometimes it is the will of another when one commands another, sometimes the will of the one who commands when he commands himself to do something.

Reply to 2: Acts precede powers, in the way objects precede acts. Now the object to be used is that which is directed to an end. Therefore, from the fact that command is directed to an end, one should rather conclude that command precedes rather than follows use.

Reply to 3: Just as an act of the will, using reason for the purpose of command, precedes command, so it can be said that a command of reason precedes the will's use of reason,[23] for the acts of these powers act reciprocally on each other.

Fourth Article

ARE COMMAND AND THE COMMANDED ACT ONE ACT OR DISTINCT ACTS?

It seems that the commanded act is not one with command itself.

1. Acts of different powers are themselves different. But a commanded

---

[20] I.e., when use is taken for an act of the will moving reason to consider and deliberate about the means, then use clearly precedes choice and, accordingly, command.

[21] Question 16, article 4.

[22] Cf. Aristotle, *Categories* 12 (14a 25-29; 14b 3-7). "Prior" first refers to time, as youth is prior to adulthood. "Prior by nature" refers to a priority of excellence, as he more honorable is prior to the less honorable. In the context here, "prior by nature" refers particularly to causality, for command as a cause is prior to what is commanded, an effect.

[23] Hence there is always some command before there is use.

act belongs to one power and command to another, for the power that commands is one power and the power that is commanded is another. Therefore the commanded act is not identical with the command.

2. Things that can be separated from each other are diverse, for nothing is separated from itself. But sometimes the commanded act is separated from the command, for sometimes a command is given and the commanded act does not follow. Therefore command is distinct from the commanded act.

3. Whatever things are related as prior and posterior are distinct. But command naturally precedes the act commanded. Therefore they are distinct.

On the contrary: The Philosopher says that "where one thing exists by reason of another, there is only one." [24] But the act commanded exists only by reason of the command. Therefore they are one.

Response: There is nothing to prevent some things being many in one respect and one in another. Moreover, all things which are many are one in some respect, as Dionysius says. [25] But a difference must be noted in that some things are many absolutely and one in a particular respect, while with others the reverse is true. Now "one" is said in the same way as "being" is. A substance is being absolutely, but an accident or even a being of reason [26] is being in a qualified sense. Consequently, whatever things are one according to substance are one absolutely and many in a certain respect. Thus in the genus of substance, a whole composed either of integral or essential parts [27] is one absolutely, for such a whole is a being and a substance absolutely, whereas the parts are beings and substances in the whole.

But things which differ in substance but are one accidentally differ absolutely and are one only in a particular respect. Thus, many men are one people and many stones are one heap; such a unity is a unity of composition or order. Likewise, many individual things which are one in genus or one in species [28] are many absolutely and one in a certain respect, for to be one in genus or in species is to be one according to the consideration of reason.

Now just as in the genus of natural things a whole is composed of

---

[24] *Topics* III, 2 (117a 18).   [25] Cf. *The Divine Names,* 13, section 2.

[26] A being of reason is that which has existence only in the mind to which nothing corresponds, at least directly, in reality; e.g., a negation, "non-man," or certain relations, such as a relation of identity ("A is A"), or such logical intentions as that of genus or species.

[27] An example of a whole composed of integral or component parts would be man as composed of head, trunk, and limbs. An example of a whole composed of essential parts, parts constitutive of a nature, would be man as composed of body and soul or, in another respect, of rational and animal.

[28] An example of many individual things one in genus would be this dog, this cat, this man, etc., as being one in the genus "animal." An example of many things one in species would be individual men as being one in species, namely, "man."

matter and form—for example, man, composed of body and soul, is one
natural being, though having many parts—so in human acts the act of
a lower power is related as matter to the act of a higher power insofar
as the lower power acts in virtue of the higher power moving it; so also
the act of the first mover is related as form to the act of its instrument.
Hence it is clear that command and the commanded act are one human
act in the way a whole is one, yet is many in its parts.

Reply to 1: If different powers are not ordered to one another, their
acts are wholly distinct. But when one power is the mover of another,
then their acts are in a certain way one, for "the act of the mover and
the moved is the same act." [29]

Reply to 2: The fact that a command and a commanded act can be
separated from each other shows that they are many as to parts. For the
parts of a man can be separated from each other, and yet they form one
whole.

Reply to 3: In things which are many in their parts and one as a whole,
nothing prevents one part being prior to another. Thus the soul is prior
in a certain way to the body, and the heart to other members.

Fifth Article

IS THE ACT OF THE WILL COMMANDED?

It seems that the act of the will is not commanded.

1. Augustine says, "The mind commands the mind to will, yet it obeys
not." [30] Now to will is an act of the will. Therefore the act of the will
is not commanded.

2. To be commanded belongs to that which can understand a command. But the will does not understand a command, for the will differs
from the intellect, to which it belongs to understand. Therefore the act
of the will is not commanded.

3. If some act of the will is commanded, with equal reason all acts of
the will are commanded. But if all acts of the will are commanded, we
are faced with an endless process, because an act of the will precedes the
act of reason commanding, and if that act of the will be also commanded,
this command will be preceded by another act of reason, and so on
without end. But it is not reasonable to proceed endlessly.[31] Therefore
the act of the will is not commanded.

On the contrary: Everything in our power is subject to our command.
But acts of the will are most of all within our power, for all acts insofar
as they are voluntary are said to be within our power. Therefore acts
of the will are commanded by us.

---

[29] Aristotle, *Physics* III, 3 (202a 18; b 20).   [30] *Confessions* VIII, 9.
[31] A process may well go on without end, as a variable converging toward a limit,
but the end is not attained in such a process.

Response: As we have said,[32] command is nothing other than the act of reason ordering, with a certain motion, that something be done. Now it is clear that reason can order an act of the will, for just as reason can judge that it is good to will a certain thing so it can order by command that a man will. It is evident from this that the act of the will can be commanded.

Reply to 1: Augustine also says in the same place that when the mind perfectly commands itself to will, it already wills, but it sometimes commands and does not will because it does not command perfectly. An imperfect command occurs when reason is moved by opposing motives to command or not to command, and so it fluctuates between the two and does not command perfectly.

Reply to 2: Just as each member of the body acts, not for itself alone, but for the whole body—thus it is for the whole body that the eye sees— so it is in powers of the soul. For the intellect understands, not only for itself, but for all powers, and the will wills not only for itself but for all powers. Hence man, inasmuch as he understands and wills, commands his own act of will.

Reply to 3: Since command is an act of reason, the act which is commanded is subject to reason. Now the first act of the will is not from the ordering of reason, but from a natural instinct or the impulse of a superior cause, as we have said.[33] Hence there is no need to be involved in an endless process.

Sixth Article

IS THE ACT OF REASON COMMANDED?

It seems that the act of reason cannot be commanded.

1. It seems unfitting for something to command itself. But it is reason which commands, as we have said.[34] Therefore the act of reason is not commanded.

2. That which is essentially such or such is distinct from what is such by participation. But a power whose act is commanded by reason is rational by participation.[35] Therefore the act of a power which is essentially rational is not commanded.

3. That act is commanded which is within our power. But to know and judge what is true, which is an act of reason, is not always in our power. Therefore the act of reason cannot be commanded.

On the contrary: What we do by free will can be done by our command. But the acts of reason are accomplished by free will, for Damascene

---

[32] Article 1.   [33] Question 9, article 4.   [34] Article 1.
[35] Cf. Aristotle, *Nicomachean Ethics* I, 13 (1102b 13; b 26).

says that "by free will, man inquires, examines, judges, and approves." [36] Therefore acts of reason can be commanded.

Response: Since reason reflects upon itself, consequently just as it directs acts of other powers so it can direct its own act. Hence its own act can also be commanded.

But we must take into account that the act of reason can be considered in two ways. One is with respect to the exercise of its act, and so considered the act of reason can always be commanded; for example, when one is told to be attentive or to make use of his reason. Secondly, with respect to the object, and in this regard two acts of reason are to be noted. The first is the act whereby we apprehend the truth about something; this act is not within our power, for it takes place in virtue of some light, natural or supernatural.[37] Hence, in this respect, the act of reason is not within our power nor can it be commanded. The other act of reason is that by which it assents to what it apprehends. Now if that which reason grasps is such that it assents naturally to it, as it does regarding first principles, it is not within our power to assent or not to assent, for such assent follows naturally and, therefore, properly speaking, is not subject to our command.[38] But other things are apprehended, which do not convince the intellect, and hence allow the intellect to assent or not assent—or at least to suspend assenting or not assenting for some reason —and in such matters to assent or not assent is within our power and subject to our command.

Reply to 1: Reason commands itself just as the will moves itself, namely, insofar as each power reflects back on its own act and from one thing tends to another.

Reply to 2: Because of a difference in the objects subject to the act of reason, nothing prevents reason from participating in this [i.e. being commanded by itself], just as the knowledge of a conclusion participates in the knowledge of principles.

---

[36] *On the Orthodox Faith* II, 22.

[37] The natural light of the intellect is simply that which makes truth manifest to it unaided. The supernatural light is the strengthening of the intellect by grace to know divine truths beyond the reach of a created intellect. On this extension of the meaning of "light" see I, question 67, article 1; question 106, article 1.

[38] Of course, one can formulate grammatically correct sentences to express dissent to, for example, the principle of non-contradiction, but these will not express what we think, but rather what we choose to say orally. As Aristotle explains, "It is impossible for anyone to believe that the same thing is and is not, as some suppose Heraclitus to say. For what a man says does not necessarily mean what he believes. And if it is impossible for contraries to be in the same subject at the same time (the usual qualifications must be presupposed here as well), and if an opinion which contradicts another is contrary to it, then it is clearly impossible for the same man to believe that the same thing is and is not at the same time; for if a man errs in regard to this point, he would hold contrary opinions at the same time." (*Metaphysics* IV, 3 [1005b 23-31].)

Reply to 3: This is sufficiently evident from what has been said in this article.

Seventh Article

IS THE ACT OF THE SENSE APPETITE COMMANDED?

It seems that the act of the sense appetite is not commanded.

1. The Apostle says, "for I do not that good which I will" (*Romans 7:15*), and the *Gloss* explains that man does not will to lust, and yet he lusts.[39] But to lust is an act of the sense appetite. Therefore the act of the sense appetite is not subject to our command.

2. Corporeal matter is subject to God alone as far as a change of form is concerned, as we have pointed out already.[40] But the act of the sense appetite is accompanied by some bodily change of form, for example, a change in warmth or coolness. Therefore the act of the sense appetite is not subject to our command.

3. The proper moving principle of sense appetite is something apprehended by sense or imagination. But something apprehended by sense or imagination is not always within our power. Therefore the act of the sense appetite is not always subject to our command.

On the contrary: Gregory of Nyssa says that "what is obedient to reason is divided into two, the concupiscible and the irascible," [41] which belong to the sense appetite. Therefore the act of sense appetite is subject to the command of reason.

Response: An act is subject to our command inasmuch as it is in our power, as we have said.[42] Hence, in order to understand how an act of the sense appetite is subject to the command of reason, we must consider how it is within our power. Now we must take into account that sense appetite differs from intellectual appetite, which is called the will, by being a power of a bodily organ whereas the will is not. Now the act of a power using a bodily organ depends not only on a power of the soul but also on the disposition of the bodily organ, just as seeing depends on the power of sight and also upon the condition of the eye, by which vision is helped or hindered. Hence, the act of sense appetite depends not only upon the appetitive power but also upon a bodily disposition.

Now insofar as an act proceeds from a power of the soul, it follows upon apprehension. But the apprehending of something by the imagination, since it is of the singular, is regulated by what reason apprehends, which is the universal, just as a particular active power is regulated by a

---

[39] Cf. Augustine, *Against Julian* III, 26.
[40] I, question 65, article 4; question 91, article 2; question 110, article 2. This point refers to the original formation of the world.
[41] Cf. Nemesius, *On the Nature of Man*, 16.
[42] Article 5, *On the contrary.*

universal active power. In this respect, accordingly, the act of sense appetite is subject to the command of reason. Nevertheless, the quality and disposition of the body is not subject to the command of reason; and in this respect the movement of the sense appetite is prevented from being wholly subject to the command of reason.

Moreover, it sometimes happens that the movement of the sense appetite is aroused suddenly with respect to something apprehended by the imagination or sense. Such a movement is then apart from the command of reason, although it might have been prevented by reason if foreseen. Thus the Philosopher says that reason does not govern the irascible and concupiscible appetite by a despotic rule, which is the rule of a master over a slave, but by a political or royal rule, which is a rule of free men who are not wholly subject to command.[43]

Reply to 1: The fact that a man does not will to lust, and yet lusts, happens because of a disposition of the body by which the sense appetite is hindered from wholly following the command of reason. Hence the Apostle also says, "I see another law in my members, warring against the law of my mind" (*Romans 7:23*). This can also happen because of a sudden movement of concupiscible desire, as we have said.[44]

Reply to 2: A bodily condition is related in two ways to the act of sense appetite. In one way as preceding, inasmuch as one is disposed to this or that passion because of his body. In another way as consequent, as when a man becomes inflamed through anger. Now the condition that precedes is not subject to the command of reason, because it is either from nature or from some previous movement which cannot at once be quieted. But a condition which is consequent follows upon the command of reason, for it follows upon the movement of the heart which is moved variously according to the different acts of the sense appetite.

Reply to 3: Because an external sensible thing is required for the apprehension of the senses, it is not within our power to apprehend anything by the senses unless what is sensible is present, and this presence of what is sensible is not always within our power. For it is in the presence of the sensible thing that a man can use his sense when he wills to, unless there is some impediment on the part of the organ. But the apprehension of something by the imagination is subject to the directing of reason in proportion to the strength or weakness of the power of imagination. Now that a man cannot imagine the things reason considers is either because they are not imaginable, for example incorporeal things, or because of a weakness of the imaginative power from some organic indisposition.

---

[43] Cf. *Politics* I, 2 (1254b 5).   [44] In the body of this article.

Eighth Article

IS AN ACT OF THE VEGETATIVE SOUL COMMANDED?

It seems that acts of the vegetative soul are subject to the command of reason.

1. The powers of sensation are of a higher order than the vegetative powers. But the powers of sensation are subject to the command of reason. Therefore much more so are the vegetative powers.

2. Man is referred to as a "small world," [45] because the soul is in the body as God is in the world. But God is in the world in such a way that all things in the world are subject to His command. Accordingly, all things in man, even the vegetative powers, are subject to the command of reason.

3. Praise and blame are attributed only to acts which fall under the command of reason. But with respect to the acts of the powers of nutrition and generation, we can speak of praise and blame, virtue and vice, as is evident with gluttony and lust, and the virtues opposed to them. Therefore acts of these powers are subject to the command of reason.

On the contrary: Gregory of Nyssa says that "the powers of nutrition and generation are not under the control of reason." [46]

Response: Some acts proceed from natural appetite, [47] some from animal appetite, and some from intellectual appetite, for every agent desires the end in some way. Now natural appetite does not follow upon some apprehension, as sense and intellectual appetite do. But reason commands in the mode of a knowing power. Consequently, acts which proceed from intellectual or animal appetite can be commanded by reason, but not acts which proceed from natural desire. Acts of the vegetative powers are of the latter kind, and hence Gregory of Nyssa says that "generation and nutrition belong to what are called natural powers." [48] For this reason, acts of vegetative powers are not subject to the command of reason.

Reply to 1: The more immaterial an act the more excellent it is and the more subject to the command of reason. It is apparent from the fact that the powers of the vegetative soul are not subject to reason that they are the lowest powers.

Reply to 2: The comparison holds only in a certain respect, namely, as God moves the world so the soul moves the body. But the comparison does not hold in all respects, for the soul does not create the body from nothing as God creates the world, in virtue of which everything is wholly subject to His command.

---

[45] Cf. Aristotle, *Physics* VIII, 2 (252b 26).
[46] Cf. Nemesius, *On the Nature of Man*, 22.
[47] Cf. question 16, article 4; also note 23.
[48] Cf. Nemesius, *On the Nature of Man*, 22.

Reply to 3: Virtue and vice, praise and blame are not owing to the acts themselves of the nutritive and generative powers, that is, digestion and the forming of the human body, but they are owed to those acts of the sense appetite which are ordered to acts of generation and nutrition. Such acts would be, for example, pleasure in the act of eating or in the act of generation, either rightly or wrongly.

Ninth Article

ARE ACTS OF THE EXTERNAL MEMBERS COMMANDED?

It seems that members of the body are not subject to reason with respect to their acts.

1. It is an established fact that the members of the body are more removed from reason than are the powers of the vegetative soul. But powers of the vegetative soul are not subject to reason, as we have said.[49] Therefore much less so are members of the body.

2. The heart is the principle of animal movement. But the movement of the heart is not subject to the command of reason, for Gregory of Nyssa says that "the pulse is not controlled by reason."[50] Therefore the movement of bodily members is not subject to the command of reason.

3. Augustine says that "the movement of genital members sometimes is importunate and not desired, but sometimes fails when sought, and though the mind glows with desire the body is left cold."[51] Therefore the movement of bodily members is not subject to reason.

On the contrary: Augustine says, "The mind commands a movement of the hand, and so ready is the hand to respond that command can hardly be distinguished from obedience."[52]

Response: Members of the body are tools of the soul's powers. Hence, in the measure in which the powers of the soul are disposed to obey reason so also are the bodily members. Consequently, since the powers of sense desire are subject to the command of reason, but not the natural powers, all movement of members which are moved by sense powers is subject to the command of reason, whereas the movement of members following upon natural powers is not subject to the command of reason.

Reply to 1: Bodily members do not move themselves but are moved by the soul's powers, and among these powers some are closer to reason than are powers of the vegetative soul.

Reply to 2: With respect to what belongs to intellect and will, that which is according to nature holds first place, and the others are derived from it. Thus, from a knowledge of principles naturally known, knowledge of conclusions is derived, and from a willing of the end naturally

---

[49] Article 1.
[50] Cf. Nemesius, *On the Nature of Man*, 22.
[51] *The City of God* XIV, 16.   [52] *Confessions* VIII, 9.

desired, choice of means to the end is derived. Likewise in bodily movements, what is first is according to nature. Now the principle of bodily
movement is from the movement of the heart. Consequently, the movement of the heart is according to nature and not according to the will,
for like a property it results from life, which follows from the union
of soul and body, just as the movement of the heavy and the light follows from their substantial form, and so are said to be moved by their
generator, as the Philosopher says.[53] Therefore this movement is called
vital. Hence Gregory of Nyssa says that just as the movements of generation and nutrition do not obey reason, so also the pulse does not,
which is a vital movement.[54] And he means by pulse the movement of
the heart, which makes itself evident through the pulse veins.

Reply to 3: As Augustine says, it is due to punishment for sin that the
movement of genital members does not obey reason,[55] that is, the soul
is punished for disobeying God by a lack of submission in that member
whereby original sin is transmitted to posterity.

But, as we shall say later on,[56] since through the sin of our first parent,
nature was left to itself by the removal of the supernatural gift bestowed
on man by God, we must consider what natural reason there is for the
insubordination of this member to the command of reason. The cause
of this is assigned by Aristotle, who says that "the movements of the
heart and the organs of generation are involuntary," [57] and for the following reason. These members are aroused by the apprehending of something, that is, inasmuch as the intellect and the imagination represent
things which arouse the passions, of which passions these movements are
a consequence. Yet they are not moved at the command of reason because these movements require some natural change, such as a change in
warmth or coldness, which is not subject to the command of reason. This
is especially the case with the two members under consideration because
each is, as it were, a separate animal insofar as it is a principle of life—
and the principle is in effect the whole. For the heart is the principle of
sense, and from the genital member proceeds the seminal principle which
is in effect the whole animal. Hence they have their own natural movements because their principles have to be natural, as we have said.[58]

----

[53] *Physics* VIII, 4 (255b 35): ". . . light and heavy things are moved either by that
which brought them into existence as such and made them light and heavy or by
that which was hindering or preventing them from being in motion." St. Thomas
identifies the *Primum Generans* with the Creator. Cf. *De Malo* question 3, article 3.
[54] Cf. Nemesius, *On the Nature of Man,* 22.
[55] Cf. *The City of God* XIV, 17.   [56] Question 85, article 1, reply to 3.
[57] *On the Motion of Animals,* 11 (703b 5).
[58] Reply to 2.

The Goodness and Malice of Human Acts in General

(*In Eleven Articles*)

Now we must consider the good and evil of human acts. First we must investigate what makes a human act good or evil; then the effects following upon the good or evil of human acts, such as merit or demerit, sin and guilt.[1]

There are three considerations with respect to the first point. The first concerns the good and evil of human acts in general; the second, the good and evil of interior acts;[2] the third, the good and evil of exterior acts.[3]

ARE ALL HUMAN ACTS GOOD OR ARE SOME EVIL?

It seems that every human act is good and none is evil.

1. Dionysius says that evil occurs only in virtue of what is good.[4] But evil is not produced by the power of good. Therefore no action is evil.

2. Nothing acts except insofar as it is in act. Now a thing is not evil according as it is in act, but as it is a potency deprived of act, whereas insofar as the potency is perfected by act, it is good.[5] Therefore, nothing acts insofar as it is evil but only insofar as it is good. Consequently, every action is good and none is evil.

3. Evil can only be a cause accidentally, as Dionysius points out.[6] But every action has an effect proper to it. Therefore no action is evil; on the contrary, every action is good.

On the contrary: Our Lord says, "Everyone who does evil hates the light" (*John 3:20*). Therefore some actions of men are evil.

Response: We must speak of good and evil in actions the way we do

---

[1] Question 21.   [2] Question 19.   [3] Question 20.
[4] Cf. *The Divine Names* IV, 20.
[5] Cf. Aristotle, *Metaphysics* IX, 9 (1051a 4; 29).
[6] Cf. *The Divine Names* IV, 20.

of good and evil in things, for a thing produces the kind of action it does because of the kind of thing it is. Now with respect to things, each thing has as much good as it has being, for good and being are convertible, as we have already said.[7] In God alone the complete fullness of His being is in something one and simple, while in everything else the fullness of being proper to it involves diverse things. Hence, some things may have being in some respect and yet lack something of the fullness of being they ought to have. For example, the fullness of a human being requires the composite of soul and body, having all the powers and instruments of knowledge and motion; hence if a man lacks any of these he lacks something of the fullness of his being. Consequently, a man has as much goodness as he has being, but inasmuch as he lacks something of the fullness of being, in that respect he falls short of goodness, and is called evil. For example, a blind man possesses goodness inasmuch as he lives, but evil inasmuch as he lacks sight. However, that which has nothing of being or goodness could not be called evil or good. Now since this very fullness of being is of the notion of goodness, if a thing lacks something of the fullness of the being it ought to have, it cannot be called good absolutely but only in a certain respect, inasmuch as it is a being; it could, however, be called a being absolutely, and non-being in a certain respect, as we have said.[8]

Therefore it should be said that every act as having something of being has something of goodness, but insofar as it lacks something of the fullness of the being a human action ought to have, it lacks goodness and to this extent is called evil, for example, if it lacks the quantity determined by reason, or a due place, or something of this kind.

Reply to 1: Evil occurs in virtue of a deficient good. For if there were nothing of the good there, there would be neither being nor the possibility of acting. On the other hand, if good were not lacking, there would be no evil. Hence the action caused is a certain deficient good, which is good in a certain respect but evil absolutely.

Reply to 2: Nothing prevents something being in act in a certain respect, so that it can act, and being deprived of act in another respect, thereby causing a deficient action. For example, a blind man actually has the power of walking, enabling him to walk; but inasmuch as he lacks vision to direct his walking, he suffers a defect in walking from bumping into things as he walks.

Reply to 3: An evil action can have a per se effect, corresponding to the goodness and being it has. For example, adultery is the cause of the generation of a human being inasmuch as it involves the union of male and female; it is not a lack in the order of reason that causes generation.

---

[7] I, question 5, articles 1 and 3; question 17, article 4, reply to 2.
[8] I, question 5, article 1, reply to 1.

Second Article

IS THE GOOD OR EVIL OF HUMAN ACTION DERIVED FROM THE OBJECT?

It seems that the good or evil of an act does not come from the object.

1. The object of an action is a thing. Now "evil is not in things, but in a sinner's use of them," as Augustine says.[9] Therefore the good or evil of a human act is not derived from the object.

2. The object is related to the action as matter. However, the goodness of a thing is not from the matter, but rather from the form, which is its act. Therefore the good or evil in actions does not come from the object.

3. The object of an active power is compared to the action as effect to cause. However, the goodness of a cause does not depend on the effect, but rather the reverse. Therefore human action does not derive its goodness or evil from the object.

On the contrary: "They became abominable, as those things were, which they loved" (*Osee 9:10*). Now man becomes abominable to God because of the evil of his action. Therefore the evil of the action is taken from the evil object which man desires. The same reason holds for the goodness of an action.

Response: As we have said above,[10] the good or evil of an action, as of anything else, depends upon its fullness of being or its lack of fullness. The principal thing that seems to pertain to fullness of being is whatever gives a thing its species.[11] Now just as a natural thing has its species from its form, so an action has its species from the object, as a movement has from its term. Consequently, just as the primary goodness of a natural thing comes from the form which gives it its species, so the primary goodness of a moral act comes from the appropriateness of its object,[12] and accordingly is called by some an action that is good of its kind,[13] for example, to make use of what is one's own.

Now just as in natural things the principal evil comes from the generated thing's not achieving its specific form—for example, if instead of a man something else were generated—so the principal evil in moral actions is derived from the object, for example, taking what belongs to another. Hence the act is said to be evil of its kind, "kind" here being taken for species, just as in speaking of the whole human species we say "mankind."

Reply to 1: Although external things are good in themselves, they are

---

[9] *On Christian Doctrine* III, 12.   [10] Article 1.

[11] I.e., its distinctive nature.

[12] Hence, the object *from which* the good or evil of a moral act is taken is not a thing considered absolutely in itself, but a thing as implying an order and relation to reason with which it is in conformity or disagreement.

[13] Cf. Peter Lombard, *Sentences* II, xxxvi, 6.

not always duly proportioned to this or that action. Hence, when considered as objects of such actions, they are not counted as good.

Reply to 2: The object is not the matter *from which,* but *about which,*[14] and in a certain respect is related to action as a form insofar as it gives a thing its species.

Reply to 3: The object of a human action is not always the object of an active power. For the appetitive power is in some way passive, insofar as it is moved by the desirable object, and yet it is a principle of human acts. Further, the objects of active powers do not always have the character of effects, but only when they are already transformed. For example, food, when digested, is an effect of the power of nutrition but food not yet digested is related to the power of nutrition as the matter upon which it acts. Now since the object is in some way the effect of an active power, it follows that it is the term of its act, and consequently gives it its form and species, for the species of a motion comes from its terms. Finally, although the goodness of an effect does not cause the goodness of an action, nevertheless from the fact that an action can produce a good effect it is said to be good. Consequently, the very proportion of an action to its effect is the reason for its goodness.

Third Article

IS A HUMAN ACT GOOD OR BAD BECAUSE OF CIRCUMSTANCES? [15]

It seems that a human act is not good or bad because of circumstances.

1. Circumstances surround an act, as being external to it, as we have said.[16] But "good and evil are in things themselves." [17] Therefore an action does not derive goodness or evil from the circumstances.

2. The goodness or evil of an act is considered most completely in moral doctrine. But circumstances, since they are certain accidents of acts, seem to be outside of the consideration of an art, for "no art considers what is accidental." [18] Therefore the goodness or evil of an action does not come from circumstances.

3. What belongs to something in terms of its substance is not attributed to it because of an accident. But good and evil belong to the substance of an action, for an action can be good or evil as to its kind, as we have

---

[14] The matter *from which,* whether permanent or changing, is that which something is made from in the sense that a house is made from wood or bricks. The matter *about which* is a thing considered as known; for example, the matter about which ethics is concerned is human or voluntary acts.

[15] The object of an act, discussed in the preceding article, concerns the nature of an act. The circumstances of an act concern the individuality of the act, i.e., those circumstances which morally, and not merely physically, affect an act and add to the moral nature of the act for better or worse. For the consideration and enumeration of moral circumstances, see question 7 above, especially articles 3 and 4.

[16] Question 7, article 1.   [17] Aristotle, *Metaphysics* VI, 4 (1027b 25).

[18] Aristotle, *op. cit.* VI, 2 (1026b 4).

said.[19] Therefore good or evil does not belong to an act because of circumstances.

On the contrary: The Philosopher says that a virtuous man acts as he should act, when he should, and so on according to other circumstances.[20] Hence, in a contrary way, the vicious man, with respect to a particular vice, acts when he should not, where he should not, and so of the other circumstances. Therefore human acts are good or bad according to circumstances.

Response: In natural things, the full perfection a thing should have does not come from the substantial form alone, which makes it be the kind of thing it is, for a good deal is added by the ensuing accidents; for example, shape, color, and things of this kind, add a good deal to man, and if any of these is not in due proportion, an evil results. The same is true of action. For the fullness of its goodness does not consist wholly in what it is essentially, but also in additional things connected with the action as accidents of it. These additional things are its due circumstances. Hence if something is lacking which is required by way of due circumstances, the act will be evil.

Reply to 1: Circumstances are external to an action in the sense that they are not of the essence of an action, but they are in the action as accidents of it. So also accidents in natural substances are outside the essence.

Reply to 2: Not all accidents are accidentally related to their subjects; some are proper accidents and these art does consider.[21] This is the way circumstances of acts are considered in moral doctrine.

Reply to 3: Since good is convertible with being and "being" is said proportionally of substance and accident, "good" also is said of a thing both with respect to its essential being and its accidental being; and this is the case both in natural things and in moral actions.

Fourth Article

IS A HUMAN ACT GOOD OR EVIL BECAUSE OF THE END?[22]

It seems that good and evil in human acts do not come from the end.

1. Dionysius says, "Nothing acts with evil in view."[23] Consequently,

---

[19] Article 2.

[20] Cf. *Nicomachean Ethics* II, 3 (1104b 26).

[21] Proper accidents imply a certain relation to their subject by their very nature, as properties, or by the intention of the one doing the act. Accidents related only accidentally to their subject are those which occur without some per se connection, or which occur by chance.

[22] By "end" here is meant the end of the agent in doing the act, and hence is the circumstance corresponding to *Why?* in the circumstances listed in question 7, article 3, although because of its importance it is often considered apart from the other circumstances.

[23] *The Divine Names* IV, 19; 31.

if action were good or evil from its end, no act would be evil, which is clearly false.

2. The goodness of an act is something that is in it. The end, however, is an extrinsic cause. Therefore an act is not called good or evil according to the end.

3. Sometimes a good act may be ordered to an evil end, as when one gives alms for his own glory; conversely, an evil act may be ordered to a good end, as when someone steals in order to give something to the poor. Therefore an act is not good or evil by its end.

On the contrary: Boethius says, "If the end is good, the thing is good, and if the end is evil, the thing is evil." [24]

Response: The disposition of things with regard to goodness and to being is the same. There are some things whose being does not depend on another, and in these things it is sufficient to consider their being absolutely. There are other things whose being depends on another, and these have to be considered in relation to the cause on which their being depends. Now just as the being of a thing depends on the agent and the form, so the goodness of a thing depends upon the end. Hence in the Divine Persons, whose goodness does not depend on something else, there is no consideration of goodness on the part of the end. But human actions, and other things whose goodness depends on something else, derive goodness from the end on which they depend, over and beyond the absolute goodness which is in them.

Hence a fourfold goodness can be considered in human action. The first is the goodness an action has in terms of its genus, namely, as an action, for it has as much of goodness as it has of action and being, as we have said.[25] Second, an action has goodness according to its species, which it has from its appropriate object. Third, it has goodness from its circumstances—its accidents, as it were. Fourth, it has goodness from its end, which is related to it as a cause of its goodness.

Reply to 1: The good in view of which one acts is not always a true good, but sometimes is a true good and sometimes an apparent good. In the latter instance, an evil action results from the end in view.

Reply to 2: Although the end is an extrinsic cause, nonetheless due proportion to the end and a relation to the end are inherent to an action.

Reply to 3: Nothing prevents an action from being good in one of the ways mentioned above,[26] and not in another. Thus it is possible that an action which is good according to its species or according to circumstances be ordered to a bad end, and vice versa. But an act is not good absolutely unless it is good in all ways, for "evil results from any one defect, while good results from the whole cause," as Dionysius says.[27]

---

[24] *On Topical Differences* II.   [25] Article 1.
[26] In the body of this article.   [27] *The Divine Names* IV, 30.

Fifth Article

IS A HUMAN ACT GOOD OR EVIL IN ITS SPECIES? [28]

It seems that good and evil in moral acts do not make them differ specifically.

1. Good and evil in acts correspond to good and evil in things, as we have said.[29] But good and evil do not differentiate things into species, for a good man and a bad man are the same in species. Therefore good and evil in acts do not make the acts differ in species.

2. Evil, since it is a privation, is a kind of non-being. But non-being cannot be a difference, according to the Philosopher.[30] Now since the difference constitutes the species, it seems that an act, by being evil, is not placed in any species. Therefore good and evil do not differentiate the species of human acts.

3. Acts different in species have different effects. But the same specific effect can follow from a good and from an evil act; for example, a human being is born from an adulterous or a lawful union. Therefore good and evil acts do not differ specifically.

4. Acts are sometimes said to be good or evil from their circumstances, as we have already pointed out.[31] But a circumstance, which is an accident, does not give species to an act. Therefore human acts do not differ in species because of their goodness or evil.

On the contrary: Like habits produce like acts.[32] But good and evil habits differ in species, for example, liberality and wastefulness. Therefore good and evil acts differ specifically.

Response: Every act has its species from its object, as we have said.[33] Hence a difference of object causes a diversity of species in acts. Now it must be noted that a difference of object which causes a specific difference in actions as they are referred to one active principle, does not cause such a specific difference in reference to another active principle. For nothing accidental constitutes a species, but only what is per se, and hence a difference of object, may be per se as referred to one active principle and accidental as referred to another; for example, to know color and to know sound differ per se in relation to sense but not in relation to intellect.

Now human acts are called good or evil in relation to reason because,

---

[28] The meaning of this question is whether good or evil constitute different species or kinds of moral action, i.e., whether they differentiate human acts specifically. The replies to *1* and *2* bring out this sense clearly, as well as the conclusion reached in the body of the article.

[29] Article 1.   [30] Cf. *Metaphysics* III, 3 (998b 22).

[31] Article 3.

[32] Cf. Aristotle, *Nicomachean Ethics* II, 1 (1103b 21).

[33] Article 2. See note 11 above.

as Dionysius says, the good of man is "to live according to reason," whereas evil is to live "apart from reason." [34] For the good of a thing is what is suitable to it according to its form; the evil, that which is in opposition to the order of its form. It is clear, therefore, that the difference of good and evil considered in regard to the object is a per se difference in relation to reason, i.e., according as the object is suitable or unsuitable to reason. Now acts are called human or moral to the extent they proceed from reason. Hence it is clear that good and evil diversify moral acts specifically, for per se differences cause a diversity in species.

Reply to 1: Even in natural things good and evil, as being in accordance with nature or against nature, diversify the species of nature, for a dead body and a living body are not the same in species. In a similar way the good, as being in accord with reason, and the evil, as being against reason, diversify the moral species.

Reply to 2: Evil implies privation, not absolutely, but as related to such a power. For an act is said to be evil in species, not because it has no object, but because it has an object which does not conform to reason, for example, appropriating another's property. Insofar as the object is something positive, it can constitute a species of evil act.

Reply to 3: A conjugal and an adulterous act, considered in reference to reason, differ in species and have different specific effects, for the one merits praise and reward, the other blame and punishment. But considered in reference to the power of generation, they do not differ in species, and thus they have one specific effect.

Reply to 4: A circumstance is sometimes taken as an essential difference of the object in reference to reason, and then it can constitute a moral act as to its species. This would be the case whenever a circumstance changes an act from good to evil, for a circumstance would not make an act evil unless it were opposed to reason.

Sixth Article

DOES AN ACT HAVE ITS SPECIES OF GOOD OR EVIL
FROM ITS END?

It seems that the good or evil an act has in terms of its end does not diversify acts specifically.

1. Acts derive their species from the object. But the end is outside the notion of the object. Therefore the good or evil coming from the end does not diversify the species of an act.

2. What is accidental does not constitute a species, as we have said.[35] But it is accidental to an act to be ordered to an end; for example, to give alms for one's own glory. Therefore acts are not diversified in species in terms of the good or evil of the end.

3. Acts that differ in species can be ordered to one end; thus acts of

---

[34] *The Divine Names* IV, 32.   [35] Article 5.

various virtues and vices can be ordered to one's own glory. Therefore the good or evil which comes from the end does not diversify acts specifically.

On the contrary: It has been shown that human acts derive their species from the end.[36] Therefore the good or evil an act has in terms of its end diversifies acts specifically.

Response: Acts are called human insofar as they are voluntary, as we have said.[37] Now there is a twofold act in voluntary action: the interior act of the will and the external act; and each of these has its object. The end is properly the object of the interior act of the will, while that with which the exterior act is concerned is its object. Hence just as the exterior act receives its species from the object it is concerned with, so the interior act of the will receives its species from the end, which is its proper object.

Now that which is on the part of the will is related as form to that which is on the part of the exterior act, for the will uses members as instruments for action; furthermore, exterior acts are not counted as moral except insofar as they are voluntary. The species of a human act, therefore, is considered formally in terms of the end, but materially in terms of the object of the external act. Hence the Philosopher says that "he who steals in order to commit adultery is, properly speaking, more an adulterer than a thief." [38]

Reply to 1: The end is also counted as an object, as we have said.[39]

Reply to 2: To be ordered to such a particular end, although accidental to the external act, is not accidental to the interior act of the will, which is related to the external act as what is formal to what is material.

Reply to 3: When many acts specifically different are ordered to one end, there is indeed a diversity of species on the part of external acts, but a unity of species on the part of the interior act.

Seventh Article

IS THE SPECIES DERIVED FROM THE END CONTAINED UNDER THE SPECIES DERIVED FROM THE OBJECT AS UNDER ITS GENUS, OR THE REVERSE? [40]

It seems that the species of goodness derived from the end is contained under the species of goodness derived from the object as a species under a genus—as when a man wills to steal in order to give alms.

1. Acts take their species from the object, as we have said.[41] But it is

---

[36] Question I, article 3. [37] Question I, article 1.
[38] *Nicomachean Ethics* V, 2 (1130a 24). [39] In the body of this article.
[40] In other words, the question is whether the good or evil of an act derives more universally from the end or from the object.
[41] Articles 2 and 6.

impossible for a thing to be contained under some other species that is not contained under its own proper species, for one and the same thing cannot be in different species if there is no subalternation between them. Therefore the species taken from the end is contained under the species taken from the object.

2. The ultimate difference always constitutes an indivisible species.[42] But the difference derived from the end seems to come after the difference derived from the object, because the end implies the notion of what comes last. Therefore the species derived from the end is contained under the species derived from the object, as an indivisible species.

3. A difference is more formal according as it is more specific, because a difference is compared to a genus as form to matter. But a species derived from the end is more formal than one derived from the object, as we have said.[43] Therefore the species derived from the end is contained under the species derived from the object as the indivisible species under a subalternated genus.

On the contrary: There are determinate differences of any genus. But an act of the same species on the part of the object can be ordered to an infinite number of ends, as stealing can be ordered to an infinite number of good or evil ends. Therefore the species derived from the end is not contained under the species derived from the object, as under a genus.

Response: The object of an exterior act can be related in two ways to the end willed. In one way, it can be ordered per se to it, as fighting well is ordered per se to victory; in another way accidentally, as taking what belongs to another is ordered accidentally to giving alms. Now the differences dividing a genus and constituting the species of that genus must divide the genus per se, as the Philosopher says.[44] But if they divide it accidentally, the division is not rightly made. Thus if someone were to divide *animal* into *rational* and *irrational,* and then divide *irrational animal* into *some with wings* and *some without wings—with wings* and *without wings* would not determine *irrational animal* per se. The division should be: *some having feet, some not having feet;* and of those having feet, *some having two, some having four, some having many,* for these determine the prior difference per se.

Accordingly, when the object is not ordered per se to the end, the specific difference derived from the object does not determine per se the species derived from the end, nor conversely. Hence one of these species is not contained under the other, and a moral act is then contained as though under two distinct species. It is in this sense we say that someone who steals in order to commit adultery is guilty of two evils in one act.

---

[42] E.g., the ultimate difference "rational" constitutes man as an indivisible or ultimate species; "three equal sides" is the ultimate difference of one indivisible species of the genus "triangle" which is a species with respect to the genus "plane figure."
[43] Article 6.   [44] *Metaphysics* VII, 12 (1038a 9).

However, if the object is ordered per se to the end, one of the differences determines the other per se. In this way, one of the species will be contained under the other.

Now we must still consider which of the two is contained under the other. To clarify this, we must note first that the more particular the form from which a difference is taken, the more specific the difference is. Second, the more universal an agent is, the more universal is the form caused by it. Third, the more ultimate an end is the more universal is the agent; for example victory, which is the ultimate end of an army, is the end intended by the commander in chief, while the ordering of this or that regiment is the end intended by a subordinate officer. It follows from all this that the specific difference derived from the end is more general, while the difference derived from an object ordered per se to that end is specific in relation to it.[45] For the will, whose proper object is the end, is the universal mover with respect to all powers of the soul, whose proper objects are the objects of their particular acts.

Reply to 1: As far as its substance is concerned, a thing cannot be in two species without one being ordered under the other. But a thing can be contained under different species with respect to what is added on to its substance. For example, this fruit is contained under one species as to its color—say, red—and is contained under another as to its odor—sweet-smelling. In a similar way, an act which is in one natural species according to its substance, can be referred to two species with respect to moral conditions added to it, as we have said.[46]

Reply to 2: The end is last in execution but first in the intention of reason, and it is in regard to the latter that moral acts receive their species.

Reply to 3: The difference is compared to the genus as form to matter inasmuch as it determines the genus. On the other hand, the genus is regarded as more formal than the species in the sense that it is more absolute and less contracted. This is the reason that the parts of a definition are reduced to the genus of formal cause.[47] And in this respect, the genus is the formal cause of the species, and the more universal it is the more formal it will be.

Eighth Article

IS ANY ACT INDIFFERENT ACCORDING TO ITS SPECIES? [48]

It seems that no act is indifferent according to its species.

1. Evil is the privation of good, according to Augustine.[49] But priva-

---

[45] This is the sense in which the goodness derived from the object is contained under the goodness derived from the end as a species under a genus.
[46] Question I, article 3, reply to 3.   [47] Cf. Aristotle, *Physics* II, 3 (194b 28).
[48] I.e., is any human act in relation to its object neither morally good nor morally bad?
[49] *The Enchiridion* XI.

tion and habit are opposites with no intermediary, according to the Philosopher.[50] Therefore no act is indifferent in species as being midway between good and evil.

2. Human acts derive their species either from the end or from the object, as we have said.[51] But every object and every end is counted as good or evil, and consequently every human act is good or evil according to its species. No act, therefore, is indifferent in its species.

3. As we have said,[52] an act is called good when it has goodness in all the respects it should have, and evil when something of this is lacking. But every act either must have the fullness of its goodness or lack it in some respect. Therefore every act according to its species must be either good or evil, and none indifferent.

On the contrary: Augustine says that "there are certain acts that are neither good nor evil which can be done with a good or evil intent, and about which it would be rash to make a judgment." [53] Therefore there are some acts which are indifferent according to their species.

Response: As we have said,[54] every act takes its species from its object; and human action, which is called moral, takes its species from the object as referred to the principle of human acts, which is reason. Hence, if the object of the act involves something which is in accord with the order of reason, it will be a good act according to its species, for example, to give alms to the poor. But if the object involves something opposed to the order of reason, it will be a bad act according to its species, for example to steal, which is to take what belongs to another. However, the object of an act may not involve anything as relevant to the order of reason, for example, to pick up a leaf from the ground or to take a walk, and so on, and such acts are indifferent according to their species.[55]

Reply to 1: Privation is of two kinds. One kind consists in having been deprived, and in this case the whole is taken away and nothing is left, as blindness totally takes away sight, darkness takes away light, and death takes away life. Between this sort of privation and the opposite habit there cannot be anything midway between in regard to the proper subject. Another kind of privation consists in being deprived as sickness is the privation of health, not that it wholly removes health, but that it is an approach to the whole losing of health, which is realized in death. Such privation, since it leaves something, is not always in immediate opposition to the corresponding habit. It is in this way that evil is the privation of good, as Simplicius says,[56] for it does not take away the good

---

[50] Cf. *Categories* X (12b 26).   [51] Article 6; question 1, article 3.

[52] Article 1.

[53] *The Lord's Sermon on the Mount* II, 18.

[54] Articles 2 and 5.

[55] "According to their species" thus means human acts considered abstractly. The next article will point out that individual human acts—acts considered in the concrete—are not indifferent.

[56] *Commentary on the Categories* X.

entirely, but leaves something. Hence there can be something midway between good and evil.

Reply to 2: Every object or end has some good or evil at least as being something natural, but this need not imply moral goodness or evil, which a thing has in reference to reason, as we have said.[57] It is this we are now treating.

Reply to 3: Not everything which an act has is relevant to its species. Consequently, although everything that belongs to the fullness of its goodness is not contained in the account of its species, an act is not thereby good or evil in species, just as man according to his species is neither virtuous nor vicious.

Ninth Article

CAN AN INDIVIDUAL ACT BE INDIFFERENT?[58]

It seems that an individual act can be indifferent.

1. There is no species which does not, or cannot, contain an individual under it. But an act can be indifferent in its species, as we have said.[59] Therefore an individual act can be indifferent.

2. Individual acts cause habits like those acts, as Aristotle says.[60] But some habits are indifferent, for the Philosopher says that those who are temperamentally placid and disposed to be lavish are not evil, and yet they are not good since they decline from virtue,[61] and hence they are indifferent as far as habit is concerned. Therefore some individual acts are indifferent.

3. Moral good relates to virtue, moral evil to vice. But sometimes a man does not order an act that is indifferent in its species to an end, either good or bad. Therefore an individual act can be indifferent.

On the contrary: Gregory says, "An idle word is one that lacks either the usefulness of rectitude, or the motive of just necessity, or usefulness as regards piety." [62] But an idle word is evil, for "of every idle word men speak, they shall give account on the day of judgment" (*Matthew 12:36*). If, however, it does not lack just necessity or utility as regards piety, it is good. Therefore every word is either good or evil, and for the same reason any other act is good or evil. No individual act is therefore indifferent.

Response: Sometimes an act may be indifferent according to its species and yet be good or bad, considered in the individual case. The reason

---

[57] In the body of this article.
[58] The question here is whether this act done by this person at this time with deliberation can be morally indifferent, i.e., neither good nor bad.
[59] Article 8.
[60] *Nicomachean Ethics* II, 1 (1103b 21).
[61] *Op. cit.* IV, 1 (1121a 26).
[62] *Homily on the Gospel* I, 6.

for this is that a moral act, as we have said,[63] has its goodness not only from the object, from which it derives its species, but also from its circumstances, which are like its accidents. So, too, something belongs to an individual man by reason of individual accidents which does not belong to man by reason of his species. Now every individual act must have some circumstance that makes it either good or evil, at least by reason of the end intended. For since it belongs to reason to bring about order, if an act proceeding from deliberative reason is not ordered to a due end, it is by that very fact opposed to reason and is counted as evil. But if it is ordered to a due end, it is in conformity with the order of reason, and so is counted as good. Now an act must either be ordered or not ordered to a due end. Hence every human act, proceeding from deliberative reason, considered as an individual action, must be good or evil.

However, if an act does not proceed from deliberative reason, but from imagination or feeling—for example, scratching one's face or moving a hand or a foot—such an act, properly speaking, is not human or moral, since a moral act must come from reason. Hence an act of this kind will be indifferent as being outside the kind of acts that are moral.

Reply to 1: An act can be indifferent according to its species in several ways. It may be such that its species necessitates its being indifferent, and the argument given proceeds along these lines. However, no act is specifically indifferent in this way, for there is no object of a human act which cannot be ordered either to good or to evil either by the end or by circumstances. Secondly, an act may be specifically indifferent because, as far as its species is concerned, it is neither good nor evil. Consequently, it becomes good or evil in virtue of something else. Thus man, as far as his species is concerned, is neither white nor black, nor does it follow from his species that he should not be white or not be black, for man is white or black because of principles other than those of the species.

Reply to 2: The Philosopher says that a man is truly evil when he is injurious to others.[64] Accordingly, he says that the extravagant man is not evil, because such a person injures only himself. The same is the case with respect to all others who do not injure their fellow men. But here we are speaking of evil in general, and this is whatever is opposed to right reason. In this sense, every individual act is good or evil, as we have said.[65]

Reply to 3: Every end intended by deliberative reason pertains to the good of some virtue or to the evil of some vice. For example, when a man's act is ordered to the assisting or resting of his body, it is also ordered to the good of virtue in one who orders his body to the good of virtue. The same applies in other instances.

---

[63] Article 3.
[64] Cf. *Nicomachean Ethics* IV, 1 (1121a 29).
[65] In the body of this article.

Tenth Article

DOES A CIRCUMSTANCE MAKE A MORAL ACT GOOD OR EVIL IN SPECIES?

It seems that a circumstance cannot make a moral act good or evil in species.[66]

1. The species of an act is derived from the object. But circumstances differ from the object. Therefore circumstances do not give an act its species.

2. Circumstances are related to a moral act as its accidents, as we have said.[67] But an accident does not establish a species. Therefore circumstances do not establish another species of good or evil.

3. One and the same thing cannot belong to many species. But there are many circumstances of one act. Therefore a circumstance does not put a moral act in some species of good or evil.

On the contrary: The place in which an action occurs is a circumstance. But a place makes a moral action be in a certain species of evil, for to steal something in a sacred place is a sacrilege. Therefore a circumstance puts a moral act in some species of good or evil.

Response: Just as the species of natural things are brought about by their natural forms, so the species of moral acts are brought about by forms as conceived by reason. This is evident from what we have said.[68] Now because nature is determined to one thing, and since a process of nature cannot go on endlessly, it is necessary to arrive at some ultimate form giving a specific difference, after which no other specific difference is possible. Hence in natural things an accident cannot be taken as a difference which establishes a species.

But the process of reason is not determined to something one, for, with whatever is given, it can still proceed further. Accordingly, what is taken in a given act as a circumstance added to the object which specifies the act, can again be taken by reason's power of ordering things, as a principal condition of the object determining the species of the act. For example, to take what belongs to another has its species from the notion of belonging to another, for this is why it is constituted in the species of stealing; but if in addition the time or place is taken into account, this will be considered as a circumstance. Now since reason can also order an act with respect to place or time, or other circumstances, it can take the condition of place in respect to the object into account as contrary to the ordering of reason; for example, the order of reason forbids an injustice being done in a sacred place. Hence to steal from another in a

---

[66] See question 7 above for meaning of moral circumstances and for an enumeration of the circumstances.

[67] Question 7, article 1.   [68] Article 5.

QUESTION XVIII, *Art. 11*

sacred place is especially and additionally opposed to the order of reason. Thus place, which was first considered as a circumstance, is now considered as a principal condition of the object and as conflicting with reason. In this way, whenever a circumstance has a special reference to the order of reason, whether "for" or "against" reason, the circumstance determines the species of a moral act, whether good or evil.

Reply to 1: A circumstance, when giving species to an act, is considered as a certain condition of the object, as we have said,[69] and so it is, as it were, a specific difference of the object.

Reply to 2: A circumstance, taken precisely as a circumstance, does not give an act its species, since it is an accident; but to the extent it becomes a principal condition of the object, it can give species to an act.

Reply to 3: Not every circumstance places a moral act in some species of good or evil, since not every circumstance implies agreement or disagreement with reason. Hence, although one act can have many circumstances, it does not follow that one act is in many species. Nevertheless, nothing prevents one moral act from being in several moral species, even diverse ones, as we have said.[70]

Eleventh Article

DOES EVERY CIRCUMSTANCE INCREASING THE GOOD OR EVIL
OF A MORAL ACT CONSTITUTE A SPECIES OF GOOD OR EVIL?

It seems that every circumstance relating to good or evil gives species to the act.

1. Good and evil are specific differences in moral acts. Therefore, that which makes a difference in the good or evil of a moral act makes it differ by a specific difference, and this is the same as making it differ in species. But everything that increases the goodness or evil of an act makes it differ in good or evil, and thus causes a difference in species. Therefore every circumstance increasing the good or evil of an act establishes a species.

2. A circumstance accompanying an act either has in itself some aspect of good or evil or it does not. If it does not, it cannot add to the good or evil of an act, for that which is not good cannot make a greater good, and that which is not evil cannot make a greater evil. But if a circumstance itself has some aspect of good or evil, by this very fact it is some species of good or evil. Therefore every circumstance increasing the good or evil of an act produces a new species of good or evil.

3. According to Dionysius, "evil is caused by any single defect." [71] Now any circumstance which increases the evil has its own defect. Therefore, any circumstance of this kind adds a new species of evil. And for the

---

[69] In the body of this article.
[70] Article 7, reply to *1;* question 1, article 3, reply to *3.*
[71] *The Divine Names* IV, 30.

same reason, any circumstance increasing the good seems to add a new species of goodness in the same way, as a unit added to a number makes a new species of number; for the good consists in number, weight and measure.[72]

On the contrary: More and less do not diversify a species. But a circumstance is something more or something less adding to what is good or evil. Therefore not every circumstance adding something by way of good or evil puts a moral act in a species of good or evil.

Response: As we have said,[73] a circumstance makes a moral act to be either good or evil insofar as it refers to the special order of reason. Now sometimes a circumstance does not have reference to the order of reason with respect to good or evil except by presupposing some other circumstance by which the act is good or evil. For example, to take something in large or small quantity does not concern the order of reason with respect to good or evil unless some other condition is presupposed by which the act is good or evil—for instance, that what is taken belongs to another, which is contrary to reason. Accordingly, to take what belongs to another in large or small quantity does not change the species of the evil, but it can increase or diminish the evil. The same holds with respect to other acts, good or evil. Consequently, not every circumstance increasing the good or evil changes the species of a moral act.

Reply to 1: With respect to things which can be increased or decreased in quality, a difference of more or less does not change the species; thus the variation of more or less white does not change the species of this color. Similarly, that which causes an act to be more or less good or evil does not change the species of the moral act.

Reply to 2: A circumstance increasing an evil or increasing the good of an act sometimes does not have goodness or evil in itself, but in relation to some other condition of the act, as we have said.[74] Hence it does not produce a new species, but increases the good or evil which comes from another condition of the act.

Reply to 3: A circumstance does not produce a particular defect by itself but only in relation to something else. Likewise, it does not add a new perfection except in relation to something else. To the extent that it does, although it adds to the good or evil, it does not always change the species of good or evil.

---

[72] Cf. I, question 5, article 5.   [73] Article 10.
[74] In the body of this article.

The Goodness and Malice of the Interior Act of the Will

(*In Ten Articles*)

DOES THE GOODNESS OF THE WILL DEPEND ON THE OBJECT?

It seems that the goodness of the will does not depend upon the object.

1. The will cannot be directed to anything but the good because evil is "outside the scope of the will," as Dionysius says.[1] Accordingly, if the goodness of the will were to be determined by the object, it would follow that every act of the will would be good and none evil.

2. Good is found first of all in the end, and hence the goodness of the end as such does not depend on something else. But according to the Philosopher, "good action is an end although good making never is," [2] for making is always ordered to the thing made as its end. Therefore the goodness of an act of the will does not depend upon any object.

3. According as a thing is of such a kind, so does it make another to be. But the object of the will is what is good by a goodness of nature. Hence it cannot give moral goodness to the will. Therefore the moral goodness of the will does not depend upon the object.

On the contrary: The Philosopher says that justice is the habit by which men will what is just,[3] and for the same reason virtue is the habit by which men will what is good. But a good will is one that is in accord with virtue. Therefore goodness of the will comes from the fact that one wills what is good.

Response: Good and evil are per se differences of the act of the will. For good and evil per se refer to the will just as what is true or false do to reason, whose act is distinguished per se by the difference of the true and the false, according as we say that an opinion is true or false. Hence good and evil willing are acts differing specifically. Now a specific difference in acts is derived from the object, as we have said.[4] Consequently good or evil in the acts of the will is properly determined according to their objects.

---

[1] *The Divine Names* IV, 32.
[3] *Op. cit.* V, 1 (1129a 9).

[2] *Nicomachean Ethics* VI, 5 (1140b 6).
[4] Question 18, article 5.

Reply to 1: The will is not always directed to what is truly good but sometimes to the apparent good, which is somehow a good but which is not desirable in an unqualified way. This is why the act of the will is not always good, but is sometimes evil.

Reply to 2: Although an action can be the ultimate end of man in a certain way, nevertheless such an action is not an act of the will, as we have already explained.[5]

Reply to 3: A good is presented to the will as an object by reason; insofar as it is in accord with reason, it corresponds to what is moral and causes moral goodness in the act of the will. For reason is the principle of human and moral acts, as we have said.[6]

Second Article

DOES THE GOODNESS OF THE WILL DEPEND
UPON THE OBJECT ALONE?

It seems that the goodness of the will does not depend upon the object alone.

1. The end has more affinity to the will than to any other power. But the acts of other powers derive their goodness not only from the object but also from the end, as we have said.[7] Therefore the act of the will likewise derives its goodness not only from the object but also from the end.

2. The goodness of an act comes not only from the object but also from the circumstances, as we have said.[8] But there can be a difference of goodness and evil in the act of the will according to the diversity of circumstances; namely, as one wills when he should, and where he should, and as much as he should, and how he should, or one wills as he should not. Therefore the goodness of the will depends not only on the object but also on the circumstances.

3. Ignorance of circumstances excuses malice of the will, as we have noted above.[9] But this would not be so unless the goodness or evil of the will depended on circumstances. Therefore the goodness and evil of the will depend on circumstances and not only on the object.

On the contrary: An act does not derive its species from the circumstances as such, as we have pointed out.[10] But good and evil are the specific differences of the act of the will, as we have also said.[11] Therefore the goodness and evil of the will do not depend upon the circumstances, but on the object alone.

Response: In any genus, to the extent something is prior, to that extent

---

[5] Question 1, article 1, reply to 2; question 3, article 4.
[6] Question 18, article 5.   [7] Question 18, article 4.   [8] Question 18, article 3.
[9] Question 6, article 8.   [10] Question 18, article 10, reply to 2.
[11] Question 18, article 5.

it is more simple and consists of fewer principles; thus the primary bodies are simple. Hence we note that those things which are primary in any genus are in some way simple and consist in something one. Now the principle of the goodness and evil of human acts is from the act of the will. Consequently, the goodness and evil of the will depend on some one thing, while the goodness and evil of other acts depend on various things.

Now that one thing which is the principle in any genus is not something accidental, but per se, for everything accidental is brought back to what is per se, as to a principle. Therefore the goodness of the will depends on that one thing alone which per se causes the act to be good, namely, the object, and not the circumstances, which are sort of accidents of the act.[12]

Reply to 1: The end is the object of the will, but not of the other powers. Hence, with respect to the act of the will, the goodness which comes from the object does not differ from the goodness which comes from the end, as it does in the acts of other powers—except perhaps accidentally, inasmuch as one end depends upon another end, and one act of the will upon another.

Reply to 2: Granted that the will is directed to a good, then no circumstance can make it evil. This is to say, then, that when someone wills a good when he should not, or where he should not, this can be understood in two ways. First, in such a way that this circumstance is referred to what is willed, and then the will is not directed to a good, for to will to do something when it should not be done is not to will a good. Secondly, in such a way that the circumstance is referred to the act of willing, and then it is impossible for someone to will a good when he ought not, for one must always will what is good; unless, perhaps accidentally, in willing this good, one is prevented from willing some other good he should will at that time. And then evil results, not from willing this good, but from not willing the other good. The same is to be said with regard to the other circumstances.

Reply to 3: Ignorance of circumstances excuses the malice of the will inasmuch as circumstances affect what is willed, that is, inasmuch as one does not know the circumstances of the act he wills.

Third Article

DOES THE GOODNESS OF THE WILL DEPEND UPON REASON?

It seems that the goodness of the will does not depend upon reason.
1. What is first does not depend upon what comes after. But the good

---

[12] Properly and intrinsically, therefore, goodness of the will depends upon the object, as just explained. Nevertheless circumstances, especially the end or motive of the agent, can provide additional goodness or evil over and beyond the intrinsic goodness or evil which comes from the object. Cf. question 18, article 3.

concerns the will before it concerns reason, as we have indicated above.[13] Therefore the goodness of the will does not depend upon reason.

2. The Philosopher says that "the goodness of the practical intellect is truth in conformity with right desire." [14] Now right desire is a good will. Therefore the goodness of practical reason depends more upon the goodness of the will rather than the converse.

3. Whatever moves something else does not depend upon what it moves, but rather the other way around. Now the will moves reason and other powers, as we have said.[15] Therefore the goodness of the will does not depend upon reason.

On the contrary: "That will is immoderate which persists in its desires in opposition to reason." [16] But goodness of the will consists precisely in not being immoderate. Therefore the goodness of the will depends upon its being subject to reason.

Response: As we have said,[17] the goodness of the will depends properly upon the object. Now the object of the will is presented to it by reason, for the good known by the intellect is the object proportioned to the will. A sensible or imaginary good is not proportioned to the will but to sense desire, for the will can tend to the universal good, which reason apprehends, whereas sense desire tends only to the particular good, which is grasped by a sense knowing power. Hence the goodness of the will depends upon reason in the same way as it depends on its object.[18]

Reply to 1: The good, understood precisely as good, that is, as desirable, pertains to the will before it pertains to reason. Nevertheless, it pertains to reason under the aspect of the true before it pertains to the will under the aspect of the desirable, for the will cannot desire a good unless it is first grasped by reason.

Reply to 2: The Philosopher here is speaking about the practical intellect as it delineates and figures out the means, and this is accomplished by prudence. Now with respect to means, rectitude of reason depends upon its conformity to the desire of a due end; however, this very desire of the due end presupposes a right understanding of the end, and this is the work of reason.

Reply to 3: The will moves reason in one way, and in another way reason moves the will, that is, with respect to the object, as we have explained previously.[19]

---

[13] Question 8, article 1; question 9, article 1.
[14] *Nicomachean Ethics* VI, 2 (1139a 29).   [15] Question 9, article 1.
[16] Hilary, *On the Trinity* X.   [17] Articles 1 and 2.
[18] Hence, while goodness of the will depends upon the object in the sense already explained, it depends likewise upon reason which, as a directing principle of human acts, specifies the object for the will. It is by reason that we distinguish one good from another.
[19] Question 9, article 1.

Fourth Article

DOES THE GOODNESS OF THE WILL DEPEND ON ETERNAL LAW? [20]

It seems that the goodness of the will does not depend on eternal law.

1. For one thing there is one rule and one measure. But the rule of the human will, upon which its goodness depends, is right reason. Therefore the goodness of the will does not depend on the eternal law.

2. "A measure is homogeneous with what is measured." [21] But the eternal law is not homogeneous with the human will. Therefore the eternal law cannot be the measure of the human will in such a way that the goodness of the will depends on it.

3. A measure should be something that is most certain. But the eternal law is not known to us. Therefore it cannot be the measure of our will so that the goodness of the will depends on it.

On the contrary: Augustine says that "a sin is a deed or a word or a desire against the eternal law." [22] But an evil will is the root of sin. Therefore, since malice is the opposite of goodness, the goodness of the will depends on the eternal law.

Response: In all causes ordered to one another, the effect depends more upon the first cause than upon a second cause, since a second cause acts only in virtue of a first cause. Now human reason's capacity to be the rule of the human will, by which its goodness is measured, is derived from eternal law, which is divine reason. Hence, "Many say: Who shows us good things? The light of Thy countenance, O Lord, is signed upon us" (*Psalms 4:7*). In other words: "The light of reason which is in us, to the extent it can show us what is good and regulates our will, to that extent is the light of Thy countenance, i.e., is derived from Thy countenance." Hence it is clear that the goodness of the human will depends much more upon the eternal law than upon human reason, and when human reason fails, we must have recourse to the eternal reason.

Reply to 1: There are not several proximate measures of one thing, but there can be several measures of one thing if one is subordinated to another.

Reply to 2: A proximate measure is homogeneous with what is measured, but a remote measure is not.

Reply to 3: Although the eternal law is not known by us as it is in the divine mind, yet it is known by us in a certain way, either through natural reason, which is derived from the divine mind as a proper image of it, or by some kind of revelation which is added over and beyond.

---

[20] Eternal law is taken generally as the divine wisdom whereby God governs all things and directs them to their end. Cf. I, question 93, especially article 1.

[21] Aristotle, *Metaphysics* X, 1 (1053a 24).   [22] *Against Faustus* XXII, 27.

Fifth Article

IS THE WILL EVIL WHEN IT IS NOT IN ACCORD WITH ERRING REASON?

It seems that the will is not evil when it is not in accord with erring reason.

1. Reason is the rule of the human will insofar as reason is derived from the eternal law. But erring reason is not derived from the eternal law. Therefore erring reason is not the rule of the human will, and hence the human will is not evil if it does not conform with erring reason.

2. According to Augustine, the command of a lower authority does not bind if it conflicts with the command of a higher authority;[23] for example, when a provincial governor commands something which is forbidden by the ruler of the whole country. But erring reason sometimes proposes something which is against the command of a superior power, namely, a command of God, whose power is greatest of all. Therefore a dictate of erring reason does not bind, and consequently the will is not evil if it is at variance with erring reason.

3. Every evil act of the will can be classified as a distinct kind of malice. But an act of the will at variance with erring reason cannot be classified as a distinct kind of malice. For example, if someone's reason errs in declaring that fornication is to be done, his will, in not willing this, cannot be classified as any distinct kind of evil. Therefore the will is not evil if it is at variance with erring reason.

On the contrary: As we have said before,[24] conscience is simply the application of knowledge to an act. Now knowledge is in reason. Therefore a will at variance with erring reason is against conscience. But all such willing is evil, for "All that is not of faith is sin" (*Romans 14:23*), that is, all that is against conscience is a sin. Therefore a will at variance with erring reason is evil.

Response: Since conscience is a kind of dictate of reason—for it is a certain kind of application of knowledge to act—to ask whether a will at variance with erring reason is evil is the same as to ask whether an erroneous conscience binds.

Apropos of this matter, some distinguished three kinds of acts;[25] some acts are good by nature, some are indifferent, and some are evil by nature. They say, consequently, that if our reason or conscience tells us to do something which is by nature good, there is no error; the same holds if it tells us not to do something which is by nature evil, for it is the same reason that prescribes good and prohibits evil. But if a man's reason or

---

[23] Cf. *Sermon* LXII, 8.   [24] I, question 79, article 13.
[25] Cf. Bonaventure, II *Sentences*, d. xxxix, a. 1, q. 3; Alexander of Hales, *Summa Theologiae* II-II, no. 388.

QUESTION XIX, *Art. 5* 183

conscience tells him that he is bound by precept to do what is in itself evil, or that what is in itself good is forbidden, then his reason or conscience errs. Likewise, if a man's reason or conscience tells him that what is in itself indifferent—for example, picking up a leaf from the ground—is forbidden or commanded, his reason or conscience errs. They say, therefore, that reason or conscience, when erring about indifferent matters, whether by commanding or forbidding, binds, so that the will which is at variance with that erring reason will be evil and sinful. But when erring reason or conscience commands what is in itself evil or forbids what is in itself good and necessary for salvation, it does not bind; and in such instances the will which is at variance with erring reason or conscience is not evil.

But this position is not reasonable. For in indifferent matters, the will which is at variance with erring conscience or reason is evil in some way because of the object, upon which the goodness or malice of the will depends—not because of the object according to its own nature, but according as the object is accidentally apprehended by reason as something evil to do or to avoid. And since the object of the will is that which is proposed by reason, from the fact that something is proposed by reason as evil, the will, by tending to it, is evil. Now this is the case not only in regard to indifferent matters but also in regard to those things that are good or evil in themselves. For not only can indifferent matters take on the character of good or evil accidentally, but also what is good can take on the character of evil, and what is evil that of good, because of reason's grasping something this way. For example, to refrain from fornication is good, but the will does not tend to this good except as it is proposed by reason. Therefore, if erring reason proposes this as evil, the will tends to it as to something evil. Consequently, the will will be evil because it wills evil, not something evil in itself but something evil accidentally, because it is apprehended as such by reason.

Similarly, to believe in Christ is good in itself and necessary for salvation, but the will tends to this only as it is proposed by reason. Hence, if it is proposed by reason as evil, the will tends to it as to an evil, not because it is evil in itself but because it is evil accidentally as apprehended by reason. Accordingly, the Philosopher says that "absolutely speaking, the incontinent man is one who does not follow right reason, but accidentally he is also one who does not follow wrong reason." [26] Hence it must be said, absolutely speaking, that every will that is at variance with reason, whether right or wrong, is always evil.

Reply to 1: Although a judgment of erring reason is not derived from God, yet such erring reason sets forth its judgment as true, and consequently as being from God, from whom is all truth.

Reply to 2: The remark of Augustine holds when it is known that the

---

[26] *Nicomachean Ethics* VII, 9 (1151a 33).

inferior authority is commanding something contrary to the command of a higher authority. But if someone believes the command of a provincial governor to be the command of the ruler of the country, then in scorning the command of the governor he would scorn the command of the country's ruler. In a similar way, if a man knew that human reason was dictating something contrary to a precept of God, he would not be bound to follow reason, but reason then would not be wholly erroneous. But when erring reason proposes something as a precept of God, then to scorn the dictate of reason is the same as to scorn a precept of God.

Reply to 3: Whenever reason apprehends something as evil, it apprehends it under some species of evil; for example, as being contrary to a divine precept or as giving scandal, or something of this kind. And then such an evil act of the will is reduced to that species of malice.

Sixth Article

IS THE WILL GOOD WHEN IT IS IN ACCORD WITH ERRING REASON?

It seems that the will is good when it is in accord with erring reason.

1. Just as the will, when at variance with reason, tends to that which reason judges to be evil, so the will that is in accord with reason tends to that which reason judges to be good. But the will at variance with reason, even erring reason, is evil. Therefore the will that is in accord with reason, even when erring, is good.

2. A will is always good when it is in accord with a precept of God and the eternal law. But the eternal law and a precept of God are proposed to us through the apprehension of reason, even when erring. Therefore the will is good even when in accord with erring reason.

3. The will is evil when it is at variance with erring reason. If, therefore, the will is also evil when it is in accord with erring reason, it seems that the willing of one having an erring reason is always evil. If such were the case, a man would be in a dilemma, and would of necessity sin, which is unreasonable. Therefore a will is good when in accord with erring reason.

On the contrary: The will of those who killed the Apostles was evil. Yet this was in accord with their erring reason according to Scripture: "The hour is coming for everyone who kills you to think that he is offering worship to God" (*John 16:2*). Therefore the will can be evil when it is in accord with erring reason.

Response: As the preceding question is the same as asking whether an erroneous conscience binds, so this question is the same as asking whether an erroneous conscience excuses. Now this question depends upon what has been said about ignorance. We have already pointed out that sometimes ignorance causes the act to be involuntary, and sometimes not.[27]

---

[27] Question 6, article 8.

And because moral good or evil consists in an act insofar as it is voluntary, as we have said,[28] it is clear that the ignorance which causes an act to be involuntary wholly removes the aspect of moral good and evil, but not the ignorance which does not cause an act to be involuntary. We have also pointed out that the ignorance which in some way is willed, whether directly or indirectly, does not cause an act to be involuntary.[29] By ignorance directly willed, I mean that to which the act of the will tends; by indirectly willed, I mean that which is due to negligence, in that a man does not want to know what he is bound to know, as we have said.[30]

Hence, if reason or conscience errs voluntarily, either directly or because of negligence, such that one is in error about what one ought to know, then such an error of reason or conscience does not excuse the will from being evil which is in accord with reason or conscience so erring. But if the error which causes involuntariness arises from an ignorance of some circumstance without any negligence, then such an error of reason or conscience excuses the will which is in accord with that erring reason from being evil. For example, if erring reason tells a man that he should go to another's wife, his will in following erring reason is evil, for this error arises from an ignorance of the law of God which he is bound to know. But if his reason errs by mistaking another woman for his wife and he thus wills to give her the marriage right when she asks for it, his will is excused from being evil because this error arises from an ignorance of circumstance, which is excusable, and causes involuntariness.[31]

Reply to 1: As Dionysius says, "good follows from the whole cause while evil follows from any particular defect." [32] Hence all that is needed to call something evil which the will inclines to is that it either be something evil according to its nature or that it be apprehended as evil. But to be called good, it must be good in both ways.

Reply to 2: The eternal law cannot err, but human reason can err. Hence the will when in accord with human reason is not always right, nor is it always in accord with eternal law.

Reply to 3: Just as in argumentation, when something unreasonable is granted, something else unreasonable necessarily follows; so in moral matters if something unreasonable is granted, other unreasonable things necessarily follow. Thus, let it be supposed that someone seeks vainglory; he will then sin whether he does what he ought to do because of the vainglory, or whether he omits doing what he ought. Yet he need not be in a dilemma, for he can put aside his evil intention. Similarly, let it be sup-

---

[28] Article 2.   [29] Question 6, article 8.   [30] *Ibid.*
[31] For example, a man and a woman might think they were married when actually the woman's former marriage was not really dissolved, and hence the man erroneously thinks she is his wife.
[32] *The Divine Names* IV, 30.

posed that one's reason or conscience errs because of an ignorance which does not excuse; evil then necessarily follows in the will. But again one need not be in a dilemma, for he can put aside the error since his ignorance is vincible and voluntary.

Seventh Article

DOES THE GOODNESS OF THE WILL IN REGARD TO THE MEANS DEPEND UPON THE INTENTION OF THE END?

It seems that the goodness of the will does not depend upon the intention of the end.

1. It was said above[33] that the goodness of the will depends upon the object alone. But in relation to the means, the object of the will is one thing and the end intended, another. Therefore, in regard to the means, the goodness of the will does not depend upon the intention of the end.

2. The desire to observe God's commandments belongs to a good will. But this desire can be referred to an evil end, to vainglory or to avarice, by willing to obey God in order to gain temporal benefits. Therefore the goodness of the will does not depend upon the intention of the end.

3. As good and evil diversify the will, so they diversify the end. But the malice of the will does not depend upon the malice of the end intended, for one who steals in order to give alms has an evil will although he intends a good end. Therefore, the goodness of the will does not depend upon the goodness of the end intended.

On the contrary: Augustine says that the intention is rewarded by God.[34] But something is rewarded by God because it is good. Therefore the goodness of the will depends upon the intention of the end.

Response: The intention can have a twofold relation to the will; first, as preceding it, secondly, as following upon it.[35] The intention precedes the act of willing as a cause when we will something because we intend a certain end. Then the ordering to the end is considered as the reason for the goodness of what is willed; for example, when one wills to fast because of God, the act of fasting takes on the character of good from the fact that it is done because of God. Consequently, since the goodness of the will depends upon the goodness of the object willed, as we have said above,[36] of necessity it has to depend upon the intention of the end.

The intention is subsequent to the act of the will when it is added to a previous act of the will; for example, when someone wills something and then afterward refers it to God. Then the goodness of the previous

---

[33] Article 2.   [34] Cf. *Confessions* XIII, 26.
[35] The Latin reads "ut concomitans" but, as the body of the article bears out, the sense is "following upon" rather than "concomitant" or "accompanying."
[36] Articles 1 and 2.

act of the will is not derived from the subsequent intention unless this act is repeated with that intention.

Reply to 1: When the intention is the cause of the willing, the ordering to the end is taken as the reason for the goodness of the object.

Reply to 2: An act of the will cannot be called good if an evil intention is the cause of the willing. Thus he who wills to give alms because of the vainglory he will gain wills something good in itself with evil in mind, and therefore as willed by him it is evil. In this way his will is evil. But if the intention follows after the act of willing, then the act of willing could be good; and this previous act of the will is not perverted by the subsequent intention, but only if the act is repeated.

Reply to 3: As we have already said, "evil follows from any particular defect while good follows from the whole cause." [37] Consequently, whether the will tends to what is evil in itself with good in mind, or to what is good with evil in mind, it will always be evil. In order that the will be good, it must tend to what is good for a reason that is good—it must will the good and will it for the sake of good.

Eighth Article

IS THERE AS MUCH GOODNESS OR EVIL IN THE WILL
AS THERE IS GOODNESS OR EVIL IN THE INTENTION?

It seems that the degree of goodness in the will depends upon the degree of goodness in the intention.

1. "The good man from his good treasure brings forth good things" (*Matthew 12:35*); the *Gloss* comments on this by saying, "a man does as much good as he intends." However, the intention not only gives goodness to the external action, but also to the act of the will, as we have said.[38] Therefore the goodness of a man's will is in proportion to the goodness of his intention.

2. As a cause is greater, the effect is greater. But the goodness of the intention is the cause of a good will. Therefore, to the extent that one intends the good, to that extent his will is good.

3. In evil actions, a man sins in proportion to his intention. Thus if one throws a stone with a murderous intent, he would be guilty of murder. For the same reason, in good actions one's will is good to the extent he intends the good.

On the contrary: The intention can be good while the will is evil. For the same reason, therefore, the intention can be greater in goodness and the will less good.

Response: We can consider a twofold quantity with respect to the act and the intention of the end. One is on the part of the object insofar

---

[37] Article 6, reply to *1*.   [38] Article 7.

as one wills or does a greater good; the other is taken from the intensity of the act, as one wills or acts intensely, and this is greater relative to the agent.

Now if we are speaking of this quantity from the point of view of the object, it is clear that the quantity in the act does not depend on the quantity in the intention. This may happen in two ways in regard to the external act. In one way, because the object which is ordered to the intended end is not proportioned to that end; for example, if someone were to offer ten dollars, he could not realize his intention if he intended to buy something worth a hundred dollars. In another way, because of the obstacles that may arise with respect to the external action which we may not be able to remove; for example, one may intend to go to Rome, and run into obstacles which prevent one from going. On the other hand, this happens in only one way with respect to the interior act of the will, because interior acts are within our power, whereas the external ones are not. But the will can will an object which is not proportioned to the intended end, and thus the will that tends to that object, considered absolutely, is not as good as the intention. However, since this intention also pertains in a certain way to the act of willing inasmuch as it is the reason for willing, the quantity of goodness in the intention redounds upon the act of the will—that is, to the extent that the will wills some great good as an end, even though that by which it wills to attain so great a good is not in proportion to it.

However, if we consider the quantity in the intention and the act according to their respective intensity, then the intensity of the intention redounds upon the interior and the exterior act of the will, for the intention is related like a form to both, as we have said.[39] But considered materially, given an intention that is intense, the interior or exterior act may not be so intense; for example, when a man does not will with as much intensity to take medicine as he wills to have health. Nevertheless, the intensity with which he wills to have health reacts formally on the intensity with which he wills to take medicine.

We must take into account, however, that the intensity of the interior or exterior act can be referred to the intention as to an object; for example, when one intends to will intensely or do something intensely. Yet it does not follow that he does will or act intensely, for the quantity of goodness in the interior or exterior act does not follow upon the goodness intended, as we have just pointed out. Hence it is that one does not merit as much as he intends to merit, for the quantity of merit is measured by the intensity of the act, as we shall point out later.[40]

Reply to 1: The *Gloss* is there speaking of good as it is in the judgment of God, who considers particularly the intention of the end.

---

[39] Question 12, article 4; question 18, article 6.
[40] Question 20, article 4; question 114, article 4.

Thus another *Gloss* says on the same passage that "the treasure of the heart is the intention, by which God judges deeds." For the goodness of the intention reacts in a certain way upon the goodness of the will, which makes the exterior act likewise meritorious in God's sight.

Reply to 2: Goodness of intention is not the whole cause of a good will. Hence the argument given does not hold.

Reply to 3: The malice alone of an intention is enough to make the will evil, and hence the will is evil to the extent the intention is evil. But the same argument does not hold for goodness.

Ninth Article

DOES THE GOODNESS OF THE WILL DEPEND UPON ITS
CONFORMITY TO THE DIVINE WILL?

It seems that the goodness of the human will does not depend upon its conformity to the divine will.

1. It is impossible for the human will to conform to the divine will, for "As the heavens are exalted above the earth, so are my ways exalted above your ways, and my thoughts above your thoughts" (*Isaias 55:9*). Consequently, if the goodness of the will required conformity to the divine will, it would follow that it is impossible for the will of man to be good. This is unreasonable.

2. Just as the source of our will is the divine will, so the source of our knowledge is the divine knowledge. But it is not necessary that our knowledge be conformed to divine knowledge, for God knows many things which we do not know. Therefore it is not necessary that our will be conformed to the divine will.

3. The will is the principle of action. But our action cannot be conformed to divine action. Therefore neither can our will be conformed to the divine will.

On the contrary: "Yet not as I will, but as thou willest" (*Matthew 26:39*), which Christ said because "He wills man to be upright and directed to God," as Augustine says.[41] Now the rectitude of the will is its goodness. Therefore the goodness of the will depends upon its conformity with the divine will.

Response: As we have said,[42] the goodness of the will depends upon the intention of the end. Now the ultimate end of the human will is the supreme good, which is God, as we have also said.[43] Therefore in order that the human will be good it must be ordered to the supreme good, which is God.

Now this supreme good is primarily and per se related to the divine will as its proper object, and that which is first in any genus is the measure

---

[41] *Commentary on Psalms,* Psalms 32:1.   [42] Articles 3 and 5.

[43] Question 1, article 8; question 3, article 1.

and explanation of everything which belongs to that genus. But everything is right and good insofar as it reaches a proper measure. Therefore, in order that the human will be good, it must be conformed to the divine will.

Reply to 1: The human will cannot be conformed to the divine will so as to equal it, but only so as to imitate it. Likewise, man's knowledge conforms to divine knowledge inasmuch as he knows the truth, and man's action conforms to divine action inasmuch as he acts in conformity with his own nature. All this is by way of imitation, not by way of equality.

The solutions for replies to 2 and 3 are evident from what has been said.

Tenth Article

IS IT NECESSARY FOR THE HUMAN WILL, IN ORDER TO BE GOOD, TO BE CONFORMED TO THE DIVINE WILL WITH REGARD TO THE THING WILLED?

It seems that the human will need not always be conformed to the divine will with regard to the thing willed.

1. We cannot will what we do not know, for the good as known is the object of the will. But we often do not know what God wills. Therefore the human will cannot be conformed to the divine will in regard to what is willed.

2. God wills the damnation of one whom He foresees will die in mortal sin. Accordingly, if man were bound to conform his will to the divine will, with regard to the thing willed, it would follow that a man would be bound to will his own damnation. This is unreasonable.

3. No one is bound to will something which is against piety. But if man wills what God wills, he would sometimes will what is contrary to piety; for example, when God wills the death of the father of a family, if his son were to will the same thing, it would be against filial piety. Therefore man is not bound to conform his will to the divine will in regard to the thing willed.

On the contrary:

(1.) "Praise becometh the upright" (*Psalms 32:1*); a *Gloss* on this says, "One has an upright heart who wills what God wills." But anyone is bound to have an upright heart. Therefore anyone is bound to will what God wills.

(2.) The will takes its form from the object, as does every act. Accordingly, if man is bound to conform his will to the divine will, it follows that he is bound to conform his will to the thing willed.

(3.) Opposition of wills occurs because of men willing diverse things. But whoever has a will in opposition to the divine will has an evil will. Therefore anyone who does not conform his will to the divine will, with regard to the thing willed, has an evil will.

Response: As we have said,[44] the will tends to its object insofar as it is proposed by reason. Now a thing may be considered in various ways by reason; hence a thing may be good from one point of view and not good from another point of view. Consequently, if one man wills that a thing take place, inasmuch as it is accounted as good, his will is good; and the will of another man when he wills that the same thing not take place, inasmuch as it is accounted as evil, is also good. For example, the judge's will is good when he wills the death of a criminal, because this realizes justice; whereas the will of someone else—the criminal's wife or son who does not wish him killed because it is an evil for the family— is also good.

Now since the will follows the apprehension of reason or the intellect, the more universal the nature of the good which is apprehended the more universal is the good which the will tends to. This is evident in the example we have just given. The judge has to guard the common good, with which justice is concerned, and as a consequence he wills the death of the criminal, which is counted as good in relation to the common welfare, whereas the wife of the criminal has to concern herself with the private domestic good, and from this point of view she wills that her husband, the criminal, not be put to death. Now God, who is the maker and ruler of the universe, apprehends the good of the entire universe, and hence whatever He wills, He wills with a view to the common good; and this is His own goodness and the good of the whole universe. A creature, on the other hand, in accord with its nature, apprehends a particular good proportionate to such a nature. Now it is possible for something to be good in view of a particular consideration which is not good in view of a universal one, or conversely. Hence it happens that one's will is good in willing something from a particular point of view which nevertheless God does not will from a universal point of view, and vice versa. Hence various wills of various men can be good in respect to opposite things, inasmuch as they will a particular thing to be or not to be for different reasons.

Now one's will is not right in willing some particular good unless he refers it to the common good as to an end, since the natural appetite of any part is ordered to the common good of the whole. Now it is the end that provides the formal reason for willing whatever is directed to the end. Hence, in order that a man will a particular good with a right will, he must will that particular good materially while willing the common and divine good formally. Therefore the human will must be conformed to the divine will, with regard to that which is willed formally, for it is bound to will the divine and common good; but not materially, for the reason just given. But in any event the human will is in a certain way conformed to the divine will in both respects. For, inasmuch as it

---

[44] Articles 3 and 5.

is conformed to the divine will with regard to the common nature of what is willed, it is conformed to the divine will with regard to the ultimate end. And in the event that it is not conformed to the divine will in what is willed materially, it is still conformed to the divine will considered as an efficient cause, for the proper inclination following upon nature, or upon the particular grasp of this or that thing, comes to it from God as from its efficient cause. Hence, in this regard it is customary to say that the human will is conformed to the divine will in that it wills what God wills it to will.

There is also another kind of conformity, from the point of view of the formal cause, such that man wills something from charity, as God wills it. This conformity is also reduced to a conformity of form, which is taken from the order to the ultimate end, which is the proper object of charity.

Reply to 1: We can know in a general way what God wills, for we know that whatever God wills, He wills it under the aspect of the good. Hence, whoever wills something inasmuch as it is good has his will conformed to the divine will with respect to the nature of what is willed. But we do not know what God wills in particular, and in this respect we are not bound to conform our will to the divine will. In the state of glory,[45] however, everyone will see in each thing he wills the order that thing has to what God wills in this matter. Consequently, he will conform his will to God in all things not only formally but also materially.

Reply to 2: God does not will anyone's damnation considered precisely as damnation, nor anyone's death considered precisely as death, for "He wills all men to be saved" (*I Timothy 2:4*); but He wills this from the standpoint of justice. In such matters, therefore, it suffices that man will that God's justice and the order of nature be observed.

Reply to 3: This is evident from what has been said.

Reply to (1) "On the contrary": One who conforms his will to the divine will with respect to the reason for the thing willed, wills more what God wills than one who conforms his will with respect to the thing willed, for the will tends more to the end than to what is for the sake of the end.

Reply to (2) "On the contrary": The species and form of an act is taken from the object considered formally rather than from the object considered materially.

Reply to (3) "On the contrary": When men will diverse things but not under the same aspect, there is no opposition of wills. There is an opposition, however, when under one and the same aspect, one man wills something which another man does not. But this is not the question at issue.

---

[45] I.e., in the state of supernatural happiness when we know and enjoy God in heaven.

The Goodness and Malice
of External Human Acts

(In Six Articles)

IS GOODNESS OR EVIL IN THE ACT OF THE WILL FIRST OR IN THE EXTERNAL ACT?

It seems that good or evil is in the external act prior to being in the act of the will.

1. The will has its goodness from the object, as has been said.[1] But the external act is the object of the interior act of the will, for a man is said to will stealing or to will giving alms. Therefore good and evil are in the external act prior to being in the act of the will.

2. Good belongs first of all to the end, for whatever is for the sake of the end is accounted as good from its order to the end. Now an act of the will cannot be the end, as we have already said,[2] but the act of some other power can be the end. Therefore the good is in the act of some other power prior to its being in the act of the will.

3. The act of the will is related formally to the external act, as we have said.[3] But what is formal comes after, for form is received into matter. Therefore good and evil are in the external act before being in the act of the will.

On the contrary: Augustine says, "it is by the will that we sin and by the will that we live rightly."[4] Therefore moral good and evil are first in the will.

Response: External acts can be called good or evil in two ways. First, according to the kind of acts they are and the circumstances connected with them; for example, to give alms under the right circumstances is good. Second, an act can be good or bad in relation to the end sought; for example, we say giving alms because of vainglory is evil. Now since the end is the proper object of the will, it is evident that the nature of good or evil, which the external act has from its ordering to an end, is found first in the will, then derivatively in the external act. However, the good or evil the external act has of itself, as being concerned with due matter

---

[1] Question 19, articles 1 and 2. [2] Question 1, article 1, reply to 2.
[3] Question 18, article 6. [4] *Retractions* I, 9.

and due circumstances, is not derived from the will, but rather from reason. Hence, if we consider the goodness of the external act as it is in the ordering and apprehension of reason, it is prior to the goodness of the act of the will, but if we consider it as it is found in the carrying out of a work, it is subsequent to the goodness of the will, which is its principle.

Reply to 1: The external act is the object of the will inasmuch as it is proposed to the will by reason as a good apprehended and ordained by reason, and in this way it is prior to the good in the act of the will. But inasmuch as it consists in the carrying out of a work, it is an effect of the will and follows upon the will.

Reply to 2: The end is prior in intention but posterior in execution.

Reply to 3: Form as received in matter is posterior to matter in the course of generation though prior in nature, but form as it is in the agent cause is prior in all respects. Now the will is related to the external act as its efficient cause. Hence the goodness of the act of the will, as existing in the agent cause, is the form of the external act.

Second Article

DOES THE WHOLE GOOD AND EVIL OF THE EXTERNAL ACT DEPEND UPON THE GOODNESS OF THE WILL?

It seems that the whole good or evil of the external act depends upon the will.

1. "A good tree cannot bear bad fruit, nor can a bad tree bear good fruit" (*Matthew 7:18*). According to a *Gloss,* the tree stands for the will and the fruit for deeds. Therefore the interior act of the will cannot be good and the external act bad, or vice versa.

2. Augustine says that there is no sin without the will.[5] If, therefore, there is not sin in the will there will not be sin in the external act, and so the whole good or evil of the external act depends upon the will.

3. The good and evil of which we are speaking now are differences of the moral act. Now differences divide a genus per se, according to the Philosopher.[6] Accordingly, since an act is moral from the fact that it is voluntary, it seems that the good and evil in an act are derived from the will alone.

On the contrary: Augustine says that "there are some acts which neither a good end nor a good will can make good." [7]

Response: As we have already said,[8] there is a twofold goodness that can be considered in the external act, one according to the due matter and circumstances, the other in relation to the end. The goodness which is derived from the ordering to an end depends wholly on the will, while

---

[5] Cf. *Retractions* I, 9.
[7] *Against Lying* VII.
[6] Cf. *Metaphysics* VII, 12 (1038a 9).
[8] Article 1.

that which is derived from due matter and circumstances depends upon reason, and from this the goodness of the will follows inasmuch as the will tends toward it.

Now we must take into account, as we have said,[9] that for something to be evil it is enough if there is a single defect, whereas to be good absolutely it is not enough for it to be good in one respect, but it must be good in every respect. If, therefore, the will is good because of both its particular object and its end, the external act is consequently good. But if the will is good because of the end intended, this is not enough to make the external act good, and if the will is evil either because of the end intended or because of the act that is willed, the external act as a consequence is evil.

Reply to 1: A good tree, taken as signifying a good will, is to be understood of the will as having goodness both from the act willed and from the end intended.

Reply to 2: One sins by the will not only when he wills an evil end but also when he wills an evil act.

Reply to 3: Not only is the interior act of the will said to be voluntary, but also the external acts according as they proceed from the will and reason. Consequently the difference of good and evil can apply to both acts.

Third Article

IS THE GOOD OR EVIL OF THE EXTERNAL
AND INTERIOR ACT THE SAME?

It seems that the good or evil of the interior act of the will and the external act is not the same.

1. The principle of an interior act is an interior knowing or desiring power of the soul, whereas the principle of an external act is the power that carries out the motion. But where there are different principles of action there are different acts. Now it is an act which is the subject of goodness or malice, and the same accident cannot be in different subjects. Therefore the goodness of the interior act cannot be the same as that of the external act.

2. "A virtue makes the one who has it good and his action also." [10] But an intellectual virtue in the power that commands is one thing and a moral virtue in the power commanded is another.[11] Therefore the goodness of the interior act, which is in the power that commands is one thing, and the goodness of the external act, which is in a power commanded, is another.

---

[9] Question 19, article 6, reply to *1*.
[10] Aristotle, *Nicomachean Ethics* II, 6 (1106a 15).
[11] *Op. cit.* I, 13 (1103a 3).

3. The cause and the effect cannot be identical, for nothing is the cause of itself. But the goodness of the interior act is the cause of the goodness of the external act, or vice versa, as has been said.[12] Therefore the same goodness cannot be in each.

On the contrary: As we have shown above,[13] the act of the will is like form in relation to the external act. Now something one results from what is formal and material. Therefore the goodness of the internal and external act is one.

Response: As we have said above,[14] the interior act of the will and the external act are one act considered morally. Now sometimes one and the same act may have several aspects of good or evil and sometimes only one. Therefore, we ought to say that sometimes the good or evil of the internal and external acts is the same, and sometimes it is different. For, as we have said,[15] the two goodnesses or evils of the internal and external are ordered to one another. Now in things ordered to something else, it may happen that a thing is good only in terms of being ordered to something else, as bitter medicine is good only because it produces health. Hence there are not two different goods, one of health and one of medicine; there is one and the same good. On the other hand, sometimes a thing that is ordered to something else has some aspect of goodness in itself even apart from being ordered to another good, as sweet-tasting medicine has the aspect of a pleasurable good apart from its producing health.

Accordingly, we must say that when the external act derives its goodness or evil only from its order to the end, then there is one and the same goodness or evil, of the act of the will which of itself is referred to the end, and of the external act which is referred to the end by mediation of the act of the will. But when the external act is good or evil of itself, according to its matter or circumstances, then the goodness of the external act is one thing and the goodness of the will derived from the end is another; but even so, the goodness of the will derived from the end carries over into the external act, and the good of the matter and the circumstances affects the act of the will, as we have said.[16]

Reply to 1: The argument given proves that the internal act and the external act are different acts physically; but, though differing in this way, they combine to form one kind of act in the moral order, as we have said.[17]

Reply to 2: Moral virtues are ordered to the very acts of the virtues, the acts being their ends, as it were;[18] but prudence, which is in reason, is ordered to things that are for an end. This is why various virtues are necessary. But right reasoning in accordance with the end of the virtues

---

[12] Articles 1 and 2. [13] Question 18, article 6. [14] Question 17, article 4.
[15] Articles 1 and 2. [16] *Ibid.* [17] Question 17, article 4.
[18] Cf. Aristotle, *Nicomachean Ethics* VI, 12 (1144a 8).

has no other goodness than the goodness of virtue, inasmuch as any virtue participates in the goodness of reason.

Reply to 3: When one thing is derived from another as from a uni-vocal efficient cause, then what is in both is different; for example, when what is hot heats, the heat of what is heated and what heats are indi-vidually different though the same specifically. But when one thing is derived from another according to analogy or proportion, then it is only one in number; for example, health as applied to medicine or urine is derived from the health in the animal's body; the health that medicine and urine refer to is none other than the health of the animal, which medicine causes and of which urine is a sign. In this way the goodness of the external act is derived from the goodness of the will and vice versa, namely, according to an order of one to the other.

Fourth Article

DOES THE EXTERNAL ACT ADD ANY GOOD OR EVIL
TO THAT OF THE INTERIOR ACT?

It seems that the external act does not add any goodness or evil to that of the interior act.

1. Chrysostom says: "It is the will that is rewarded for doing good or punished for doing evil." [19] Now the deeds we do testify to our will. Therefore, God does not require deeds on His own account in order to know how to judge, but for the sake of others so that all may know that God is just. But good or evil is to be evaluated according to the judg-ment of God rather than the judgment of man. Therefore the external act adds nothing to the good or evil of the internal act.

2. The goodness of the internal and external act is one and the same, as has been said.[20] But increase is brought about by the addition of some thing to another. Therefore the external act does not add any good or evil to that of the internal act.

3. The whole goodness of created things adds nothing to the divine goodness, for all of it is derived from the divine goodness. But sometimes the goodness of the external act is derived entirely from the goodness of the internal act, and sometimes conversely, as said above.[21] Therefore neither of them adds any goodness or evil to the other.

On the contrary: Every agent intends to accomplish good and avoid evil. If, therefore, no good nor evil is added by the external act, it would be futile for one who has a good or evil will to do a good work or refrain from one that is evil. This is unreasonable.

Response: If we speak of the goodness the external act has from the goodness of the end, then the external act adds nothing to this good-ness unless it happens that the will itself becomes better in what is

---

[19] *Homily* XIX.   [20] Article 3.   [21] Articles 1 and 2.

good, or worse in what is evil. It seems that this may happen in three ways. In one way, numerically; for instance, if one wills to do something for a good or evil end, and then does not do it, but afterward does will and do it, the act of the will is doubled and in this way there is a twofold good or twofold evil. Secondly, by way of prolongation. For example, suppose a man wills to do something for a good or evil end but abandons it because of some obstacle, while another perseveres until the deed is accomplished; it is clear that the latter wills good or evil for a longer time, and in this respect is better or worse. Thirdly, by way of intensity. For there are some external acts which, as pleasurable or painful, naturally make the will intend something more or less strongly, and it is evident that the more intensely the will tends to a good or an evil, the better or worse it is.

If, however, we speak of the goodness the external act has from its matter and due circumstances, then the external act, since it is related to the will as its term and end, does add to the good or evil of the will, for every inclination or motion is perfected by achieving its end or attaining its term. Hence the will is not perfected unless it be such that, given the opportunity, it acts. But if there is no possibility of action, and the will is in fact perfect in the sense that it would carry out the act if it could, the lack of the perfection that comes from the external act is wholly involuntary. Now just as the involuntary does not merit reward or punishment in accomplishing good or evil, so neither does it lessen reward or punishment if a man, wholly involuntarily, fails to do good or evil.

Reply to 1: Chrysostom is speaking of man's will when it is fully realized and desisting only because powerless to act.

Reply to 2: The argument given refers to the goodness which the external act has from the goodness of the end. But the goodness of the external act derived from its matter and circumstances is different from the goodness the will has from the end, but it is not different from the goodness the will has from the act itself which is willed, which is related to it as its reason and cause, as we have said.[22]

Reply to 3: The reply is evident from what has been said.

Fifth Article

DOES THE CONSEQUENCE OF AN EXTERNAL ACT INCREASE ITS GOOD OR EVIL?

It seems that the consequence of an external act adds something to its good or evil.

1. An effect pre-exists virtually in its cause. But consequences follow upon the act as effects upon causes. Therefore they pre-exist virtually in acts. But a thing is judged to be good or evil according to its power or

_____
[22] Articles 1 and 2.

virtue, for "a virtue makes whoever has it good." [23] Therefore consequences add to the good or evil of acts.

2. The good deeds of his listeners are effects that are consequences of
the words of the one preaching. But such goods redound to the merit of
the one preaching, as is clear from Scripture: "So then, my brethren, be-
loved and longed for, my joy and my crown" (*Philippians 4:1*). Therefore the consequences of an act add to its good or evil.

3. Punishment is not increased unless guilt is increased, for "According
to the measure of the sin shall the measure also of the stripes be" (*Deu-
teronomy 25:2*). But the punishment is increased because of the consequences, for "if the ox was wont to push with his horn yesterday and the
day before, and they warned his master, and he did not shut him up, and
he shall kill a man or a woman, then the ox shall be stoned, and his
owner also shall be put to death" (*Exodus 21:29*). But he would not have
been put to death if the ox, though not tied up, had not killed a man.
Therefore the consequence adds to the good or evil of an act.

4. If someone does something that may cause death, by striking a person or by passing sentence on him, and death does not ensue, he does not
contract irregularity. But he would contract irregularity if death ensued.
Therefore the consequence of the act increases its good or evil.

On the contrary: A consequence does not make an act which was good
evil, nor an act which was evil good. For example, if someone gives alms
to a poor man who makes bad use of the alms by committing sin, this
does not undo the good done by the one who gave the alms; likewise, if
someone bears patiently a wrong done to him, the one who does the
wrong is not thereby excused. Therefore the consequence of an act does
not add to its good or evil.

Response: The consequence of an act is either foreseen or it is not. If
it is foreseen, obviously it adds to the good or evil. For when one foresees
that many evils may follow from his act, and yet does not refrain from
doing the act, his will is clearly the more disordered.

But if the consequence of an act is not foreseen, we must make a distinction. If the consequence follows per se from the kind of act it is and
for the most part, in that case the consequence adds to the good or evil
of the act, for clearly an act from which many good things can follow is
of its nature better, and of its nature worse if from it many evils follow.
However, if a consequence follows accidentally and seldom, then it does
not add to the good or evil of the act, for we do not make a judgment
about a thing in terms of what belongs to it by accident, but only in terms
of what belongs to it per se.

Reply to 1: The power or virtue of a cause is judged according to its
per se effect, not according to its accidental effect.

Reply to 2: The good acts which the listeners do, follow from the

---

[23] Aristotle, *Nicomachean Ethics* II, 6 (1106a 15).

preacher's words as per se effects. Hence the good deeds redound to the merit of the one preaching, especially when such deeds were his intention.

Reply to 3: The consequence for which the man is ordered to be punished follows per se from the nature of the cause and is also supposed as foreseen. Hence it is judged to be punishable.

Reply to 4: The argument would hold if irregularity were the result of fault. But it is not a result of a fault, but of the fact, because of a faulty decision.

Sixth Article

CAN ONE AND THE SAME EXTERNAL ACT
BE BOTH GOOD AND EVIL?

It seems that one and the same act can be both good and evil.

1. "A motion is one which is continuous." [24] But one continuous motion can be both good and evil; for example, a man while going to church may first intend vainglory and then later on intend to worship God. Therefore one act can be both good and evil.

2. According to the Philosopher, action and passion are one act.[25] But the passion can be good, such as Christ's, and the action evil, such as that of those Jews who crucified Him. Therefore one and the same act can be both good and evil.

3. Since a servant is a sort of instrument of the master, the action of the servant is the action of the master, just as the action of a tool is the workman's action. But it can happen that the action of the servant proceeds from the good will of the master, in which respect it is good, and also from the bad will of the servant, in which respect it is evil. Therefore the same act can be both good and evil.

On the contrary: Contraries cannot be in the same thing. But good and evil are contraries. Therefore one act cannot be both good and evil.

Response: Nothing prevents something being one insofar as it is in one genus and being multiple as referred to another genus. Thus a continuous surface is one as considered in the genus of quantity, but multiple as referred to the genus of color if it is in part white and in part black. Accordingly, nothing prevents an act being one as referred to the natural order, but not as referred to the moral order, or conversely, as we have said.[26] Thus an uninterrupted walk is one act according to the natural order, but it may be multiple from a moral point of view if the will of the one walking changes, for the will is the principle of moral acts. If, therefore, an act is considered to be one according to the moral order, it is impossible for it to be morally both good and evil. But if it is one in natural unity, and not in moral unity, it can be both good and evil.

---

[24] Aristotle, *Physics* V, 4 (228a 20).   [25] *Op. cit.* III, 3 (202a 18).
[26] Article 3, reply to *1;* question 18, article 7, reply to *1.*

Reply to 1: The continuing motion which goes on with a varied inten-tion is one as to natural unit, but not one as to moral unity.

Reply to 2: Action and passion belong to the moral order insofar as they are voluntary. Hence to the extent they are voluntary as coming from different wills, they are two morally, and good can be in one of them while evil is in the other.

Reply to 3: The act of the servant, as proceeding from his own will, is not the act of the master, but only insofar as it results from the com-mand of the master. Hence the bad will of the servant does not make the act evil in this respect.

What Follows upon Human Acts by Reason of Their Being Good or Evil

(In Four Articles)

First Article

IS A HUMAN ACT RIGHT OR SINFUL INSOFAR AS IT IS GOOD OR EVIL?

It seems that a human act is not right or sinful as good or evil.

1. "In nature, monsters are mistakes." [1] Monsters, however, are not acts, but something generated outside the course of nature. Now what comes from art and reason imitates what comes about by nature.[2] Therefore an act is not sinful by reason of being disordered and evil.

2. A mistake happens in nature and art when the end intended by nature or art is not attained.[3] But the good or evil of a human act depends chiefly on the intention of the end and on pursuing it to its completion. Therefore it seems that the evil of an act does not make it sinful.

3. If the evil of the act makes the act sinful, it would follow that whenever there is evil there is sin. But this is false, for punishment is not counted as sinful though it is counted as something evil. Therefore an act is not counted as sinful by reason of being evil.

On the contrary: As we have shown above,[4] the goodness of a human act depends principally upon the eternal law; consequently, the evil of an act consists in its going against the eternal law. But this is what sin is, for, as Augustine says, "a sin is a word, deed, or desire for something against the eternal law." [5] Therefore a human act is sinful by reason of its being evil.

---

[1] Aristotle, *Physics* II, 8 (199b 4). The Latin translation of Aristotle reads: "Peccata sunt monstra in natura." The Greek word for peccatum in this passage is ἁμάρτημα. In Aristotle, this word means a failure or mistake and is midway between ἀδίκημα ("intentional wrong") and ἀτύχημα ("a fault of ignorance"). Hence, ἁμάρτημα cannot be strictly translated as "sin" in this passage; this meaning of the word arose, by way of extension, only with the Stoics. One could apply this extended meaning to this passage insofar as this argument, and the following one, rest upon the extended meaning, but it seems preferable to keep to the sense Aristotle had in mind.

[2] Cf. Aristotle, *loc. cit.* (199a 16).

[3] Cf. Aristotle, *loc. cit.* (199a 33). See note 1.

[4] Question 19, article 4.   [5] *Against Faustus* XXII, 27.

Response: Evil is wider than sin just as good is wider than right. Any privation of good, in anything whatever, is an evil, whereas sin consists in an act done for a certain end and lacking the right order to that end. Now the right ordering to an end is measured by some rule, and in things which act according to nature this rule is the power of nature itself, which inclines to a given end. Therefore, when an act proceeds from a natural power according to the natural inclination to the end, rectitude is observed in the act, for the mean does not deviate from beginning to end; that is to say, it does not deviate from the order of its active principle to the end. But when an act loses this right order, it is accounted as a sin.

However, in voluntary actions the proximate rule is human reason and the supreme rule is eternal law. Consequently, when a man's act tends to the end according to the order of reason and eternal law, the act is right, but when it deviates from such rectitude, it is said to be a sin. Now it is clear from what we have said above,[6] that every voluntary act is evil from the fact that it departs from the order of reason and the eternal law, while every act is good which is in accord with reason and eternal law. Hence it follows that a human act is right or sinful by reason of being good or evil.

Reply to 1: Monsters are called mistakes insofar as they follow from a failure in an action of nature.

Reply to 2: There is a twofold end, an ultimate one and a proximate one. In a mistake of nature, the act fails with respect to the ultimate end, the perfection of the thing generated, but it does not fail with respect to a proximate end, for in acting nature forms something. Similarly, in the sin of the will, there is always defection from the ultimate end intended, because no voluntary evil act can be ordered to the happiness which is the ultimate end. However, the act does not fail with respect to the proximate end which the will intends and achieves. Hence, since the intention of the proximate end is ordered to the ultimate end, this very intention can be accounted as something right or sinful.

Reply to 3: Each thing is ordered to its end by its own act, and hence sin, which consists in a deviation from the order to the end, consists properly in an act. But punishment relates to the person who has sinned, as we have said.[7]

Second Article

DOES A HUMAN ACT, AS GOOD OR EVIL,
DESERVE PRAISE OR BLAME?

It seems that a human act, as good or evil, does not deserve praise or blame.

---

[6] Question 19, articles 3 and 4.
[7] I, question 58, article 5, reply to *4:* article 6, reply to *3.*

1. "Mistakes are possible even in the operations of nature," [8] but things that are natural are not culpable or praiseworthy, as Aristotle points out.[9] Therefore a human act, when evil or sinful, does not deserve blame; nor, consequently, does a good act deserve praise.

2. Just as sins occur in moral acts so mistakes occur in the activity of art, for "the grammarian makes a mistake in writing, and the doctor pours out the wrong dose." [10] But an artist is not blamed for doing something wrong, for it belongs to the artist's skill to produce a good or bad work as he pleases. Therefore it seems that a moral act, when evil, is not blameworthy.

3. Dionysius says that evil is "weak and powerless." [11] But weakness or inability either removes or diminishes blame. Therefore a human act is not blameworthy by being evil.

On the contrary: The Philosopher says that "virtuous acts are praiseworthy, while acts contrary to them deserve censure and blame." [12] But good acts are acts of virtue, for "virtue makes good the one who has it and makes his action good," [13] and hence acts opposed to virtue are evil. Therefore a human act, as good or evil, deserves praise or blame.

Response: Just as evil is wider than sin, so sin is wider than blame.[14] For an act is said to be culpable or praiseworthy and this is imputed to an agent, since to praise or to blame is simply to impute to someone the good or evil of his act. Now an act is imputed to an agent when it is within his power in such a way that he has dominion over it, and this holds for all voluntary acts because man has dominion over his acts through his will, as we have said.[15] Hence it follows that only in voluntary acts do good and evil take on the character of praise and blame, and in such acts evil, sin, and blame are the same.

Reply to 1: Natural acts are not within the power of the natural agent, since nature is determined to one thing. Hence, although there are mistakes in natural acts, there is no blame.

Reply to 2: Reason directs works of art in one way and moral actions in another. In art, reason is ordered to a particular end which is devised by reason, whereas in moral matters, reason is ordered to an end that is common to all human life. Now a particular end is ordered to the common end. And, since a sin or mistake occurs through a deviation from the order to the end, as we have said,[16] a mistake can occur in two ways in art. First, by a deviation from the particular end intended by the

---

[8] Aristotle, *Physics* II, 8 (199a 35). See note 1 above.

[9] *Nicomachean Ethics* III, 5 (1114a 23).   [10] Aristotle, *Physics* II, 8 (199a 33).

[11] *The Divine Names* IV, 31.

[12] *Nicomachean Ethics* III, 1 (1109b 31). Cf. *On Virtues and Vices* (1249a 28).

[13] Aristotle, *Nicomachean Ethics* II, 6 (1106a 15).

[14] "Sin" in this context is taken widely to extend to a mistake as well as a moral fault.

[15] Question I, articles 1 and 2.   [16] Article 1.

artist, and such a mistake is proper to art; for example, an artist, in-tending to produce a good work, produces something bad, or intending to produce something bad, produces something good. Second, by deviat-ing from the end common to human life, and then he is said to sin if he intends to produce a bad work and does produce a bad work for the sake of misleading someone. But such a sin does not belong to the artist as artist, but as a man. Hence, for the former fault the artist is blamed as an artist, but for the latter he is blamed as a man. In moral mat-ters, however, where we consider the ordering of reason to the common end of human life, there is always sin and evil when there is deviation from the ordering of reason to the common end of human life. Hence a man, as man and a moral being, is blamed for such a sin. Thus the Philosopher says, "in art, he who errs willingly is preferable, but in prudence, as in the moral virtues," which prudence directs, "he is the reverse." [17]

Reply to 3: That weakness which is in evils that are voluntary is sub-ject to man's power, and hence it neither removes nor diminishes blame.

Third Article

DOES A HUMAN ACT, AS GOOD OR EVIL,
HAVE MERIT OR DEMERIT?

It seems that a human act does not have merit or demerit because of being good or evil.

1. Merit and demerit are said in relation to recompense, which is rele-vant only in matters relating to another person. But not all good or evil human acts relate to another, for some refer to oneself. Therefore not all good or evil human acts have the nature of merit or demerit.

2. No one deserves reward or punishment for doing as he wishes with that over which he has dominion, for a man who destroys a possession of his own is not punished, but he would be if he destroyed the possession of another. But man has dominion over his own acts. Therefore he does not merit reward or punishment by determining his own act in a good or evil way.

3. In acquiring a good for himself, a man does not thereby deserve to be benefited by another, and the same applies in regard to an evil. But a good act is itself a good and a perfection of the agent, and a disordered act is an evil of his. Therefore a man does not merit or demerit by doing a good or evil act.

On the contrary: "Say to the just man that it is well, for he shall eat the fruit of his doings. Woe to the wicked unto evil, for the reward of his hands shall be given him" (*Isaias 3:10-11*).

Response: We speak of merit and demerit in relation to recompense,

---

[17] *Nicomachean Ethics* VI, 5 (1140b 22).

which is rendered in accord with justice. Now a recompense is made to someone in accordance with justice by reason of his doing something for the benefit or injury of another. But in connection with this we have to consider that anyone living in a society is in some way a part and member of the whole society. Therefore, any good or evil done to one of those constituting a society redounds to the whole society, just as an injury to the hand injures the man. Accordingly, when someone does good or evil to another person, there is a twofold merit or demerit in his act. The first is the recompense owed him from the single person whom he helps or injures; the second is the recompense owed him from the society as a whole. However, when someone orders his act directly to the good or evil of the whole society, recompense is owed to him, first and above all, by the society as a whole, secondarily by all the members of the society. Moreover, when someone does that which contributes to his own good or evil, again recompense is owed to him insofar as it also affects the community according as he is a member of society. However, recompense is not owed him insofar as the good or evil belongs to a single person, who is the very person acting, unless perhaps a man owes recompense to himself, according to a kind of similitude, insofar as it can be said that man owes justice to himself.

It is thus evident that a good or evil act is counted as praiseworthy or blameworthy insofar as it is within the power of the will; that an act is right or sinful according as it is ordered to the end; and that the merit or demerit of an act is taken according to the rendering of justice to another.

Reply to 1: A man's good or evil acts, although they are sometimes not ordered to the good or evil of some other person, are still ordered to the good or evil of another, the community itself.

Reply to 2: Man does have dominion over his act; but in addition, as he belongs to another—that is, to the community of which he is a part— he merits or demerits inasmuch as he disposes his acts well or badly, just as if he were to dispense well or badly other possessions of his in respect to which he is bound to serve the community.

Reply to 3: The good or evil which someone acquires for himself by his own act redounds to the community, as we have said.[18]

Fourth Article

DOES A HUMAN ACT, AS GOOD OR EVIL, ACQUIRE MERIT OR DEMERIT BEFORE GOD?

It seems that a good or evil human act does not acquire merit or demerit in the sight of God.

1. As we have said,[19] merit or demerit implies the relation of compensation for good or harm done to another. But a man's good or evil act

---

[18] In the body of this article.   [19] Article 3.

does not become a good or harm to God Himself, for "If thou sin, what shalt thou hurt Him? . . . And if thou do justly, what shalt thou give Him?" (*Job 35:6-7*). Therefore a man's good or evil act does not have merit or demerit before God.

2. An instrument acquires no merit or demerit for the one who uses it, for the whole action of the instrument belongs to the user. But when man acts, he is an instrument of the divine power, which is the principle mover in his action, and hence it is said, "Shall the axe boast itself against him that cutteth with it? or shall the saw exalt itself against him by whom it is drawn?" (*Isaias 10:15*). In this passage, man as an agent is evidently being compared to an instrument. Therefore man, whether doing good or evil, does not merit or demerit in the sight of God.

3. A human act acquires merit or demerit inasmuch as it is ordered to another. But not all human acts are ordered to God. Therefore not all good or evil acts have merit or demerit before God.

On the contrary: "All things that are done, God will bring into judgment . . . whether it be good or evil" (*Ecclesiastes 12:14*). But judgment implies recompense, in respect of which we speak of merit or demerit. Therefore all man's acts, both good and evil, acquire merit or demerit in the sight of God.

Response: As we have said,[20] a man's act inasmuch as it is ordered to another, either to another person or to the community, acquires merit or demerit, and in both ways our good or evil acts have merit or demerit before God. This holds in relation to God inasmuch as He is man's ultimate end, and we are bound to refer all our acts to the ultimate end, as we have pointed out.[21] Hence whoever does an evil act, an act that cannot be referred to God, does not give God the honor owed to Him as our ultimate end. It holds on the part of the whole community of the universe, because in any community the one who governs the community cares particularly for the common good, and hence it is his concern to allot recompense for whatever is done well or ill in the community. Now God is the governor and ruler of the whole universe, as we have said,[22] and especially of rational creatures. Hence it is clear that human acts have merit or demerit in relation to God, otherwise it would follow that God has no concern for human acts.

Reply to 1: God in Himself neither gains nor loses anything by man's action; nevertheless man, as considered in himself, does take something from God or gives something to Him when he observes or does not observe the order established by God.

Reply to 2: Man is moved in such a way as an instrument by God that this does not exclude his moving himself by free choice, as we have said.[23] Hence by his own act man acquires merit or demerit before God.

---

[20] *Ibid.*   [21] Question 19, article 10.   [22] I, question 103, article 5.
[23] Question 9, article 6, reply to 3.

Reply to 3: Man is not ordered to the political community according to his whole being and according to all that he has, and hence it is not necessary that every act have merit or demerit in relation to the political community. But all that man is, and what he is capable of, and what he has, must be ordered to God; consequently, every act of man, good or evil, acquires merit or demerit in the sight of God by very reason of the act.